WITHDRAWN

THE INFLUENCE OF WEALTH
IN IMPERIAL ROME

THE MACMILLAN COMPANY
NEW YORK · BOSTON · CHICAGO
ATLANTA · SAN FRANCISCO

MACMILLAN & CO., Limited
LONDON · BOMBAY · CALCUTTA
MELBOURNE

THE MACMILLAN CO. OF CANADA, Ltd.
TORONTO

THE
INFLUENCE OF WEALTH
IN IMPERIAL ROME

BY

WILLIAM STEARNS DAVIS

PROFESSOR OF ANCIENT HISTORY
UNIVERSITY OF MINNESOTA

New York
THE MACMILLAN COMPANY
1910

All rights reserved

Norwood Press:
Berwick & Smith Co., Norwood, Mass., U.S.A.

PREFACE

This book attempts to consider various phases in the economic and social life of Ancient Rome; such as has not been treated, except incidentally, in any English work, nor in any French or German work from precisely the same standpoint; a fact which gives justification for the present essay.

The purpose is to consider the influence of money and of the commercial spirit throughout the period of Roman greatness. Sometimes a liberal interpretation has been given to the term "Money Power," and certain subjects have been discussed not at first sight closely connected with public finance or private industry and commerce. Yet the idea that the Romans owed much, both of their greatness and of their ultimate failure, to the supreme estimate they put upon wealth and its concomitants has never been lost from view.

This essay makes no claim to exhaustive or original learning. The evidence of the ancient authors, supplemented by much testimony from the great *Corpus Inscriptionum Latinarum,* is however carefully used, and from what is possibly a somewhat new point of departure. Yet modern investigators on one point or another have put the author under a great debt—Friedlaender, Grupp, Mommsen, Marquardt, Voigt, Schiller, Seeck, Hirshfeld, Schanz, Bloch, Boissier, Duruy, Arnold, Dill and many more, as well as the able contributors to Smith's *Dictionary of Classical Antiquities,* and to the Pauly-

Wissowa *Real-Encyklopaedie der classischen Alterthums-wissenschaft.*[1]

Since this book does not claim to be a critical compendium for the advanced scholar, it has not seemed wise to encumber the pages with foot-note references and citations of the classical and modern authorities. The only notes given are to complete or elucidate the statements in the text.

Much of the book naturally is taken up with a discussion of the prosperous period of the early Empire; yet the "Influence of Wealth" began its dominance far back under the Republic, and many references must be made to this period. Also the testimony of Cicero is too important to be ignored in a great many matters. Abundant use is made of the evidence of the younger Pliny, as one of the most illuminating and entertaining witnesses to the social life of the Empire.

If this essay shall succeed, in scant measure, in making plain that within the Roman world, amid which Cicero thundered his eloquence, Caesar led his legions, and Nero indulged his passions, there was another world, less voluptuous and glittering, less famous in history, but no less real and important to the men of the day—the realm of the great god Lucre,—the attempt will not have been in vain.

For much kind revision and criticism of this work while it was in manuscript, I am extremely indebted to my friend, Professor Joseph B. Pike of the University of Minnesota.

University of Minnesota
    Minneapolis
                                          W. S. D.

[1] The recent works of Messrs. Ferrero and Heitland came to hand after the preparation of this volume was well under way. I have not always agreed with Signore Ferrero's conclusions, but Roman history owes him a debt for the marked accent he has placed upon the economic factor. His book, however, has mainly to do with the Republic, while I am chiefly concerned with the Empire.

CONTENTS

vii

CHRONOLOGICAL REFERENCE LIST

201 B.C. End of Second Punic War; final defeat of Hannibal.

146 B.C. Destruction of Corinth and Carthage, commercial rivals of Rome.

133 B.C. Attempt of Tiberius Gracchus to reform the state.

123-121 B.C. Attempt of Gaius Gracchus to reform the state.

90-88 B.C. "Social War," attempt of the Italians to secure equal rights with the Roman citizens.

82-79 B.C. Dictatorship and Reforms of Sulla.

73-71 B.C. Spartacus' Slave Revolt in Southern Italy.

66-61 B.C. Pompeius' Conquests in the East.

63-62 B.C. Conspiracy of Catiline.

58-51 B.C. Conquest of Gaul by Julius Caesar.

49-45 B.C. Civil War between the Pompeians and Caesar; dictatorship of Caesar.

44 B.C. Murder of Caesar.

42 B.C. Battle of Philippi. Octavius Caesar (West) and Antonius (East) practical rulers of the world.

31 B.C. Battle of Actium; fall of Antonius.

27 B.C. Octavius Caesar takes title of *Augustus*. Organization of the "Principate"—monarchy with veneer of republican forms.

9 A.D. Successful revolt of German Tribes against the Roman Rule.

14-37 A.D. *Tiberius* (step-son of Augustus.)

37-41 A.D. *Gaius* (*Caligula*) insane.

41-54 A.D. *Claudius* (governed by his freedmen).

54-68 A.D. *Nero* (tyrant, matricide, aesthete) good government in first part of reign, thanks to Burrhus and Seneca.

68-69 A.D. *Galba*
69 A.D. *Otho* ⎬ Short-lived emperors; mutinies in armies; civil war.
69 A.D. *Vitellius*

69-79 A.D. *Vespasian* (risen from humble origin); reorganization and regeneration.

79-81 A.D. *Titus*, son of Vespasian.

81-96 A.D. *Domitian*, son of Vespasian (tyrant, but not incapable).

The five   ⎧ 96-98 A.D. *Nerva* (aged senator).

good | 98-117 A.D. *Trajan*(adoptive son of Nerva), conquest of Dacia

Emperors. | and Parthians.

Empire | 117-138 A.D. *Hadrian* (adoptive son of Trajan), traveler,

at | builder, reformer.

its | 138-161 A.D. *Antoninus Pius* (adoptive son of Hadrian), very

highest | peaceful reign.

seeming | 161-180 A.D. *Marcus Aurelius* (adoptive son of Antoninus),

pros- | philosopher; beginnings of decline and barbarian inva-

perity.   ⎩   sions.

180-192 A.D. *Commodus* (son of Marcus), degenerate; ruled by freedmen.

193 A.D. *Pertinax* (able ruler, murdered by praetorian guard).

193 A.D. *Didius Julianus* (bought Empire at auction from praetorian guard).

193-211 A.D. *Septimius Severus* (African), stern, energetic, able.

211-217 A.D. *Caracalla* (son of Severus), tyrant.

217-218 A.D. *Macrinus* (usurper).

218-222 A.D. *Elagabalus* (worthless Syrian).

222-235 A.D. *Alexander Severus* (cousin of Elagabalus), well-meaning, gifted but weak prince; army getting out of hand.

[After 235, rapid succession of worthless rulers, raised and pulled down by army; longest reign *Gallienus* 260-268, A.D.; barbarian invasion; pestilence; general disorganization and misery. Regeneration thanks to several able army officers raised to purple.]

268-270 A.D. *Claudius II* (Goths repulsed).

270-275 A.D. *Aurelian* (Dacia abandoned, but Gaul and Palmyra re-con-quered).

275 A.D. *Tacitus* (last Emperor who favored the Senate).

276-282 A.D. *Probus.* (Barbarians beaten back).

282-283 A.D. *Carus* (Persia invaded).

284-305 A.D. *Diocletian* (Reorganization of Empire on basis of absolute monarchy. Unsuccessful attempt to provide series of coadjutor Emperors—Augusti and Caesars).

305-312 A.D. Empire divided among many claimants. Civil wars.

312-337 A.D. *Constantine the Great* ruler of the West. Toleration of Christianity.

323 A.D. *Constantine* overthrows Licinius, Emperor of the East.

330 A.D. *Constantine* founds Constantinople.

375 A.D. Beginnings of Teutonic Migrations into the Empire.

378 A.D. Goths slay the Emperor Valens at Adrianople.

379-395 A.D. *Theodosius the Great* (at first rules only the East; in 394 recovers the West; *last reunion of East and West* 394-5); barbarians checked.

395-423 A.D. *Honorius* (son of Theodosius), Emperor of the West.

395-408 A.D. *Arcadius* (son of Theodosius), Emperor of the East. Permanent division of Empire.

410 A.D. *Alaric plunders Rome.*

476 A.D. *End of Western Roman Empire* (steady loss of provinces through preceeding seventy years).

1453 A.D. End of Eastern Empire at Constantinople.

Note on the Values assigned Roman Money.

In the course of this book the following values are usually assigned the money therein discussed.

Sesterce=4 cents.

Denarius=16 cents.

Talent=about $1,000.00.

I am entirely aware that these values are merely approximate, also that a given coin fluctuated from age to age, e.g., the *denarius* of Augustus weighed 60 grains, that of Nero only 52; but the nice questions involved in the valuation of ancient coins can hardly be taken up in a book like this, and it is not likely that any reader will be led into serious error.

CHAPTER I

OF the year 33 A.D. it may possibly have been recorded in the diaries of certain Roman business men, that there was a disturbance in the remote province of Judaea—a tumult quickly quelled by the energy of his excellency Pontius Pilate, the governor, who seized and crucified one Christus, the chief malcontent, and two bandits, his accomplices. It is more probable, however, that they only remembered this year as marking one of the severest panics which ever shook the foundations of Roman credit.

As with most panics, the causes of this were not obvious. About a year before, the firm of Seuthes & Son of Alexandria, lost three richly laden spice ships on the Red Sea in a hurricane. Their ventures in the Ethiopian caravan trade also were unprofitable, ostrich feathers and ivory having lately fallen in value. It soon began to be rumored that they might be obliged to suspend. A little later the well known purple house of Malchus & Company (centered at Tyre, but with factories at Antioch and Ephesus) suddenly became bankrupt; a strike among their Phoenician workmen, and the embezzlements of a trusted freedman manager being the direct causes of the disaster. Presently it became evident that the great Roman banking house of Quintus Maximus & Lucius Vibo had loaned largely to both Seuthes and Malchus. The depositors, fearing for their

1

money, commenced a run on the bank, and distrust spread because men, experienced on the Via Sacra (the first century Wall Street), said that the still larger house of the Brothers Pettius was also involved with Maximus & Vibo. The two threatened establishments might still have escaped disaster had they been able to realize on their other securities. Unfortunately the Pettii had placed much of their depositors' capital in loans among the noblemen of the Belgae in North Gaul. In quiet times such investments commanded very profitable interest; but an outbreak among that semi-civilized people caused the government to decree a temporary suspension of processes for debt. The Pettii were therefore left with inadequate resources. Maximus & Vibo closed their doors first; but that same afternoon the Pettii did likewise. Grave rumors obtained that, owing to the interlacing of credits, many other banks were affected. Still the crisis might have been localized, had not a new and more serious factor been introduced.

In a laudable desire to support the Italian agricultural interest—then in a most declining way—the Senate, with the assent of Tiberius, the emperor, had ordered one third of every senator's fortune to be invested in lands within Italy. Failure to comply with the ordinance invited prosecution and heavy penalties. The time allowed for readjustment had almost expired, when many rich senators awoke to the fact that they had not made the required relocation of their fortunes. To find capital to buy land, it was necessary for them to call in all their private loans and deposits at the bankers. Publius Spinther, a wealthy nobleman, particularly was obliged to notify Balbus & Ollius, his bankers, that they must find the 30,000,000 sesterces he had deposited with them two years before. Two days later Balbus & Ollius had closed their doors, and their bankruptcy was

being entered before the praetor. The same day a notice
in the *Acta Diurna*, the official gazette posted daily in the
Forum, told how the great Corinthian bank of Leu-
cippus' Sons had gone into insolvency. A few days
later it was heard that a strong banking house in Carthage had suspended. After this all the surviving banks
on the Via Sacra announced that they must have timely
notice before paying their depositors. The safe arrival
of the corn fleet from Alexandria caused the situation at
the capital to brighten temporarily; but immediately
afterward came news that two banks in Lyons were
"rearranging their accounts," as the euphemism ran;
likewise another in Byzantium. From the provincial
towns of Italy and the farming districts, where creditors
had long allowed their loans to run at profitable interest,
but were now suddenly calling in their principals, came
cries of keen distress and tidings of bankruptcy after
bankruptcy. After this nothing seemed able to check
the panic at Rome. One bank closed after another.
The legal 12% rate of interest was set at nought by any
man lucky enough to possess ready money. The praetor's
court was crowded with creditors demanding the auction-
ing of the debtor's houses, slaves, warehouse stock, or
furniture. The auctions themselves were thinly attended,
for who could buy? Valuable villas and racing studs
were knocked down for trifles. Caught in the disaster,
many men of excellent credit and seemingly ample fortune
were reduced to beggary. The calamity seemed spreading over the Empire, and threatening a stoppage of all
commerce and industry, when Gracchus, the praetor,
before whom the majority of the cases in bankruptcy
came, at his wits' end to decide between the hosts of
desperate debtors and equally desperate creditors,
resorted to the Senate-house; whence, after a hurried
debate, the Conscript Fathers dispatched a fast mes-

senger with a full statement of the danger to their lord and master Tiberius, in his retreat at Capri.

While the Caesar's reply was awaited, the business world of the capital held its breath. Four days after the dispatch from the Senate, an imperial courier came pricking back from Campania. The Senate assembled in the Curia with incredible celerity. A vast throng—slaves and millionaires elbowing together—filled the Forum outside, while the Emperor's letter was read, first to the Senate, then from the open Rostrum to the waiting people. Tiberius had solved the problem with his usual calm, good sense. The obnoxious decrees were for the time to be suspended; 100,000,000 ses. were to be taken from the imperial treasury and distributed among reliable bankers, to be loaned to the neediest debtors; no interest to be collected for three years; but security was to be offered of double value in real property. The law being relaxed, and the most pressing cases cared for by the government loan, private lenders began to take courage and offer money at reasonable rates. Dispatches from Alexandria, Carthage and Corinth indicated that the panic had been stayed in those financial centers. The moneyed world of the Via Sacra began to resume its wonted aspect. A few banking houses and individuals never recovered from their losses, but the majority escaped permanent suspension—and so the panic of the "Consulship of Galba and Sulla," i.e. of 33 A.D., passed into half-forgotten history.

Such—a little expanded from Tacitus and Suetonius —is the tale of the great panic under the third Caesar. A narrative like this would have no verisimilitude unless placed in a society extending over seas and continents, with a great internal and foreign commerce, rapid means of communication, complex and vast credit transactions, an elaborate system of banking; in other words, with conditions not unlike many of those of the twentieth century. Great was the Roman Empire—in its military glory, its system of law and administration, its preservation of the artistic and intellectual heritage from Greece, its elimination of clan patriotism and local prejudices— but it was also great, in that it fostered the development of an economic life such as has not come again to the world until very recent times. It is of this Roman commerce, communication, banking, credit, and of a society largely founded on such a "money basis," that we propose to write.

CHAPTER II

1. *The Increasing Scramble for Wealth.*

"WITH us the most reverend majesty is that of
Riches: even though, Foul Lucre! thou dwellest
in no temple, and we have not reared altars to Coin, as we
have for the worship of Peace and Faith, Victory, Virtue
and Concord." Thus the satirist Juvenal writes one
hundred and fifty years after the Roman Republic had
become the Roman Empire. He might have written the
same words in praise of the *"sanctissima divitiarum
majestas,"* whether he had lived in the days of Cicero or
in those of Theodosius I. Claudian and Ammianus.
Marcellinus give ample witness that the scramble after
wealth—honest or fraudful,—the tricks of the legacy
hunter, the client, the parasite, lasted down to the last
glitter of the Empire. At all ages of Rome, after the
Republic went forth conquering and to conquer, this love
for Mammon existed, and we can discover it almost at its
worst a hundred years before Julius Caesar toppled
down the decayed edifice of the Republic.

The Roman seemingly was in all his business relations more devoid of sentiment than the most abused
Semite. He was in money matters either oppressor or
oppressed, either hammer or anvil. In his private life
his sympathies extended only to a very narrow circle of
associates. His instincts as a moral being were always

6

subordinate to his instincts as a financier, and a financier whose code was that of unmitigated commercialism. If he kept his old Latin religion—and with the spread of Greek philosophy in Italy it is likely he did not,—he regarded the gods as he did his customers and commercial correspondents. He gave so much in prayer and sacrifice, in return for which he expected a given amount of favor. If the divine favor was not forthcoming, heaven had broken its contract; and it was a misfortune that the faithless god could not be brought into court to be compelled to make good his promise or refund the offering.

The average Roman indeed realized that from a selfish standpoint "honesty was the best policy;" even if his honesty was usually of a deplorably narrow and literal kind. Nevertheless, the love of gain and of the enjoyments which followed gain, too often blunted his vision utterly; and made him a harsh father, an unfilial son, a faithless husband, a brutal master, a corrupt citizen. At his best a Roman could rise to the heights of civic and personal virtue. At his worst, he could show examples of avarice, cruelty and vice to the basest peoples he had conquered. To what a condition the "gilded youth" of Rome could come was well shown during the great proscription conducted by the Second Triumvirs (43 B.C.). One Thoranus, an ex-praetor, had been denounced. He pleaded with the centurion, come to slay him, to delay until his son, a favorite of Marcus Antonius, could beg him mercy. "He has already appealed," laughed the officer, "but on the other side." The son, in other words, had sought the reward offered the betrayers of the proscribed. The old man called for his daughter, begged her not to claim her share of the inheritance after he was dead, or her brother would ask for her life, too,—then submitted to his doom.

The causes which made tragedies like this possible lie outside the scope of this volume. Whether the Romans would have continued chaste, honest, and simple, had they never spread their dominions beyond Italy, is a question no historian can answer. "I do not know," writes Florus, "whether it would have been better for the Roman people to have been content with Sicily and Africa, or even to have been without them, while still enjoying Italy, than to grow to such greatness as to be ruined by their own strength. For what else produced those intestine distractions but excessive good fortune?" And he adds that it was the Conquest of Asia from Antiochus the Syrian, presently followed by the annexation of the Kingdom of Pergamus, which wrought the special havoc in the old-time morality and simplicity.

It is perfectly certain that in the second century B.C. the Romans changed from a people predominantly agricultural to one predominantly commercial. The change —as will be explained in later chapters—wrought grievous harm to Italy, and ultimately to the whole world. The ruling Roman classes ceased to ask how much they could get out of the soil, and asked how much they could get out of their subjects. The Forum, and the basilicas around it, became a regular stock exchange; the most influential men in the state were directly or indirectly the speculators. A few steps from his banker's stalls brought the Roman nobleman to the Curia, where as an august senator he and his class handed down decrees enforced by the legions upon Syria or Spain. The commercial motives in public policy were often highly obvious. Corinth and Carthage were both destroyed in 146 B.C. Both were dangerous commercial and financial rivals. The fear of Carthaginian moneylenders, competing with Roman money-lenders, was at least equal to the dread of the rise of a second Hannibal.

The removal of these great cities drove capital to Rome more than ever before. Her only real commercial equal now was Alexandria; and Alexandria was remote, and circumstances made her more an ally than an enemy to the money-kings by the Tiber.

The process of commercializing the Romans, which had begun probably before the Second Punic War, went on through the later Republic, and reached a climax in the Age of Augustus. By that time the old noble families had largely run out. Their scions, who had not earned but had inherited riches, were more anxious for spending than for getting. Luxury and squandering rose to ever greater excesses, and culminated under Nero. After him several things began to produce a reaction. The emperors undertook to set a more frugal example; the Stoic philosophy and, more slowly, Christianity, began to establish other ideals than those of getting and enjoying. The high-born families who had amassed the riches had nearly all died out, thanks to a childlessness caused by luxurious living and to the slaughters of the civil wars and of the tyrants; and property was passing into the hands of ex-slaves and provincials who had a juster knowledge of the use of riches.

Unfortunately the leaven that had begun to work among the Roman upper classes during the Republic, had spread into the whole social lump. The ex-slaves and subject nations had now learned, if not before, to worship the golden god so eagerly invoked by their masters. Under the Empire the forms and expressions of the commercial spirit changed in some details from those under the Republic. The underlying essence was the same. Money continued to be the leading power in the world until the coming of the barbarians and of Christianity.

* * * * * * *

To justify the broad generalizations of the preceding paragraphs, it will be necessary to examine the influence of money upon the forms of human interest and activity usual in the Roman Age. By the Roman Age is meant the last century of the Republic, and the first two centuries of the Empire. We are not concerned with the Romans while they were purely an Italian power, before they became the dominators, and finally actual masters of the ancient world. Again, when we pass too far beyond the Age of the Antonines we find forces intruding themselves into the Empire that are distinctly alien to the genius of Ancient Society. We have nothing to do with the economic development of the early Church, or with the institutions of the invading barbarians, although occasionally a reference to conditions in the third, fourth or fifth centuries will be illuminating. On the other hand, to understand how the money power stretched its tentacles over society one must examine many things apart from mere financiering. One must ask how the money power affected marriage, home life, slavery, the getting and holding of public office. One must examine ancient benevolence and its tendencies. In short, the question must be, how did money or the "sense" of money affect the relations of man to man? Thus there need be no apologies for discussions that seem to touch only slightly on the fortunes of Crassus and the poverty of Manes.

2. *Bribery and Political Corruption.*

If a state becomes thoroughly commercialized, this fact will probably betray itself in the public life. It will be increasingly difficult for officials to quit office with clean hands. The receipt of what is to-day called "graft" will affect both magistrates and citizens. If this tendency to make the public loss the private gain is not ultimately checked, it is likely there will be needed some violent change in the structure of government by which political bribery and corruption will be left less opportunity for their sinister work. Not all the evils that cursed the dying Roman Republic were due to this illicit passing of money. Not a few of the oligarchs who did their best to make the rule of the Roman Senate intolerable went through their public careers without directly filching or unlawfully receiving a denarius. This can be said of Cato Minor, of Cicero, of a good many more. On the other hand, Julius Caesar, the founder of the better regime of the Empire, would undoubtedly have assented to Walpole's alleged maxim, that "all men have their price." He bought up votes and opposing statesmen shamelessly—witness his purchase of Curio; and probably the other leaders of the democratic party were no more free from malpractices than their senatorial opponents.

But the direct influence of money upon elections in the Comitia, upon questions of policy in the Senate, or upon the relations of Rome with foreign princes, commenced almost as soon as Rome became a great power, and hardly ended when the Empire dissolved the phantom of a "Free Republic." And even under the Caesars, who shall say that the bribe to the prominent palace official, the confidential freedman-secretary, did not often have as great effect on the public weal as the direct purchase of so many thousand *quirites* in the Comitia of the days of Pompeius?

The Second Punic War—that gigantic contest which actually decided the destinies of the ancient world—gave opportunity for the rich men of the Republic, as well as for its soldiers, to display their patriotism. On one occasion when the government was in the most direful financial straits, the Roman moneyed classes came forward with a large loan to replenish the empty treasury, on no other security than a bare promise to repay when the government had the money; while other companies undertook the public works which had been suspended, and told the bankrupt state they would expect repayment when the war was over.

Such exhibitions of disinterested patriotism were seldom afterwards called for. From the day when the great war indemnity wrung out of Carthage began to fill the Roman treasury, whatever else the Senate's government lacked, it seldom lacked money. The public service, especially the foreign service, with its chances for the plunder of conquered kings, the loot of conquered cities, the "gifts" of trembling Asiatics and Greeklings, was no longer likely to cost the general or propraetor a farthing; on the contrary, he was an exceptional man if he laid down his unsalaried office without being far wealthier than when he took it up. In 171 B.C. occurred the first case of a Roman official—a commissioner to Illyria—taking bribes from a foreign potentate; an example only too eagerly followed by the succeeding generations, until the scandals culminated in Jugurtha's bribery of a large fraction of the actual rulers of Rome (111 B.C.), and his memorable words as he cast his eyes backward when quitting the sovereign city, *"Urbem venalem, et mature perituram, si emptorem invenerit."*

Unfortunately for Jugurtha he did not possess treasures enough to purchase *all* his enemies; and he discovered too late that there were limits at Rome beyond which even gold could not carry him. But while bribery was often a determining factor in the Republic's foreign relations, the influence of money was equally decisive upon home politics. A great noble craved office to enrich himself by a war, an embassy, a governorship. An Italian farmer craved the franchise more humbly to fatten on the favors handed him for electing the great noble to office. The results were almost inevitable.

The abuses of the *Ambitus*—the canvassing for election—were patent to the Roman fathers before the city ceased to be a weak commonwealth. The custom of a candidate's walking around the Forum, saluting the farmers come to trade, and asking their votes, was not to be supplemented by adventitious helps. Thus in 432 B.C. a law forbade such candidates from wearing a conspicuous white dress to attract attention. In 358 B.C., they were forbidden to go about on market days when the people would be especially thronged together. These laws appeared to be sufficient for nearly two centuries; then it seemed that their edge needed to be sharpened. In 181 B.C. a new law declared that persons convicted of illicit convassing should be ineligible as candidates for ten years. Here matters were again allowed practically to sleep, while the laws themselves insufficient, considering the highly organized party-system developing at Rome, were more honored in the breach than in the observance. Finally in the last two decades of the Republic the trading in votes rose to such a height that the law was repeatedly strengthened—though, it would seem, to deplorably little purpose. By an act of 67 B.C. the "treating" of voters was made punishable; in 63 B.C. (the year of Cicero's consulship) the penalty for violating this act was set at ten years of exile; it was also forbidden to candidates to give any public games for the two years previous to standing for office, or to hire persons to attend them while they made their rounds of vote seeking. In 55 B.C. a new law struck at what was probably the most flagrant form of corruption—a form that to an American has a painfully familiar aspect. The wealthy candidate would quietly arrange for his election to the desired office with a band of political

"go-betweens" (*interpretes*). These professional gentlemen would proceed to mark out the Roman tribes into
smaller and more wieldy sections, arrange the voters
into clubs and fraternities, compound with each section
for its votes, marshal the faithful henchmen to the electoral comitia, and duly pay over the stipulated honorarium upon delivery of the election. The details of such
arrangements were—it may be imagined—seldom committed to writing. We are left to guess at the workings
of these voters' collegia by a few hints from Cicero. It
is sufficient to remark that under the later Republic
almost any man of noble family and deep purse seems
to have been able to rise fairly high in the scale of offices,
provided he was willing to spend freely. In times of
great excitement, to be sure, mere money might fail to
prevail against an approved party leader; but the latter,
it can be assumed, would himself hardly prove niggardly.[1]
The law of 55 B.C., declared these voters' collegia unlawful, and arranged special methods for trying offenders
against the election statutes. That this new law was
ineffectual is shown by still another act in 52 B.C., against
political clubs, making the penalties still heavier. Soon
after this came the Caesarian regime, and elections
became mere registrations of the will of Julius Caesar,
and later of the Triumvirs. Under Augustus[2] a modi-
cum of freedom returned to the electoral comitia, and
that the old methods were being pursued and the old
evils returning, is shown by the law of 18 B.C., which
required a candidate, before beginning his canvass, to

---

[1] The large number of annual offices at this date—those of two consuls, ten tribunes, eight praetors, four aediles and twenty quaestors—
gave an ample opportunity for the candidate to find at least one post
to which he could be elected.

[2] Augustus ought to have had knowledge of bribes and bribers. His
own father had been a professional agent to distribute the fees among
the voters at the Campus Martius.

deposit 100,000 sesterces as security that he would keep the laws. With the death of Augustus, however, and the transfer of the elections by Tiberius from the Comitia to the Senate, election bribery practically ceased to be a crime. At least if a Roman Father was open to a gratuity from a candidate, the consideration would be conveyed in a way too delicate for the law to find an entrance.

It would be easy to present details of the venality of the Roman government during the later Republic. The notorious case (61 B.C.) of the trial of Clodius for sacrilege, when thirty-one judges out of fifty-six voted him "not guilty" of a crime all knew he had committed, is a good instance of the way gold could blind the eyes of Roman *judices*. The manner in which the infamous Egyptian King, Ptolemaeus Auletes, bought the friendship of the Senate in 58 B.C., was almost as glaring as the bribery by Jugurtha. Too often the person to buy was not the voter or the influential party leader, but the party leader's mistress. This was true in the instance of the concubine of that Verres, whose knaveries were immortalized by Cicero; and of Praecia, the mistress of Cethegus, a powerful tribune, whose favor was necessary to Lucullus when he wished the Cilician province.

The gifts an Asiatic prince might be expected to send a Roman general and his staff, can only be compared to the fortunes acquired by the Anglo-Indian "nabobs" in the days of Clive and Hastings. Even petty potentates would pay richly for the privilege of keeping life and power. Thus Aristobulus, a Jewish Prince, sent Pompeius a golden vine worth 500 talents; he gave a legate, A. Gabinius, 300, a quaestor 400 talents. Ptolemaeus "Mennai," lord of a robber state in Lebanon, bought immunity for himself from Pom-

peius for 1,000 talents, which—with unusual honesty for
a Roman general—Pompeius used to pay his troops.
Ariobarzanes of Cappadocia paid the same conqueror
thirty-three talents monthly, which, however, did not
reach to the interest on his debts. Gabinius again while
proconsul of Syria pressed out of the province 400,000,-
000 sesterces. Finally Crassus the Rich is said to have
taken from the Temple of Jerusalem, treasure worth
10,000 talents.

These great hoards, however, could not, in the
nature of things, come to every general and governor.
These had a far more reliable mine in the regular
pickings which all Roman officials could find among the
rich and unfortunate subject-populations in their provinces.

3. *The Plundering by Governors in the Provinces.*

From the first conquest of Sicily the Romans admin-
istered their provinces with no altruistic notions as to
the uplifting of the governed. The provinces were so
many farms of the sovereign people. The only question was how to raise the largest possible crops of
tribute. Should the new farm be forced, its soil quickly
exhausted by a few huge harvests, or should it be carefully cultivated, preferring smaller but permanent
returns? The question seemed merely one of expe-
diency. It was only after bitter experience that the
rulers of the ancient world could assent to the Emperor
Tiberius's maxim,—"a good shepherd clips his sheep,
but does not flay them."

Sent forth to govern while such motives obtained at
home, it required more than ordinary strength of
character on the part of a pro-magistrate not to extend
also to the filling of his private coffer, the mandate to fill
the public aerarium. With him would go a suite of

friends, usually young spendthrifts, and with their fortunes to make. If he and they were truly honest, still they would return after one to three years with their fortunes vastly bettered. If they were men of easy consciences they would return, as Varus—the victim of Arminius—did from Syria, who "as a poor man entered a rich country, as a rich man left the country poor."

As early as 198 B.C. Cato, the censor, had to put a stop to certain unjust exactions in Sardinia. In 171 B.C. delegates from the two Spains made formal complaint in the Senate of the avarice and insolence of their governors. Before this there had been outcry from the Ambraciots of Greece and the Cenomani of Gaul. In 149 B.C. came the *Lex Calpurnia,* the first of the almost fruitless laws devised to prevent provincial oppression.

As a rule the Roman governor—especially if he was set over the more civilized, hence more wealthy and desirable provinces—had little to fear from that usual check to despotism—the revolt of the oppressed. In the East the Diodochi and their long series of wars and tyrannies had almost stamped out the sentiment of local patriotism, and it is a fair question whether the rule of the average Roman governor was worse than that of the average local despot to which those regions had been accustomed. Greece, the one country where local spirit ought to have been strong, had been emasculated by the great draughts on her population for the Hellenistic colonies and armies, and by the systematic pressure from Macedonia. The defeat at Sellasia in 221 B.C. of Cleomenes of Sparta ended perhaps the last genuine attempt of the home *Hellenes* to live for themselves, and to pursue their own policy; forAratus and Philopoemen were barely able to keep their much vaunted Achaean League from becoming the victim of Macedonia; and the deathlike quiet that settled over Greece after the destruction

of Corinth (146 B.C.) shows how little political vitality
was left in a country which three centuries before had
seemed one high-school of active politics. That Roman
misrule might be resented, could be shown by the ready
welcome Mithridates of Pontus received from the Greek
and Asiatic cities; but, except as the help came from
without, things seldom passed beyond mere grumblings.
It was usually cheaper and safer to pay the fee to the
Roman governor and his quaestor than to engage in
conspiracies against the power which had worn down
the genius of Hannibal. Besides, as was said—bad as
were Roman governors—the dynasts preceding them had
been very bad also. The woes of the Jews arose largely
because of the misdeeds of the houses of the Maccabees
and of the Herods. Those Agrippas who held sway over
much of Palestine down to the great Jewish War, had
to pay tribute to Rome and support their own ostentatious courts—no small expense for the governed; which
expense partly ended when the royal household with its
harem, eunuchs and greedy chamberlains was replaced
by the simpler praetorium of a Roman governor. The
average proconsul, in short, could seldom oppress to the
extent of a covetous, unscrupulous, degenerate princelet
only indirectly under the supervision of Rome.

And yet the oppression of the provinces, those "estates
of the Roman people" (*praedia populi Romani*), was
very great. The provincial was regularly spoken of as
a *stipendarius,* "the man who must pay." If he was to
be defended from attack and fostered, it was only
because leaving him defenseless cut off his sovereign's
revenue. The governors sent out to him were clothed
with the power of Turkish pashas. In theory the governor was not allowed to purchase anything in his province "because," we are naïvely informed by Cicero, "it
was thought a theft, not a purchase, when the seller

could not sell at his own price"; for a governor would be able to take anything he pleased whether for sale or not, once he began to purchase. A Lucius Piso, governor of Further Spain, having lost a ring, sent for a goldsmith to come to his tribunal in the open Forum at Corduba, weighed out the necessary gold, and had the man make the ring in the sight of every one; but that an honest governor should feel the need of such precautions is a sorry comment on the general practice. A new governor, in fact, entering his province, came to his subjects almost as a strange demi-god, who might prove to be a benefactor or a demon. They would await eagerly his "edict"—his announcement of his attitude towards the dreaded tax-farmers and money-lenders, and as to how he would deal with the matter of usury. Would he exact the *aurum aedilicium,* a supposedly voluntary offering, sent from the provincial cities to pay for the aediles' games at Rome?[1] Finally, would he exact large fees from litigants, and consistently give the judgment to the man with the freest purse?

In theory a governor was usually sent out for one year only—time enough to amass a fair fortune; but the supply of eligible ex-consuls and ex-praetors was so small that with a little managing at Rome the term was usually prolonged.[2] Verres held Sicily three years; Fonteius, Gaul for three; Quintus Cicero, Asia for three; Marcus Cicero held Cilicia only one, but he had much trouble in getting away at that time, when he wished to be in Rome, and finally had to leave a deputy. In those years the new pasha could suck his victims and grow fat; to

---

[1] Caelius seems to have written to his friend Cicero, begging for some of this money from the Cilician cities, as if it were a dependable income.

[2] In Cicero's day there were two consuls, eight praetors and fourteen provinces; while not all of these officials would desire to go at once abroad.

repeat the boast of Verres in Sicily—in the first year he could gain enough for himself, in the second enough to reward the friends who got him the office, in the third enough to silence the accusers and mollify the judges, should he be brought to trial for oppression at the end of his service. If the governor did not find mere presents from timid cities and fees from wealthy litigants sufficient, he had plenty of other means of oppression. A favorite means of inducing the money to flow out of the strong boxes of provincials was found in the quartering of troops upon them—dragonades worthy of Louis XIV. It would sometimes be stipulated in city charters (*e.g.* Thermesus in Pisidia) that this should not be done without the special vote of the Senate; but not many communities were so favored. The provincials usually avoided this calamity by regular payments to their ruler. This was done by the rich towns of Cilicia, and Cicero tells how the people of Cyprus set aside two hundred talents for the purpose. At Salamis in Cyprus there was a "Praetor's Fund," a sum appropriated yearly by the municipality to buy the good will of the governor. When Cicero refrained from taking it, the astonished burghers used the money for paying the city debt.

The laws upon *repetundae,* for the recovery or punishment of sums extorted from provincials, were sufficiently numerous, but so long as the Republic lasted about equally ineffective. The evil governor could only be attacked at the *end* of his period of rule, when the plunder was in the thief's possession. He was tried before a numerous jury, usually containing a large percentage of ex-magistrates as corrupt as he, or of Roman Knights—who, as will be made plain, might be still more corrupt. His conviction as a rule depended as much on the political influence of his chief accuser—the Roman advocate who undertook the provincials' cause—as on the evidence. If he was convicted, he had usually to fear only an easy exile, and a fine that was but a fraction of his plunderings. Therefore, while in power he could wisely gamble upon immunity at the end of his office, and regard it as exceptional cruelty of fortune—as no doubt Verres did—if some Cicero, able, eloquent, and unbribable, stood across his path finally to bring him to partial justice.

We hear of a good many trials for maladministration in the provinces, but except in Verres's case it is seldom that we feel the verdict was a just one. Many guilty men were acquitted. In at least one case an upright governor was convicted because he had not allowed his subalterns and the ubiquitous Roman tax-farmers and usurers to plunder the provincials in his name. With the coming of the Empire much is changed. The emperor is wise enough to know that if the provinces are his farms, no one must grow rich from them but himself. Governors are his agents. They are given ample salaries. Let them not then steal from their employer's property! If there is a fair case against them, a trial before the Senate is certain, and the presiding Caesar will see to it that there is no undue leniency.

In all of Tacitus, and of the younger Pliny, we find that twenty-seven governors were set on trial for misrule; of these only seven were acquitted, perhaps justly. Under the Republic the conditions had been practically reversed.

How much could a provincial governor gain during a term of office? Fortunately we are well informed about Cicero and his year in Cilicia. He was supposed to serve without salary, and to levy only enough in money and kind to cover his expenses and no more. Cicero was an extraordinarily honest Roman. He made fair boasts of how he turned away tempting perquisites. His province—Cilicia—was small and poor compared with many others. He was only in it a year. Yet he brought back from Cilicia 2,100,000 sesterces, or counting the difference in purchasing power of coin, say $250,000 to-day. Cicero was an "honest" governor—how much could one less scrupulous make in three years!

Cicero surely did not make full use of his opportunities. The fashionable circles at Rome were so certain that he would come back princely rich that Tullia, the proconsul's daughter, was beset by noble young suitors who wished her hand—and her father's plunder. We are left to imagine their disgust when Cicero returned with only his beggarly two millions.

Cilicia, however, if it received a year of respite, was destined soon to disgorge all the wealth that this over-lenient governor had neglected to take away. In 43 B.C., Cassius, Caesar's murderer, descended on the province. He was engaged in a life and death struggle with Antonius and Octavius the avengers. Under the justification of extreme public peril, his exactions rose to sheer confiscation. At Tarsus he ruthlessly quartered soldiers on the city folk till the huge sum of 1,500 talents had been paid. The miserable citizens sold all the public property, coined all the sacred vessels and precious ornaments in the temples, and finally the despairing magistrates "sold free persons into bondage, first boys and girls, later women and wretched old men, who brought a very small price, and finally young men. Many of these committed suicide." Finally Cassius' heart "was touched" (did he have true scruples, or did he fear a desperate insurrection?). He remitted a part of the contribution, and presently marched away to his doom. In the great province of Asia during this destructive civil war the contributions levied by both sides were almost as merciless.

It has been said that the rule of the emperors in the provinces was milder and juster than that of the Republic. This is true; but all abuses were by no means at an end. In Tiberius' reign the formidable revolt of Julius Florus and Julius Sacrovis in Gaul was directly traceable to "the excessive debts of the states of Gaul," and the rebel agitators argued against the domineering and cruelty of the government, and "the tribute without end and the excessive usury" of the Romans. Juvenal, writing about 100 A.D., again would have one feel that "the very marrow is drained from the empty bones of kings"; that it is folly to complain at Rome; that the governor's wife often abuses her influence; that the lictors' rods and axes are always busy, and that judgments are sold for bribes. But this, in his age, we can say on better authority than his statement, was the exception, not the rule. Under the early Empire the average governor was not a great extortioner; but, better than that for the provincials, the still more grievous exactions of the tax-farmers and Roman money-lenders were largely curbed or swept away. What these crying evils were under the later Republic it is now time to see.

4. *The Tax-Farmers and Usurers Under the Republic.*

If it were possible to find complete statistics of the money unjustly wrung from the provinces and communities subject to Rome, it is very probable that while the extortions of the governors would appear great, the extortions of the Roman tax-farmers and money-lenders would be found greater.

The rulers of the Republic were fond to a marked degree of the practice of farming out the revenues. The method certainly had advantages. Each pair of cen-

sors could readjust the state finances for five years.
For this *lustrum* the government receipts could be estimated to a certainty, and consequently the expenditures
arranged to match. The income of the Republic came
largely from lands—held in Italy, or in the conquered
provinces. The petty business details, the rent collecting and the like, could be done much better by the
experienced agents of the great tax-farming syndicates
than by the kid-gloved, noble magistrates who did not
like the smell of vulgar business. So long as Roman
domains were small, and a reasonable watch could be
kept over the doings of the tax-farmers, their system
was not open to very gross abuses.

But when the provinces rose one by one to fourteen;
when shares in one of the five-year tax-syndicates became
a favorite form of investing much of the floating capital
at Rome, it was inevitable that the system—unless carefully supervised—should become a burden, and very
often a frightful curse to the provincials.

The tax-farming companies early in the second century B.C. had become large and powerful. The shareholders were many—influential politicians, still more
influential capitalists. The Senate in 184 B.C. undertook
to cancel the tax-farming contracts, awarded by the
censors, as unjust to the successful bidders, and it is a
reasonable guess that some of the Conscript Fathers
were indirect shareholders and feared for their profits.

As the Roman dominions grew, the tax-farming contracts grew correspondingly. The *publicani* bid in
almost every state monopoly. The right to take oysters
in the Lucrine lake was held by a syndicate; the right to
work the salt mines,[1] the gold mines, the forests, to collect the customs revenues—all fell into this category.

---

[1] This was an extremely old monopoly, perhaps the most ancient in
Rome. Its beginnings have been dated back as far as 508 B.C.

But the most important business was undoubtedly the collection of the land taxes, especially in the conquered provinces.

The Romans had formed the convenient theory that most of the subjected territories had become the real as well as the political property of the conquerors. In place then of mere *taxes,* the unlucky provincials were now required to pay the new owners *rent* for the lands of which they remained mere tenants. Being tenants, it was largely a matter of condescension on the part of their landlords if the rentals were not made ruinously high. The technical details of the provincial system of taxation under the Republic are of no moment here. Suffice it that a system of rentals like the above was open to the gravest abuses, and that it was left for the tax-farmer practically to be his own assessor; to determine how much the provincial ought to pay, then to collect it. If the tax-farmer had been caught in brisk competition before the censors, and had his bid run up to dangerously high figures, his temptation to ensure against loss by arbitrary assessments would naturally be overpowering. It is true the contract with the censor determined the rate at which the publican could collect. One tenth of the produce of sown land was usually set apart for him; one fifth from the planted. A shepherd must pay so many lambs or kids out of his flocks, etc. The governor was supposed to act in the manner of arbiter between publican and tax-payer. He was to restrain the extortionate collector, to coërce the laggard debtor. But considering the character and motives of the average governor, it would be easy to predict which way his influence would tend. A round present from the company would commonly close his eyes to the most systematic plundering; if he were an unwontedly scrupulous man, he could be reminded that

the shareholders at Rome were very influential and
that his political future depended on their good graces.

To the organization of these tax-farming syndicates,
the Romans brought their usual capacity for practical
business. The companies had to be formed for the five
years of the *lustrum;* at its end wound up or organized
afresh. The shares were numerous. They could be
bought directly; or loans might be made to the *socii*
(shareholders) of the company, the interest being
dependent on the success of the venture. The shareholders' liability was limited, and they could dispose of
their shares from time to time, which were subject to
the fluctuations of the market. More important, however, were the direct managers and promotors of the
concern. At Rome there must be a central manager and
banker, the *magister societatis,* elected annually, and his
account subject to yearly audit; he had a corps of secretaries and clerks under him. In the province, where the
revenue was being gathered, was the deputy of the chief,
—the *pro magister,* with more clerks. There was a staff
of regular messengers, *tabellarii,* to carry the volu-
minous correspondence necessary between the province
and the capital. The legal head of the company was
not, however, the *magister,* but the *manceps,* a financier
of repute and responsibility, who had bid in the contract
from the censors, had deposited the security for per-
forming its provisos, and who was responsible to the
government for the engagements of the company. In
the province itself, beneath the *pro magister,* would be
the actual tax gatherers, agents often native and natives
of no very high class, so odious were their duties. These
were the ill-famed "publicans" of the New Testament,
not the purple-hemmed *equites* at Rome.

As intimated, not all the *publicani* got in their handiwork in the provinces. They made the Italian custom-

houses, where they collected the *portoria,* more odious than the most exacting in the United States. Their extortions in searching for dutiable goods were notorious. "Imagine," writes Cicero to his brother, "what is the fate of our allies in the remote provinces, when even in Italy I hear the complaint of Roman citizens." In the provinces again their powers for plundering were not always equal. Tax-farming was not a new invention of the Romans. The Greeks knew of it. An elaborate system of farming the revenues is found in Ptolemaic Egypt. In Sicily the *Lex Hieronica,* instituted by King Hiero and confirmed by the Romans, fixed—so far as Sicily was involved—the tax-farming on a very careful basis. Verres to be sure in his three years of rule, let the laws be set at defiance;[1] but a commission of the Senate investigating Sicily about his time confirmed these laws as the best possible. Again, in Syria, the teeth of the *publicani* were blunted by the institution—soon after the conquest—of a fixed tax-payment. But in Sardinia, Greece, and especially the rich Asiatic provinces, their system reached its fullest development. The taxes here were merely a fluctuating tithe, and the profits through over-valuing the harvest and collecting a quota of a crop which the land had never borne can be conjectured.

The power of the *publicani* in the eastern provinces was such that Marcus Cicero deliberately tells his brother Quintus—governor of provincial Asia—to urge the natives not to stand too much upon their bare legal rights lest worse befall them.

"Wherever the publican penetrates," says Livy, solemnly, "there is no justice or liberty for any one—" unconscious, it would seem, that he was penning a griev-

[1] Verres even owned shares in the Sicilian tax syndicate, which was directly forbidden by law.

ous indictment against the Republic he so tried to glorify.

The system of tax-farming is said in some modern books to have been abolished by the emperors. This is not, strictly speaking, true. *Publicani* continued to manage the public mines and forests, and the customs duties; but the government now had a strong motive for curbing their rapacity, just as it had for curbing the governors. The substitution of direct taxation in the provinces for the collecting of an uncertain tithe through middlemen, stopped the largest channel for abuses. Nero issued edicts making the penalties for illegal exactions by the farmers more severe and certain. The system, however, had become almost hopelessly bad, so that "publicans and sinners" could indeed be grouped together in popular speech as one in kind. A tax-farmer who was honest and uncovetous was indeed such a wonder as to leave a name and fame behind him. Such a man was Sabinus, the father of Vespasian, a tax-farmer in Asia engaged in collecting "the tax of the fortieth penny." The cities of Asia erected statues to him, "to the honest publican"—a more unique honor than those heaped upon proconsuls, nay! upon emperors.

It may be presumed that some of the subordinate "publicans" of the New Testament were not agents of Rome at all, but farmers of the revenues of the vassal Herods. Whatever their origin, they all shared the popular hatred. In Rabbinical literature the tax gatherer is commonly treated as a robber. The chances of even a subordinate to grow rich by over-appraisement of articles was usually irresistible. "If I have taken any thing from any man by false accusation [as to its value] I restore him fourfold;" cries Zacchaeus, "the chief among the publicans" of Jericho, after Jesus had conversed with him; but it was not often that the stony heart of a tax gatherer was thus melted.

How the agents of the tax-farmers were regarded by the subject peoples is shown again by the ordinances of the Rabbis. Such men could give no testimony in a Jewish court of law; it was forbidden to receive gifts from them in charity. No money was to be changed at their treasury.[1] They were ranked with highwaymen and murderers, and below harlots and heathen. It was even allowed in dealing with them to swear falsely and to make false returns—to do anything in short to avoid paying their demands. And it is very possible that Jesus gave greater offense to his countrymen when he led about "Matthew the Publican" in his company, than when he refused to condemn Mary Magdalene.

If the Greeks, the Syrians, the Phrygians, and the other races under the iron heel of Rome, had left us similar records, there is no doubt similar sentiments would have pervaded them. The system, to repeat, was incurably bad. However, it was one of the chief arteries by which gold was pumped into Rome, until the city became the financial as well as the political capital of the ancient world.

The tax-farming system, nevertheless, did not stand alone. Along with it went a system of octopus-like usury which tended every year to make the vassal states and provinces more completely the helpless victims of their conqueror.

The Roman genius seems to have run to credit-transactions, banking and money handling to an extent hardly surpassed by that of the Jew. The hard-handed, hard-headed, shrewd, covetous race that had wrested the crops out of the stony soil of Latium, that had worn away the armies of Hannibal, now diverted its talents from farm-

[1] They often combined money-changing and banking with the tax-collecting.

ing and fighting to money getting, and with equal or greater success.

The trade of the usurers was not so genteel as that of the general, the magistrate, the Forum orator. A certain social stigma fell upon the money-lender, as will be explained in a later chapter; but the vast gains of his calling made it an attractive one, and *very successful* usurers could pose as boon companions of consulars and triumphators. As a class, the money-lenders were called *negotiatores*. They were usually of the equestrian order, and the line of cleavage between them and the *publicani* was never very clear. It was more genteel to farm the taxes than to lend on interest; but many a tax-farmer, if outbidden before the censors, must have spent the vacant *lustrum* in placing loans, many a lucky lender having diverted his capital to a tax syndicate. A man could not be both a *publicanus* and a *negotiator* at once, but nothing prevented him from changing his calling frequently, while sometimes the lender would be a man of great social consequence at least in a province; as Cnaeus Calidius for example, who in Sicily could entertain the governor and provincial officials seemingly on terms of equality.

As a rule, again, the *negotiator* and the *publicanus* acted together as brethren. The lender's chief booty often came in loans to provincials trying to satisfy the demands of the rapacious tax gatherers. The *negotiator* could work with less capital than the *publicanus;* he usually represented a pettier class of interests, and on very rare occasions the ambitions of the two orders clashed. Once we find Cicero writing to Atticus of how the *publicani* were demanding that the customs duties be increased, while the lenders were as anxious that they be lessened. But such conflicts are quite exceptional.

The payments and presents of vassal princes were

the richest gold mines for many Roman diplomats; but the humbler *negotiatores* found in kings and kinglets also a goodly prey. It was worth while to finance a pretender to a throne; to push his fortunes before the Senate; to induce the Roman government to "restore" him with the legions. The friendly money-lender in such cases would not let himself be forgotten. He would plunge his hands deep in the treasury of the vassal state. If, after the "restoring" general and the kindly financier had been rewarded, the luckless prince had a drachma left, and had not driven his subjects to a fresh revolt by grinding taxation, he was a happy man. Publius Sittius, a well known financier of the later Republic loaned heavily to the King of Mauretania. Brutus and Pompeius themselves did not hesitate thus to put in leading strings the unfortunate Ariobazanes III of Cappadocia.

But besides an occasional king to "assist," the negotiator could depend more surely on getting whole provincial municipalities in his debt; and woe to the city that could not repay. Nicaea in Bithynia owed 8,000,000 ses. to a ward of Cicero. Apollonia owed so much that it was worth while for the municipality to bribe the local governor with two hundred talents not to allow payment to be enforced. That loans to provincial towns were a source of grave abuses was realized at Rome. In 67 B.C. a *Lex Gabinia* was passed forbidding such lending; but the law was not enforced. The Senate also weakened it by various votes. The practice continued under the early Empire, and was one of the motives in Sacrovir's Gallic revolt, previously mentioned.

A municipality, in normal times, was surely entitled to borrow a reasonable amount of money on reasonable security. The evil came in the fact that the pressure of the *publicani* made such loans painfully frequent, and that no law regulated the rate of interest as in Italy. The community must pay its taxes; otherwise the tax gatherers supported by the governor's lictors—if need be, cohorts—would be seizing the holy statues in the local temples, and perhaps the estates of the town council. Recourse must be had to the nearest man with ready money—an Italian *negotiator,* sage, sly, unscrupulous. He would not hesitate to demand 24, 36 and even 48%. The trembling provincials could do nought but accept his terms. Henceforth they were a community of serfs. The load of interest would become intolerable. No stony Janus at the highway would be more implacable than the lender. The governor would be on his side. If by a great good providence one or two communities managed to discharge the loans before they became unendurable, many succumbed. It would have been better to have submitted to the tax gatherer and avoided several years of civic misery.

The workings of the money-lenders' system is well illustrated by a concrete case. Brutus, the tyrannicide, was one of the last individuals to be imagined soiling his hands with vulgar usury; but he was rich and possessed two friends, Scaptius and Mantinius, able to act as his agents, and keep his name from appearing too often in a profitable business. Some time before 51 B.C., the town of Salamis in Cyprus borrowed money on bond at 48% interest. Pressed for payment the town tried to raise the sum at Rome, assigning the bond as security. The Roman lenders refused to take this, since by Roman law only 12% was recoverable—insufficient, they thought, on a provincial loan.[1] Brutus' two agents, however, offered to advance the money, provided the 48% rate was authorized by a special decree of the Senate. The

---

[1] The new loan was to be negotiated at Rome, and so would be subject to local Roman law.

Conscript Fathers, influenced by the pressure Brutus could bring to bear, did pass such a decree. But a mere *senatus consultum* could not put aside a solemn Roman law, and a new decree of the Senate, the Fathers having reconsidered the matter, declared the lenders were to have no special privileges. In course of time, when Appius Claudius, Brutus' father-in-law was governor of Cilicia and Cyprus, Scaptius went out to his province and was soon made one of Claudius' praefects. He now used all means in his power to coërce the Salaminians into paying the uttermost farthing of the unlawful bond. Though the Roman Senate had practically repealed its own unconstitutional decree, Scaptius filled Salamis with cavalry, shut up the local councilors in the city hall, and kept them imprisoned there till five died of sheer starvation. When Cicero started for Cilicia and Cyprus,[1] he was met at Ephesus by a deputation from Salamis imploring his protection. He at once ordered Scaptius to send away his cavalry. Brutus meantime wrote to Cicero about "the debt due to his friends," but saying not a word as to who was the true lender. Scaptius likewise came to Cilicia begging to be re-appointed praefect, but Cicero declined to give high office to a man engaged in trade; still the proconsul told him he should have his money. By this time Cicero was aware that Brutus, his intimate friend, was the real usurer; however, he could not avoid being judge in the case of "Scaptius vs. Inhabitants of Salamis," that soon came to trial at Tarsus. That the Salaminians would have to pay something on the bond there was no doubt. But what amount? And at what interest? In his edict on assuming office Cicero had announced he would never permit more than 12% to be collected with compound interest. Scaptius claimed his 48% and produced the

[1] They formed together but one province in 51 B.C.

3

first invalid decree of the Senate justifying such a demand. But the later decree and the standing, unchangeable law was also in evidence. Cicero pointed out to Scaptius the weakness of his case, whereupon Scaptius the plaintiff, took Cicero the judge *aside,* said that it was quite so, that the town really did not owe him so much as was contended. "Let it pay him two hundred talents." Cicero then asked the deputies from Salamis how much they claimed they owed. One hundred and six talents was the answer. Scaptius protested, but the sums were verified then and there in the praetorium. The Salaminians were right. Then Scaptius again took Cicero aside and asked not to be forced to take the money. In other words Brutus's agent wanted to delay, until a new and more compliant governor would let him have his full 48%. Cicero tells us that "the request was an impudent one, but he yielded to it." He even prevented the Salaminians from depositing their money in a temple, and so stopping the heaping up of interest. He said he did this out of regard for Brutus. And thus—so far as the great orator was involved—the case ended. No doubt that noble young Stoic, Brutus, felt that his older friend had been decidedly unfriendly in not awarding the full 48%. Cicero, however, prided himself on the way he disposed of the case. As Fowler, one of Cicero's most lenient biographers remarks, "if one of the most upright of Roman governors could allow himself thus to trifle with equity, what may not be believed of the conduct of others?" "For if they do these things in a green tree, what shall be done in the dry?"

The *negotiatores* were ubiquitous; they were the Phoenicians of the first century B.C. In Africa they formed large and prosperous colonies. "All Gaul," says Cicero in his speech for Fonteius, "is full of traders—Roman citizens. No Gaul does any business without a Roman's aid.'' He avows that ''he does not declare this rashly,'' though we must never forget that it is an orator and not a statesman who is talking. They were in Egypt long before Augustus' conquest—witness that case of Gaius Rabirius Postumus, a rich money-lender, who in 55 B.C. believed he had grasped all the revenues of the Lagidae, thanks to the loans he had advanced Ptolemaeus XI, who to collect his fortune became *diocetes,* chief treasurer of Egypt, and whose extortions finally were so terrible that Ptolemaeus cast him into prison, lest the people revolt; and who with some difficulty escaped stripped to Rome, where a law-suit and banishment awaited him. And Asia Minor, with its rich and defenseless industrial cities was as fair a prey for the money-lenders as for the *publicani.* Lucullus—an honorable exception among proconsuls of Asia—tried to stand out against their rapacity. He found parents selling their children, cities their art treasures and ancestral gods. Individuals, says Plutarch, were so tortured and beset by their Roman creditors, that the very slavery they fell into was a relief. The province was groaning under the effect of Sulla's war fine of 20,000 talents. To pay this sum the provincials had turned in despair to the Roman lenders. In a few years usury and sheer outrage had swollen the alleged debt to 120,000 talents. Because Lucullus struck off their worst demands, and arranged for a fair settlement, the *negotiatores* never forgave him, ''and by their money's help'' says Plutarch, ''as they were very powerful and had many of the statesmen in their pay, they stirred up several leading men against him.''

Lucullus was finally recalled, more because he failed to bow to the financial magnates than because he could not end the Pontic War. It is to be hoped that Cicero's

fortune was not enlarged by a round fee for that speech
"Pro Manilia Lege" which did so much to send Pompeius
out to replace the money-lender's enemy.

Not every Roman money-lender, any more than every
publicanus, was invariably extortionate. Later we shall
speak again of the fortune of Atticus, Cicero's friend,
and some questionable transactions he engaged in; but
at Athens where he spent so much of his life, he delighted
to play the accommodating friend and easy creditor. He
loaned the city of Athens money for a long term, and
took no interest; and on one occasion he presented every
Athenian citizen with seven *medimni* of wheat. These,
however, are not the acts of a financier, but of a rich
benefactor. Other communities that borrowed of Atticus did not find him so obliging.

Finally it should be said that much of the business of
the *negotiatores* was, no doubt, quite legitimate. The
coming of the Empire put an end to most of the peculiar
abuses of the republican regime, nor would the mis-
doings of governors, *publicani* and usurers have permanent significance save for two reasons.

First: These abuses tended to concentrate the capital
of the world at Rome and made possible the vast fortunes and prodigal spending of the later republic and
the early Empire.

Second: These extraordinary opportunities for ill-
gained and easily gained wealth deepened the lust of
the ruling classes for money, and their willingness to
gauge honor, happiness, love, religion, in terms of
money.

The result, under the early Caesars, was a cult of
Mammon which has no counterpart in history.

CHAPTER III

1. *Prosperity of the Early Empire, and the Process of Romanization.*

O N the wall of the temple of Latopolis is the head of an Egyptian king. Above it appear to be the customary hieroglyphics of a cartouche—a royal inscription. The monarch wears the tall, pointed hat of a Pharaoh, his hands are outstretched, adoring some god of the Nile in the stilted, formal attitude inseparable from Egyptian art. An observer unlearned in the hieroglyphics might well conjecture that here was one of the mighty Ramesidae, or Thothmes the Conqueror of Syria in the days before the Exodus. A reading of the inscription, however, tells us that this is Decius, the Roman emperor whose brief reign was marked by the great persecution of the Christians, and who perished in battle with the Germanic Goths in 251 A.D.

The relief at Latopolis is then instructive. It reminds the student that the Roman Empire was not a nation but a world; that old conditions and local customs lingered long; and that it is unsafe to generalize from data secured from one part of the vast Empire as to things which obtained in the rest of it.

Nevertheless, considering its bulk and the population which entered into the huge fabric, how many jarring races, languages, creeds; how violent was the process of

assimilation; how Rome bought every acre of her empire
with her own blood and that of the conquered; it is
marvelous what unity was ultimately attained—until,
when the Empire was dissolving in wreck, the Britons
—almost the last race to bow to the legions—could
mourn the departure of those guardian eagles, which
had so long stood as the representatives of a law and
order men had never seen before.

But the process of trampling down weak and decaying nationalities had been mainly done before the corrupt
Senate passed its powers over to the abler Caesars.
The brutal cut-and-thrust of conquest had been accom-
plished by the now vanished Republic. Carthage was
conquered; Mithridates was conquered; Egypt was ripe
to fall, hardly struggling, into the hands of the heir of
Julius Caesar. Only Parthia, of all the lands within the
circle of "Antiquity," preserved a sullen independence.
Attacks might come from without, from the German and
Scythian barbarians; but a successful revolt against
Rome had become almost impossible. Vercingetorix the
Gaul was practically the last national champion to con-
front the eagles with the least hope of success, until Arminius the German should succeed where the chief of the
Averni, the king of Pontus and the general of Carthage
had failed. Come good, come ill, the ancient civilized
world must endure the fates allotted by its Roman
masters. So that world suffered during the weary
years of senatorial misrule, and suffered still more during the three civil wars of Caesar against Pompeius, of
the Triumvirs against Brutus and Cassius, and of Octavius against Marcus Antonius. The battle of Actium
(31 B.C.) did more than decide that Antonius and Cleopatra were not to transfer the center of empire from
Rome to Alexandria. The victory of Octavius was followed by a peace and prosperity that seemed almost

miraculous to men who from the first outbreak of Mithridates (88 B.C.) had forgotten what peace was in the East, while in the West war had seemed the normal condition for still longer generations. The "Closing of the Temple of Janus" was no idle ceremony. It meant that the old days of violence were at an end; that life, property and manly honor were safe; that two centuries were coming in which men could draw breath and enjoy the sunlight before the coming of the shadows of the later Empire and of the wrack of the Middle Ages.

The Romans—as has already been suggested—had been anything but merciful conquerors. Worse than the exactions of rapacious governors and *publicani* had been the levies made upon the defeated powers at the end of every war. Many instances might be cited of this wringing of vast sums from the unfortunate. At the end of the First Punic War, Carthage had been obliged to pay Rome 3,200 Euboic talents[1] in ten years. After the Second War, Carthage had to bind herself to pay 200 talents[2] per year for fifty years. And if a rich city-state like the Queen of North Africa could discharge this burden with an ease alarming to the elder Cato, the fines which the Romans collected from the eastern dynasts must have been direful to those kings' unlucky subjects. Fifteen thousand talents[3] must Antiochus the Great tell out after his defeat at Magnesia. Mithridates had to pay roundly for the peace he obtained in 84 B.C. from Sulla; but the chief punishment in this case fell on the luckless Asiatic cities that had joined his cause. Their plight after his great levy of 20,000 talents has been described. It

---

[1] Decidedly over $3,200,000.

[2] Something under $250,000.

[3] Considerably over $15,000,000.

was decades before Asia Minor recovered from the plundering.

But after the foreign wars came the civil wars. Because Roman fought Roman, did not make the lot of the provincials happier, especially if their Italian governors had espoused the losing side. Thus Antonius, after the battle of Philippi, assembled all the representatives of Asia Minor at Pergamus and informed them that though they had already given Brutus and Cassius ten years' tribute in two years, now they must pay Antonius and his army ten years' tribute in one. The abject groanings of the deputies that this demand would result in their absolute ruin resulted in the demand being reduced to nine years' tribute payable in two. How unstable property was in such countries and times; how paralyzing to all commercial and industrial enterprise were such calamities, need not be told. It is bad to be subject to rigorous inequable taxation; but civilized life becomes difficult when property rights become almost a farce.

The lot of Italy had hardly been better than the provinces. The civil wars had ruined thousands in a society where the struggle for economic independence was already fierce. The climax seemed reached in the proscription and confiscation conducted by the Second Triumvirs (43 B.C.). The confiscations then were so wholesale that it was almost impossible to find buyers. "Some," says Appian, "were ashamed to add to the burdens of the unfortunate. Others thought that such property would bring them ill luck, or that, as they were not free from dangers with their present holdings, it would be doubly dangerous to increase them. Only the boldest spirits dared to purchase. Thus it befell that the Triumvirs, who had hoped to realize enough for all their war preparations, fell short by 20,000,000 drach-

mas.[1] To make good the deficit, fourteen hundred of
the richest women had been ordered to put a large portion of their property at the disposal of the rapacious
government, a proceeding which caused such a feminine
protest[2] that the number of women liable was reduced
from fourteen hundred to four hundred; and all men
possessing over 400,000 sesterces[3] were ordered to lend
the triumvirs one fiftieth of their property, and contribute one year's income to the cost of the war against
Brutus and Cassius.

Some years later when Octavius was very popular,
and was just beginning his war on Antonius to defend
the honor of Rome, he ventured again to lay on his
countrymen the incredibly heavy war tax of 25% of the
income of all real estate owned by freemen; and 12½%
of the entire property of ex-slaves.

Then after the wars, the contributions, the taxes and
confiscations came peace; and for a time men forgot
that great calamities could ever return to vex the world.

The greatness of the gift of the *Pax Romana* by
Augustus is hard to realize in an age when war is happily the exception not the rule. In the second Caesar's
own day men cheerfully recognized the boon. Late in
his life the *Princeps* was chancing to sail by the bay of
Puteoli. The passengers and sailors of a ship of Alexandria, just then arrived, came to him, clad in white,
and with chaplets on their heads, loading him with
praises and glad acclamation. "By you," they cried,
"we live, by you we sail securely; by you we enjoy our

---

[1] About $3,200,000.

[2] The triumvirs ordered their lictors to drive a band of ladies, come
to protest, from their tribunal; but the mob took up the women's cause,
the lictors hesitated, and the triumvirs reconsidered.

[3] About $16,000.

liberty and our fortunes.'' The Emperor, greatly
pleased, gave each one forty gold pieces, pledging them
all to spend it only on Alexandrian merchandise. No
doubt this was a piece of oriental adulation, but it was
adulation almost deserved. It was better—at least for
the decade—to earn such praise than to conquer Arminius the German.

And a whole chorus of applause for the Empire and
its benefits went up during the next generations. At
Halicarnassus, in Caria, an inscription praises Augustus
and his rule as ''the healing for the whole human race,
whose providence not merely fulfils the prayers of all,
but surpasses them; by land and sea we are at peace,
the cities flourish in law and order, unity and prosperity;
and there is overflow of everything good.''

About a hundred years later Plutarch is willing to
take up the grateful story. He tells us a state ought to
supply two things—peace and liberty; and then adds,
''As to peace there is no need to occupy ourselves, for
all war has ceased; as to liberty, we have that which the
government [of Rome] leaves us, and perhaps it would
not be good if we should possess any more.'' A wise
saying, indicating—what is abundantly indicated elsewhere—how intelligent men, outside the old senatorial
circle at Rome, realized that the Empire gave all sufficient liberty to the average non-servile individual—
seemingly as much personal liberty as is granted in such
a semi-free country as present-day Germany.

In the times of the Antonines, Aristeides the rhetor
is able to follow in the path of Plutarch. ''The entire
continent,'' he assures us, ''is in a state of repose, and
men no longer believe in war, even when it is raging
at some distant point.'' Finally, about half a century
after Aristeides, Tertullian, bitter Christian that he is,
and opposed to all things pagan, still has his praise for

the Empire. "Every day the world is better known, better tilled, more wealthy. The roads are open to commerce. The deserts are changed into fruitful dominions. Tillage supplants forests. Everywhere are houses, people, cities; everywhere is life." But perhaps the concisest tribute to the imperial system is Appian's, written about the same time as that of Aristeides. "From the coming of the emperors to the present time, nearly two hundred years, the city (of Rome) has been adorned in a marvelous manner, the revenues of the Empire have increased, and in the long enduring peace the peoples have advanced to the very height of happiness."

Soon after Tertullian the clouds began to darken. The Empire became more and more an oasis of civilization, amid a wilderness of barbarism, with the desert sands ever encroaching. Finally the sands were to choke out the life-giving waters. But for long these evil days seemed never to come. The civilized world was under one government—remarkable and intelligent as human institutions go. The extortions of corrupt governors and usurers had notably abated. The barriers of race and prejudice were steadily declining. Hampering customs tariffs appear happily absent.[1] Wars were mainly police expeditions on a distant frontier—glorious to the commanders, but not important to civilians. The rumor of battle with the Picts of Caledonia would alarm a Syrian purple-merchant almost as little as the tale of a Moro outbreak would a New England cotton weaver. So it was for the two hundred and more years from the battle of Actium to the death of Marcus Aurelius. The abolition of war and the coming of the brotherhood of man were far away, yet the peoples were justified in rejoicing in so much sunlight.

How great was the population of this "World of

[1] Ancient customs duties were "for revenue only."

Rome?" Data are lacking. Conjectures differ widely. The ancients seldom appreciated the precise values of figures; and the copyists of the old manuscripts have committed amazing blunders with numerals. So the little information we seem to have is unreliable. No one ever appears to have made a complete census, in the modern meaning of the word, of the entire Empire; although reliable lists were drawn up of the persons variously liable to taxation. We know how many Roman citizens there were at several periods, but unfortunately we do not know just who were included in these numbers;[1] how many dwelt in Italy, or outside thereof; nor is it easy to conjecture how large a percentage of the entire population could boast themselves to be "Romans."

As the figures stand we are told that in 28 B.C. Augustus took a census of the Roman citizens, and found they amounted to 4,164,000; in 8 B.C. they had risen to 4,233,000; in 14 A.D. (just before his death) they were 4,937,000.[2] Since the Emperor was somewhat chary in awarding the Romans franchise to provincials, we may set down this steady increase to the freeing of a great number of slaves by Italian masters and to the natural growth incident to prolonged prosperity. The upward movement did not cease with Augustus. In 48 A.D. Claudius' census showed that over a million citizens had been added in about a generation; the number was now 5,984,072. In other words, the "Romans" of the Empire may be set at about 25,000,000, assuming the foregoing figures show simply adult males. But how of the non-Romans, the peasants of Gaul and Spain, the

---

[1] E.g., whether persons without taxable property were included, etc.

[2] These numbers, from the Monumentum Ancyranum, a practically contemporaneous inscription, are probably reliable so far as they go. There is a theory that the total is for the *full* number, including women and children, but this seems unlikely.

Moors of Numidia, the tribesmen by the Danube, the swarming populations of the Levant, the decaying communities of Greece? Not many individuals of these could boast *"Civis Romanus sum!"* and claim the rights of the toga.

We are thus driven upon mere conjectures, and conjectures differ almost hopelessly. Dean Merivale has attempted to estimate the population under Augustus; the German, Beloch, writing later than Merivale has tried the same problem with greater parade of assembling all available data and extreme conservatism in estimates, while adhering strictly to scientific method.[1] The differences between these scholars can best be shown in a table.

Roman Province or District	Beloch's Estimate	Merivale's Estimate
The Gauls and Narbo	4,900,000	6,000,000
Spain	6,000,000	8,000,000
Italy	6,000,000	13,500,000
Sicily, Corsica and Sardinia	1,100,000	2,500,000
The Danubian Lands, Balkan Peninsula and Greece	5,000,000	10,000,000
Total for Europe	23,000,000	40,000,000
Asia Minor and Syria	19,000,000	27,000,000
Cyprus	500,000	1,000,000
Egypt	5,000,000	8,000,000
Cyrene and North Africa	6,500,000	9,000,000
Total for Asia and Africa	31,000,000	45,000,000
Total population of Roman World	54,000,000	85,000,000

There seems little profit in trying to reconcile these two totals. Thirty-one millions make an extremely wide gap! Besides other scholars of authority have their guesses also. Schiller's estimate for Imperial Italy is of fourteen to seventeen million freemen, and adding

[1] Beloch's conclusions are contained in an entire book devoted to the question *"Die Bevölkerung der Griechisch-Römischen Welt."* The summary of his estimates is on page 507.

in the slaves he would make Italy scarcely less populous than to-day. Mommsen concedes to Egypt, in Vespasian's reign, at least 7,500,000 inhabitants liable to the poll tax; and adding the exemptions he cannot accept less than Merivale's guess of 8,000,000. French scholars have computed that the Gallic provinces and their German adjuncts contained 12,000,000. When experts thus disagree it is folly for others to try to pick the knot. This much however can be safely said: that the figures of Beloch are extremely conservative; that the population of the Roman world assuredly was not less, but was probably much more than he allows.[1] We may say the Empire contained in aggregate approximately as many souls as does the United States. What this means will become clearer on recalling that never since the fall of Rome till the expansion of the American republic have so many persons lived together in a single highly civilized unit—unless "highly civilized" can be applied to India, China, or the czardom of Russia.

In the Roman Empire, as in every wide dominion, the bulk of the people, of course, lived as peasants in the country, yet the proportion of dwellers in sizable cities was perhaps as large as in America to-day. The population of Rome itself presents peculiar problems to be attacked later; but if Rome was the undoubted metropolis, she was not without her rivals in size, if not in prestige. Alexandria, the commercial capital of the East, had hardly less than 600,000. Antioch could boast of almost as many; Caesarea in Cappadocia is, perhaps with slight exaggeration, set at 400,000. Pergamus in Asia Minor had at least 120,000. Of about the same size or even greater must have been Corinth, Ephesus, and possibly Athens. Carthage, after its restoration by

[1] Certainly his estimates for Italy, Egypt and, less certainly, Gaul are altogether too low.

the first Caesars, was able to rank well up with Alexandria and Antioch; of course the reconstructed city could not boast the 700,000 she claimed before 146 B.C., but she had at lowest 300,000, or even 400,000. In the West, naturally, cities were less numerous and less populous than in the longer and more stably settled East. As years went on Milan became the metropolis of northern Italy. As late as the sixth century A.D. she was given over 300,000. The Gallic capital, the modern Lyons, was comparatively large, though not able to compare in size with the great Eastern centers. No city of Italy, save Milan, could rival Rome, even so feebly as Liverpool rivals London; but the number of prosperous smaller cities was great. Pola was a thriving town of 30,000. Aquileia, a prominent seat of the northern trade, had 100,000. In Padua 500 persons wore the gold ring of the *eques*,[1] a number unrivaled by any other Latinized city save Rome and Spanish Gades. This last city —a bulwark of ancient civilization, flung out against the untraversed Atlantic—was proverbial for its riches, luxury and refinement. Its merchant princes were renowned for their prosperity. Their intercourse with Rome was constant. "Gaditanian songs" were sung at many a refined Roman supper party, or in the less refined music hall. As the Empire spread its influence wider, and the shadow of the *Pax Romana* more completely covered the nations, London, in half-wild Britain, not to mention Paris in North Gaul, and Treves almost on the bulwarks against Germanic savagedom, were to become cities of no meager dimensions.

The conditions then for a complex and highly developed civilization were fully presented. Men of action or ideas could be assured of the stimulus that comes from having their subjects or their audience, not a petty

[1] And therefore proclaiming themselves personages of wealth.

city in some corner of Hellas, but an Empire that could justly claim to be the civilized world. What could semi-barbarous Parthia, or that *terra ignota* called India, really add to a realm stretching from the Firth to the Euphrates? Beyond a few spices and precious stones, in no way needful to human happiness, or even to the highest luxury, almost every natural product useful to man was within this one Empire. There had never been such a day before. It is not too much to say there has never been such a day since.

The first age then of the Empire was one of extra-ordinarily rapid material enterprise and expansion. Undoubtedly much that was done was performed in a hurried and superficial spirit, promising little perma-nence. The command of Constantine the Great, who bade a provincial governor to "send word, not that you have begun your new buildings, but that you have finished them," must have been spoken many times by other over-hasty magnates in the earlier centuries. In Bithynia, about 100 A.D., there was such building activity among the cities in carrying out magnificent public works, that the governor was fain to apply to Trajan at Rome for an expert engineer. The Emperor could send none —there were none to be spared; and he was compelled to urge that a man be found in provincial Asia, where there seems to have been considerable building also.

Another proof of the prosperity is the rapid spread of strange fruits over the Empire. Cherries were intro-duced into Britain in 47 A.D., only four years after Claudius' conquest. In Pliny's time "Lusitanian cherries"—an import clearly of the Tagus region—were growing in Belgica and along the Rhine. A Roman knight, Pompeius Flaccus, introduced into Spain the pistachio which Lucius Vitellius had already brought into Italy. Peaches were soon raised in Narbonensis.

The olive and the vine, both children of the South and of the sunny Mediterranean, pressed steadily north into Gaul, working up from Massilia and winning away part of the territory of "Beer and Butter." The wines of the later Burgundy and Bordeaux regions were well known in imperial times. In Claudius' reign a lively wine-growing industry was springing up in the Danube valley.

Peace and good government thus made commerce easy; and commerce, it is a mere axiom, makes for the unifying of the nations. It was the Roman Empire that made Spain, Gaul, and for a brief space Britain, loyal and valuable co-workers in civilized society. In the West the task was one of directly Romanizing, the Latin language driving out the Celtic dialects; the superior Latin culture destroying the habits of Gallic barbarism. But in the East the Romanizing process went on slowly, and presently ceased altogether, while a recrudescence of Hellenism gradually won its way over much of the declining Empire.

The Greek and the Grecianized Oriental would not willingly admit the superiority of any thing Roman, save that of the Scipionic legions over the degenerate Macedonian phalanx. The number of "Roman citizens" in the eastern half of the Empire who knew not a word of Latin was probably great. Claudius—a great stickler for Roman dignities—felt called upon to strike from the list of jurors, and to disfranchise a Greek of high rank because he was ignorant of the language of his adopted country;[1] and Suetonius records this as something exceptional. Greek was usually the official language in the proconsuls' court east of the Adriatic.[2] Greek was the

[1] Mommsen thinks that even so educated a man as Plutarch had only a superficial knowledge of Latin.

[2] The local population considered it an insult if the government sent a proconsul who did not understand Greek.

language probably understood by most of the readers of Pilate's inscription set above Jesus, in preference to the perfectly novel Latin, and the almost forgotten priestly Hebrew. As Mahaffy and many another modern scholar have made clear, the age of the Empire was in one sense the age of Hellenistic expansion, of new conquests—under the fostering favor of Rome—for the tongue and the ideas of Homer and Plato.[1]

Yet when all this is said, even in the East there was a considerable Latin influence; still more there was a Romanizing influence—the citizens of Athens, Ephesus, Tyre or Palmyra merging their local patriotism into the pride of being subjects—and, as time advanced,—citizens of the world Empire. Here and there in the Greek world were veritable Latin islands—veteran colonies of which Philippi in Macedonia is the most familiar example. But besides that, in the eastern cities the number of Italian merchants, bankers, commercial men generally was very great. They preserved a local civic life of their own apart from the native government; their *conventus,* which managed their affairs, was a corporation of Roman citizens, and had a recognized and privileged place in the city. In certain parts of the East the Italian element was surely very great. In 88 B.C., 80,000 Italians, resident in Asia Minor, perished in the massacres inaugurated by Mithridates; or according to another account, fully 150,000. Twenty-two years later Cicero represents Asia as full of all sorts and conditions of Italian merchants and bankers. A little later the same could probably be said of Syria and of Egypt.

But after all, the work of Romanizing went forward

---

[1] The Greek pressed the Aramaic very hard in Syria, and it is needless to suggest how it forced an entrance into the synagogue. The Parthian "Great King" struck his coins with Greek legends, and affected the forms of Greek culture at his court.

most rapidly in the West, where the natives were more willing to acknowledge the superior arts as well as the superior arms of the conquerors. Here indeed the Roman genius could accomplish its most perfect work. Roman traders were everywhere the missionaries of civilization. In 46 B.C. there were three hundred Roman bankers and wholesalers in African Utica, and many important Roman trading firms in the neighboring cities of Thapsus and Hadrumentum. In 61 A.D.—eighteen years after the conquest of South Britain—there was a large settlement of merchants and traders in London, and seventy thousand Romans and Romanized allies then perished in the revolt of the natives. Seneca, writing at about this time, voices the consciousness of the Romans themselves in the matter: "How many colonies has this (Roman) people sent out into every province! Wherever the Roman conquers, there he dwells. These migrations have always found people eager to take part in them, and veteran soldiers desert their native hearths and follow the flag of the colonists across the seas. . . . You will scarcely find any land which is still in the hands of its original inhabitants; all peoples have become confused and intermingled; one has come after another."

It has been calculated that only about one hundred years was required after the conquest of an outlying province before it should become genuinely Romanized, and the natives become loyal and zealous in putting down any revolt. Trade, of course, was the prime civilizer; but in the train of commerce came the cultured literature and philosophy for the upper classes, and the Latin theater for the many. The theater cannot be despised as a Romanizer. The giving of Latin dramas and farces, even if not highly refined, must have worked mightily on audiences of swart Moors or blonde Gauls. The mimes showed often much keenness of observation.

Seneca could find more wisdom in the farces of Publius Syrus than in the lore of most of the philosophers. It must not be forgotten that, when they danced in the theaters of Trier or Gades or Carthage, it was often to the lines of Vergil or Ovid.

The progress of the armies carried civilization as well as protection to the very verge of the frontiers. Mainz, Cologne, Trier, Sirmium, Carnutum, Aquincum, and many another outpost of the legions along the Rhine and Danube changed in a few generations from half-besieged "lagers" of the legions into thriving cities, usually with stately theater, amphitheater and forum, a vigorous civic life, and a brisk trade with the unsubdued peoples of the North. A permanent camp always meant a nucleus for a city; a city meant a center of civilization in lands just redeemed from savagery.

In 74 A.D. Vespasian awarded the "Latin Right" to the whole free population of Spain, obviously a token that he considered that peninsula essentially Roman in speech and customs. Gaul, too, was almost equally loyal despite the outbreak of Civilis along the Rhine. The provincials by the third century had come to feel the advantages of partnership in the Empire so keenly that, even when anarchy was at its height under the feeble Gallienus,—when in self-protection against the barbarians the provincials set up local emperors to ward off the peril—the very rebels would only rebel against Gallienus, not against Rome. "*Roma Aeterna*" is the most frequent legend on the coins of Postumus, the "Gallic Emperor," and the same potentate made haste to create a senate on the regular Roman model.

As a matter of fact, national revolts against the imperial authority were extraordinarily rare. Ambitious generals—not discontented provincials—were what the Lords of the Palatine dreaded. Tacfarinas the

Moor, Sacrovir the Gaul, Civilis the Batavian, were rebels indeed, but rebels in half-civilized or recently annexed provinces. The Jewish revolts are also exceptions, for religious fanaticism can defeat the best endeavors of statecraft. The most prominent *national* anti-Roman revolt in a civilized and long subject province was in 172 A.D. in Egypt, when the native "Bucolic" troops defied for a while the government, and were at length put down with some difficulty by Avidius Cassius, Marcus Aurelius' able governor of Syria. But how many persons—even tolerably familiar with history—know of this "Bucolic" uprising, and of Isidorus, the Egyptian priest, its leader?

The process of fusing the races into a single type, therefore, went on with startling rapidity. "The same gods were prayed to from the Tigris to the Atlantic; and if Rome already at the end of the first century was more Greek and Semitic than Roman (as Juvenal bewailed), by the end of the fourth, Britons, Africans, Hellenes, Egyptians, when face to face with the barbarians, called themselves *Romani* or Ῥωμαῖοι."[1]

Very rapidly the native, after securing the coveted Roman franchise, would conceal his non-Italian origin with a new name worthy of the peers of Claudius the Censor. A tomb in Africa records one Quintus Postumius Celsus. This Celsus, however, was not born on the Esquiline, for it soon appears that his father was a certain African Iudchad. But after a few generations this new line of Postumii Celsi would forget that their ancestors were Moors, and evidence seems to point out that native names were at a discount, and out of social pride provincials would cover their lowly origin by names stolen straight from the capital.

Africa indeed was not at first the most rapidly

[1] *Seeck: Geschichte des Untergangs der antiken Welt:* Vol. I. p. 323.

Romanized of the western provinces. Carthage rose from its ruins but slowly. Pomponius Mela, in Claudius' time, speaks of it deprecatingly; but Aurelius Victor (about 370 A.D.) can call it "the wonder of the universe." We know also that Thysdrus, afterward a large city, was merely a straggling hamlet in Caesar's age. The bloom of Africa was late, but it was one of the fairest flowers of Latin civilization; and it was a grievous calamity to the world when Vandal, Moor and Saracen blasted North Africa, and sent her back into the barbarism whence she is barely emerging. A rich soil, a beautiful country, a remarkable variety of natural products—made the African provinces the peers of any others. Carthage belongs to universal history; but not many readers know of Thamugade, that magnificent ruin in Numidia where to-day, almost amid a desert, the pavements still show the deep ruts worn by the wheels of a mighty traffic. Trajan had founded the colony in 100 A.D. A stately triumphal arch rises in honor of Septimius Severus. The streets were wider, and much more spacious than at Pompeii. Another African city, Thysdrus in southern Tunis, must have had 100,000 people. It was the center of the Byzacium, a wonderfully fertile region with many prosperous towns. North Africa is to-day a treeless country. Sallust, writing of conditions before the Empire, calls it treeless also; but thanks to Roman cultivation, it became covered with luxuriant forests, and towards the end of the Empire was able to ship to Italy considerable timber and fuel wood. This was all done in an arid country by one of the most perfect systems of irrigation ever seen.

Another almost forgotten African city is Iol Caesarea (the modern Shershell in Algiers). Juba II, the vassal-king of Mauretania, and his Queen Selene, the daughter of Antonius and Cleopatra, were its sponsors. It was a city adorned with a superb Greek art—a cultured, luxurious capital—a smaller Alexandria on the confines of Mauretania. From it have been taken many of the statues that are the present glory of the Louvre.

Roman roads, Roman aqueducts spread over Tunis, where of late, till the recent French occupation, all was desolation. In one case an aqueduct forty-three miles long brought water to the plain-cities from the hills. So great was the lost Latin civilization of Africa!

Gaul was equally the subject for this peaceful after-conquest, a conquest undoubtedly in full progress in those second and third centuries when the legions were no longer marching forward, and were even beginning to draw back. Aquitania had made the least resistance to Romanizing, says Ammianus Marcellinus, for it was the first to be opened to trade. But the Latin influence ran rapidly northward. Along the Danube again the ubiquitous Roman traders pressed in, outrunning or accompanying the legions. In 6 A.D. (only fifteen years after the conquest) the region swarmed with them; and one hundred years later they were ready to flock into Dacia at the heels of Trajan, where by one stroke a barbarian population was rooted out and a Romanized one introduced.

Hadrian's age was another in which Romanism gained steadily on barbarism. The expansion was now quite as much in the East as in the West. In 105 A.D. Cornelius Palma had conquered Arabia; and Felix had spread over the caravan routes and desert region the *Pax Romana*. Jews, Syrians, Egyptians, Arabs all flocked thither to trade and prosper. Hadrian commenced the Temple of the Sun at Baalbec; Septimius Severus built the Temple of Jupiter there—a sign of the imperial fostering. In Hadrian's time, while the army centurions were busy in Egypt directing the porphyry quarries for the temples in Rome and in Athens, the same Emperor's freedmen also conducted mining in the Carpathians. Along the Rhine the *Agri Decumates* were filling with Latinized settlers. Egypt had so prospered during the preceding period that it had been needful greatly to expand the volume of her coinage. Everywhere were beneficent government supervision, peace, and an intense, peaceful activity.

A few generations later a Roman colony was created by Septimius Severus almost in the center of the Syrian desert—Palmyra. It commanded the caravan trade to the East. Its merchant princes were bound by close ties of interest to Rome. In the evil days of Gallienus it was the bulwark of the Empire against reviving Persia. It gave to history Zenobia, the second Cleopatra. It was a cruel fate that Aurelian had to destroy it.

Inevitably under this benignant *Pax Romana* almost every legitimate form of money-getting increased.

2. *The Ancient Attitude Towards the Means of Gain.*

If the Roman world offered great advantages for the increase of material welfare, it labored also under severe handicaps. Social proscription made it often difficult for the ablest, the most progressive class to use their talents for the full benefit of either themselves or the world. The modern age owes much to antiquity; one thing which it does not owe is the present-day conception of the dignity of labor. A Roman of genteel family found extremely few opportunities for the exercise of his educated abilities. As will be pointed out, he was almost cut off from participating directly in trade. The Emperor preferred to advance "self-made men" rather than aristocrats in the army. A nobleman would perhaps have a seat in the Senate, but that was a body which talked much and did little. He was thrown back upon the practice of advocacy in the courts, or upon a polite idling with letters and philosophy, or too often upon a life of riotous excitement and dissipation.

It ought to be said again that the ancients had a rather hazy conception of the employment of specialists in public life. The man who was a good legislator was usually counted good enough for a command in the army. Gaius Flaminius, who led the legions to disaster at Trasemene, owed his military appointment to his putting through a popular land bill. Cicero, the advocate, thought it only proper that he should govern Celicia and command the local army. A land-general might suddenly be appointed admiral of the fleet in all the naval wars from the first contest with Carthage to the sea-battles of Crispus, son of Constantine. And, of course, Julius Caesar—who is rightly set beside Alexander, Hannibal and Napoleon as strategist and tactician—was little more than a successful politician before he went to Gaul.

All this tendency made against the development of highly trained professional classes—except in the field of the law. On the other side, the prejudice of aristocrats against more plebeian forms of livelihood was highly circumscribing. Cato Major took pains to point out that the usurer was branded by the Roman law as a greater evil than the common thief, and he made the dishonesty of loans sufficient grounds for declining them as investments. Indeed Cicero makes him avow that "usury is a form of homicide." The foregoing pages have perhaps proved that this prejudice against money-lending was undoubtedly more avowed than real; yet many a stiff Roman noble scorned the money-lender as a mere bargainer of the vulgar Forum although he himself might employ that lender as private agent, and might also be growing rich by bold undertakings in real estate that hardly agreed with Aristotelian ethics.

Against distant and maritime commerce, the old-time prejudice was almost as inveterate. It crops out in the speech assigned to Censorinus, the consul, when he urged the Carthaginians to surrender to Rome in 149 B.C. "The sea always begets a grasping disposition by the very facilities it offers for gain. . . . Believe me, country life with the joys of agriculture and freedom from danger is much more wholesome. Although the gains of agriculture are less than come from commercial pursuits, they are surer and a great deal safer. . . . A maritime city is to me more like to a ship than to solid ground, being tossed about on the waves of trouble, and so much exposed to the chances of life, while an inland city enjoys all the security of the firm earth."

For a Roman patrician to descend to "trade" would indeed have been a humiliation greater than a like calamity to an English "My-Lord" or a German "Freiherr." To a Claudian, reckoning in Tiberius' time twenty-seven consulships, five dictatorships, seven censorships, seven triumphs and two ovations, or even to a Livian with only eight consulships, two censorships, three triumphs and a dictatorship, such a descent from a lordly eminence to vulgar commerce was unthinkable. It would have meant social ostracism and probably imperial censure. How stern the sentiment was, is shown by Augustus, who in his census of the *equites*—themselves distinctly of the moneyed class—deliberately degraded members who had borrowed money at a low interest in order to reloan it at a higher; and punished a man of high rank for quitting his lodgings shortly before the appointed moving day, in order to hire them again at a lower rent a little later. Such practices were not worthy of Roman knights and nobles, and must be left to the freedmen scarce out of bondage!

Cicero in his *De Officiis* has summed up the opinion of his day on the callings and professions in a wonderfully suggestive passage. He ranks as ungenteel and unworthy of a gentleman the business of tax gatherers or money-lenders because "they come into collision with the ill-will of men." He bans all sorts of hired labor and men who are paid, not for skill but for mere work; small retailers also, because "they make no profit except by a certain amount of falsehood;" all mechanics, "for a workshop can have nothing respectable about it;" all the trades that minister to the sensual pleasures, " 'fishmongers, butchers, cooks, poulterers and fishermen' as Terence says;" also perfumers, ballet-dancers and acrobats.

More honorable are the professions that call for skill and benefit the community at large. Medicine, architecture, the instruction of the young in liberal studies, "are respectable for those whose rank they suit" (i.e. they are, however, unworthy of a senator or *eques*). Commerce on a small scale is vulgar, but on a large scale and "importing much from all quarters and making large sales without fraud *is not so very discreditable.*[1] Nay, it may justly claim the highest regard if the merchant satiated or rather contented with his profits, leaving the sea, betakes himself, not merely to a port-town, but to an estate in the country. But of all means of acquiring gain nothing is better than agriculture, nothing more productive, more pleasant, more worthy of a cultivated man."[2]

Certain callings fell under a peculiar stigma, not always undeserved; especially auctioneers, undertakers,

[1] A remark worthy of a British "gentleman."

[2] This partiality for agriculture is warp and woof of almost all ancient and modern aristocracies. The aristocracies of England, Prussia, Russia, not to name other countries, have been almost synonymous with "the landed interests."

bakers, bath-keepers, lessees of river and customs duties, and such public servants as sewer-cleaners were under the ban. The auctioneer was particularly unpopular, because he was the middleman in a great number of petty transactions, often involving considerable chicanery. The proportions of sales by auction in ancient times was much larger than to-day. The auctioneer received 1% of the price, and no doubt it took careful watching to see that he did not get more.

The actor's profession, too, suffered disrepute. A certain Damasippus who had run through his wealth, but who had a good voice, went upon the stage. The proceeding sent Juvenal—that mouthpiece of the conventionalities—into a horrified rage. Undoubtedly to a conservative Roman the "dramatics" of American college societies, especially where the male actors assume female parts, would have been unspeakably disgusting, and would have blasted in his eyes all claims of Cambridge or New Haven to produce an intellectual aristocracy.

As early as the beginning of the Second Punic War, the conservative majority of the nobility undertook to check by law any efforts of their fellow aristocrats to meddle in commerce, and tied them forever to the land. This *Lex Clodia* forbade any senator or senator's son from owning a ship of over three hundred amphorae[1] burden. The small ships would be enough to carry the produce of their estates along the coast, but they would be barred from distant commerce, especially from the over-sea corn trade. The law indeed became a dead letter. It was *"antiqua et mortua"* in Cicero's time; but it was not repealed, and undoubtedly had an important effect in shaping Italian economy in the age succeeding Hannibal.

[1] An amphora was a Roman cubic foot.

The real business of a cultured, high-born man—in the opinion both of Greek theorists and Roman statesmen—was the service of the public. To be quaestor at thirty-one, curule aedile at thirty-seven, praetor at forty, consul at forty-three,[1] i.e., to get the great state magistracies at the earliest age permitted by law—that for the average Roman aristocrat was a "successful life." Money undoubtedly was necessary, but it must come from ancestral estates, from the gifts of rich clients defended in the court, from the proconsulships in unlucky provinces or from the presents of unluckier vassal-kings. The actual handling of the capital accumulated must be turned over to the lower class of *equites*, or the still lower class of freedmen. But even public service in the stormy days preceding the downfall of the Republic was becoming distasteful to refined and sensitive men. The coarse caballing and riotous comitias disgusted many men of family, and they shut themselves up in slothful obscurity and idleness. Cicero in vain railed against the indolent rich, who were comforting themselves over the impending ruin of the Republic by thinking they would at least save their beloved fish-ponds.

Of course this indifference to trade and commerce was largely a pretense; it was necessary simply to avoid appearances of touching the accursed thing and to employ capable middlemen.

Pompeius Magnus invested his funds in an important bank and shared in the profits. Cicero did not do this, and perhaps Pompeius did it a little too openly; but the thing went on. As a public officer a Roman official had to handle very considerable sums, and it seems likely that, great as was the corruption in many quarters, direct embezzlement from the treasury was not a sin of Roman magistrates. In the second century B.C. Polybius

[1] The exact legal age for these offices is sometimes disputed.

could draw his famous comparison between them and
the Greeks of his day. "If but a talent of money were
entrusted to a magistrate in a Greek state, ten audi-
tors, as many seals, and twice as many witnesses are
required as security of the bond, but even then no faith
is observed; while the Roman official who handles vast
sums adheres to his duty, through mere obligation of
the oath which he has sworn."

Likewise in the transactions of the Roman banking
and tax-farming companies, business honor (despite
some deplorable lapses) seems to have been fairly high.
The *publicani* might grind the provincials, but they had
learned that honesty was the best policy, at least among
themselves. Large credit transactions could therefore
be undertaken, and the foundation was laid for those
more stable conditions which came in under the Empire.

Beyond a doubt the Roman *nobilitas* affected to dis-
pise the more vulgar methods of gain, but the Roman
nobilitas was a decaying class. The Empire was the
age when men with short ancestries or no ancestries
rose to great offices, commands, and finally to the purple.
If the greed for gold was fierce under the Republic, conditions did not change when the *princeps* replaced the
oligarcy. Rather the pursuit of gain was easier, its
enjoyment more certain.

When men cease to boast of birth, they commonly
begin to boast of possessions, usually of a very material
kind. Juvenal with customary over emphasis declares
that in the second century A.D. when a man's testimony
was given at Rome, not his character but his wealth decided his creditability. "How many slaves has he? How
many acres of public land does he occupy? How expensive are the dishes on his table? [For] in exact proportion
to the money in his chest is the credit given to his oath."

While the age was one of social shifting, it was not

one of increased democracy. On the contrary, new barriers were being set up which were to grow ever more rigid till they paralyzed the decaying later Empire. A freedman who had showed himself a useful informer to Nero, was rewarded by the gift of a seat in the theater "among the tribunes' runners;"[1] showing how already honors and caste distinctions were being reduced to a science.

Undoubtedly the most rough and ready means of testing an unknown man's worth is his wealth. This was inevitable in the new imperial society at Rome; it was even more inevitable in the less hide-bound provinces. On the threshold of a house in Pompeii is an inscription welcoming the patron god, "Salve Lucrum!" And this deity surely never lacked his myriad worshippers.

As the scramble for wealth grew fiercer, the conventional barriers against mingling in trade grew ever weaker. Even the city aristocracies in the imperial age did not share the prejudices against commerce prevailing in the old Roman military oligarchy—witness Dion Chrysostom, who shows how his grandfather, his father and finally himself all returned to business after almost ruining themselves in the service of the community, and recovered their lost fortunes.

Dion Chrysostom was of good equestrian family, and an intimate of the Senate's emperor, Nerva. If this could be true of him, what must not have been true of the average rich man of the imperial period—a freedman or the son of a freedman?

Trimalchio, the vulgar successful ex-slave, has figured in too many books of late to make the rehearsing

---

[1] In a speech of political advice which Cassius Dio alleges Livia delivered to Augustus, she is made to recommend "degradation in public seats" as a wholesome discipline to malcontents.

of his alleged career profitable; still Petronius' summary can hardly be omitted.

"Yet this Trimalchio is only a freedman. Till quite recently he carried wood upon his shoulders. Whence this respect with which he is surrounded?—He is possessor of 18,000,000 sesterces.[1] And how did he get them? Nobody knows; but he has them—that is the important matter. . . . He speaks loud and men listen. He will say plenty of foolish things—what matters it?—his fortune is full substitute for his lack of brains!"

But money and able effrontery could rise higher yet; we need not turn to Petronius' clever romance, but to the sober pages of Tacitus. Few men, save the wearers of the purple, were ever so fawned upon as was Pallas, the clever freedman of Claudius and Nero. And yet this quondam slave, who had nothing but his ill-gotten money and his backstairs influence at court to commend him, could testify during a trial, that touching his own freedmen "at home he always signified his pleasure by a nod, or motion of the head; or if he had many directions to give he wrote them out to avoid the familiarity of exchanging words with them."

The Yankee and the Jewish races have been by varying enemies declared to be money-seekers *par excellence*, and to be delivered body and soul to the quest of material wealth. No age or race can rightly compare itself with those behind it. Yet it may not be prejudice to assert that never was the quest for gold more furious than in the age of the early Caesars. If the great republic is the Land of the Almighty Dollar, *Rex Denarius* was not less potent in the great empire.

---

[1] Nearly three quarters of a million dollars cash, but much more counting the relative purchasing power of money in the ancient days.

3. *Great Fortunes and Millionaires.*

The philosopher Seneca, whose time-serving career stands in such marked contrast to his puritanical preachments, once undertook to explain the view of a superior man towards riches. The wise man, he thinks, should not despise them: "They give him a wider field for his development than if he be poor, seeing that then the only virtue he can show is that of not being crushed or perverted by his poverty; whereas, if he has riches, he will have a wide field for the display of temperance, generosity, laboriousness, methodical arrangement and grandeur."

Seneca ought to have been a singularly virtuous man then, for he had one of the greatest fortunes of his day. Charges were brought against him, to be sure, by one Suilius, a slippery advocate, that he had committed adultery with Julia, the daughter of Germanicus; that he made 300,000,000 ses.[1] in four years by imperial favor; that in Rome he clutched at the legacies of the childless; that the provinces were sucked dry by his usury. These charges probably were exaggerated, but no doubt there was a basis. Seneca was perhaps no better than many another of his time who did not try to combine the multimillionaire and the teacher of ethics in one person. His fortune was huge for his generation, but it was not unique. How were the other great properties amassed? At first, no doubt, by the mere use of opportunities as generals and proconsuls in the provinces. In Republican times this was in most cases certainly true. Only under the Empire did this easy road to riches become increasingly inaccessible. The methods of corrupt magistrates, *publicani* and *negotiatores,* have already been examined, but something should be said of

[1] Over $12,000,000.

the *mere sums* collected by the lucky plunderers. We hear, for example, of the wealth drained out of Gaul. About 106 B.C. Quintus Caepio plundered a temple at Tolosa of a treasure worth 15,000 talents. Julius Caesar is alleged to have brought from Gaul nearly $70,000,000, and consequently let loose so much new bullion that the value of gold sank from 4,000 to 3,000 ses. to the pound, i.e., 25% in its relation to silver. Pompeius Magnus also, despite his fame as a marvelously cleanhanded conqueror, did not come from his wars empty handed. Appian tells how the Senate voted Sextus his son, 200,000,000 ses. as indemnity for his paternal estates, or, to believe the text of Cicero, the vast amount of 700,-000,000 ses. Again Octavius' conquest of Egypt brought huge treasures both to the state and to individuals.

The generation following the death of Sulla was that in which the great fortunes ran up most rapidly, thanks to the conquests of Caesar and Pompeius, and also to those of Metellus Creticus, Servilius Isauricus and others. Bithynia, Pontus, Crete, Cilicia and Syria were all bent under the Roman yoke, as well as Gaul, and often the countries most easily conquered proved highly rewarding to the Roman. Almost without effort every conqueror, every lucky subordinate of a conqueror, would grow rich; an example to the point being Demetrius, Pómpeius' freedman, who left 4,000 talents (over $4,000,000) behind him as a "business fortune."

But of course, many of the Roman millionaires owed their prosperity only indirectly, at least, to the conquests. The case of Atticus, Cicero's principal correspondent, is one which shows how far a man of excellent family could stretch the prejudices against vulgar moneyhandling, and still remain in his caste. He had inherited a fortune of 2,000,000 ses.[1] On making his home in

---

[1] About $80,000.

Athens he found real estate in Greece to be very cheap, owing to the devastations of the Mithridatic wars. Thus he bought up many landed properties, and grew rich selling corn and cattle. He found another very gentlemanly source of income by maintaining a large force of slaves, and employed them copying books which he sold at good profit to Cicero and many others. He gathered gangs of gladiators, trained them carefully, and hired them out to cities seeking amusements. He was a banker and loaned money to great Roman nobles, who were, no doubt, glad of an urbane creditor. He also placed loans in Macedonia, Epirus, Ephesus, Delos and probably elsewhere. He likewise loaned money to cities —a somewhat shady transaction in which, as seen, it was necessary to use discreet agents. These municipal loans were profitable, but also hazardous. Once the Senate passed a decree protecting Sicyon against his extreme demands for repayment and he had to compromise at a loss. Finally from his uncle, Q. Caecilius, a famous money-lender, he inherited 10,000,000 ses.[2] When he died, Atticus, no doubt, had a very large fortune, gained as honorably as most Roman fortunes.

Some men, of course, bettered themselves by wealthy marriages; Cicero's Terentia—hardly a very rich catch— brought her husband nearly half a million sesterces, and she owned houses in Rome and a forest near Tusculum. But the whole matter of mercenary marriages and dowries must be taken up later.

Generally speaking, the advance in size of fortunes was proportionately as great during the last century of the Republic as during the nineteenth century in the United States. At the end of that time a man worth in the Marian period 2,000,000 ses., could be spoken of slightingly as "rich according to the circumstances of

[2] About $400,000.

that day;" and Lucius Domitius Ahenobarbus, Caesar's most implacable enemy, was wealthy enough to be able to promise to 20,000 soldiers four *jugera* of land per man, all out of his own property. At the same time the number of surpassingly rich men in Rome was not then so very great. About 100 B.C. L. Marcius Philippus, a statesman of moderate democratic views, declared there were hardly two thousand wealthy families in the whole citizen body of the Republic, and until Caesar destroyed the Republic it is not likely the number increased, although those rich before grew richer still. Data for the early Empire are somewhat lacking, but probably not the least blessing it brought was a more even distribution of wealth.

As an instance of a rich man of the older type, Sextus Roscius may be taken. He was a wealthy, though not an extraordinarily wealthy, landowner. When he was murdered in 81 B.C. he was worth 6,000,000 ses.,[1] divided among thirteen different estates. These he managed himself, seldom coming to Rome, and when he did, displaying very clownish manners. No doubt he was a fairly typical country gentleman, of a class that long survived in Italy; and which had many of the traits of the eighteenth century English squirearchy.

At the other pole stood Publius Licinius Crassus, the king of all republican millionaires, whose name is still something of a byword. He began life with less than 300 talents. Just before going on his ill-fated Parthian expedition, he found he had 7,100 talents,[2] most of which he gained "by taking advantage of public calamities." He succeeded in getting hold of the goods of numbers of the proscribed, when Sulla was trying to implicate as many confederates as possible in his mas-

---

[1] About $240,000.

[2] Over $7,100,000.

sacres. He had a band of five hundred trained slaves, with which he would go to a region where there was a fire, and buy up the property burning or that next to the blaze, at a moment when the owners were delighted to sell for a trifle. The bargain once struck, these private firemen at once fell to work to save the new property of their master. In this way the greater part of Rome at one time or another fell into his greedy hands. He had silver mines and valuable lands with gangs of men working them; also a host of slaves which he was at personal pains to train as skilled readers, copyists, silversmiths, stewards, and table waiters. In fine, his prosperity reached such a pitch that he was able—thanks to the mere influence of his money—to unite himself to Caesar, and become the makeweight to Pompeius in the First Triumvirate; and he had the arrogance to declare that "no man was to be accounted rich that could not maintain an army at war at his own charges."

We come now to the question of the size of the greatest of Roman fortunes. They reached their height under the early Empire. The largest fortunes we find on record are those of 300,000,000 ses. and 400,000,000 ses. There are only two known cases of the latter amount— that of the Augur, Cnaeus Lentulus (a man whom Tiberius forced to make him, the Emperor, his heir), and that of Narcissus, the powerful and rapacious freedman, secretary of Claudius. Probably family estates were kept together more carefully than in America to-day. The greatest ancient income we know of is that of a Roman family, who, at the beginning of the fifth century, had an income of 4,000 pounds weight of gold yearly in cash, and natural products each year of about one third that sum. This would make the total income approximately $1,200,000. Then again it must be remembered the average returns on investments in ancient days were certainly much higher than to-day—at least 6% as against 4%; so a fortune worth $10,000,000 would yield as much as one of $15,000,000 at present.

But when all is said it is perfectly plain that the greatest fortunes of the first cannot compare with those of the twentieth century. The fortune of Narcissus presents an extreme case; he was worth about $16,000,000 actual money values, or, allowing for interest charges, $24,000,000. If we assume that the purchasing power of money was three times as great under Claudius as at present—a very uncertain proposition—we get a modern equivalent of $72,000,000—a great fortune, but in several cases surpassed in America—without examining Europe. It is only when we recall how scarce coined money really was in the earlier centuries of antiquity; how simple conditions of life had been in earlier Rome, that we begin to realize the great effect produced on the public mind by these huge fortunes. When we turn to the question of the expenditure of wealth, it will be easier to explain how the limited opportunities of a Roman for spending his fortune made a moderate patrimony *seem* greater than at the present day.

All wealth of course was not centered in the capital. We cannot name the incomes of the merchant princes of Alexandria, Antioch or Ephesus. Yet undoubtedly those commercial capitals must have been able to show not a few rivals to the richest houses in Rome. Gaul also was an extraordinarily wealthy country. The amphitheater and sarcophagi at Arles, the theater at Orange, the temples and bridges near Avignon all testify to departed opulence. "In Gaul," says Josephus, "the sources of wealth are at home [in the land] and flood the earth with their abundance." "Nowhere else," thinks Mommsen, "were equally numerous and magnificent country houses, especially along the Rhine and its affluents where the Gallic nobility lived in princely ease." Vine culture and cattle rearing must have been the basis of many great Celtic fortunes. If means would allow, we could doubtless make similar generalizations for almost every province under the early Empire.

There is another side to this question of great fortunes. Many nobles of long pedigree fell upon evil days, and found it hard to keep up the state of a Roman aristocrat. The emperors—despite their small love for the senatorial class—appear often to have "saved the face" of these men suffering from gilded poverty. In Tiberius' time Propertius Celer, an ex-praetor, wished to resign his senatorship, not having means to maintain the dignity. The Emperor gave him 1,000,000 ses. on proof that Celer had inherited the incumbering debts from his father. In other like cases Tiberius seems to have required that these noble applicants for charity should first prove their worthiness to the Senate. Nero was similarly generous, though hardly as circumspect. In 58 A.D. he awarded a pension of 500,000 ses. per year to Valerius Messala, his colleague in the consulship, "to sustain his honest poverty;" and to Aurelius Cotta and Haterius Antoninus he also gave pensions, although they had squandered their patrimonies in riotous living. Other like instances could be found, if they were needed, of how rich fathers had poor sons, and how sometimes the emperors relieved them.

But the prosperity of the Roman world did not depend on the rise and fall of noble families and millionaires; rather on the millions of hard-working, honest folk—farmers, tradesmen, merchants, mariners, manufacturers, who are the backbone of every civilization. While the Empire had these, it was great; when these declined, it declined also.

4. *Banking and Interest.*

An extensive commerce and great fortunes in personal property almost of necessity imply an elaborate system of banking and business credit. These were not lacking in the world of Rome. The mere necessity of having a safe place for the deposit of money, without regard to its profitable increase, could indeed be provided for otherwise. The innumerable "treasure-troves" unearthed everywhere in what was once the classical world, testify to the earliest means of safe deposit. Jesus' parable of the talents has more than religious importance; it clearly indicates what was the primitive method of keeping funds left in trust, and how that method had already become obsolete. "Thou wicked and slothful servant," speaks the master to the recipient of the one talent, who had hidden it in the ground, "thou oughtest to have put out my money at the banker's; then when I came, I should have received what was mine with interest."

As time advanced, safer places than mere holes in an obscure field were felt to be necessary. The temples became favorite places of deposit—at Athens the cella of the Parthenon, at Rome the sacred house of the Vestal Virgins. The boldest thief would hesitate before violating the treasures in such a sanctuary; but the gods could not often be expected to pay interest. Besides, even such a refuge was not absolutely secure. In the evil days of Antonius' and Octavius' general proscription, they compelled the Vestal Virgins to give up to the government the deposits entrusted to them—an act which Plutarch ranks among the greatest of Antonius' iniquities—and centuries before the imperial age, banking, interest, and a great credit system had become part and parcel of the ancient world.

If Assyriologists are to be believed, the banking house of Egibi of Babylon was a power during the last years of the Babylonian kingdom, and well down into the supremacy of Persia. Into Italy banking had penetrated from Greece, and transmitted through the cities of *Magna Graecia* had become fairly implanted in Rome before the period of the Second Punic War.[1] The *argentarius* and his compeer, the *nummularius*, were soon people of no small importance. The former class appear to have been private individuals working for themselves with little relation to the government; the latter were primarily officers of the mint who assayed the new coins, and distributed them to the people. But their functions naturally gave them large opportunities for private business, and the terms are frequently used interchangeably, e.g., Suetonius calls the father of Augustus now an *argentarius*, now a *nummularius*.

But, even if a private person, a Roman banker was too important an individual to be free from governmental control. In imperial times the bankers of the capital were supervised by the city praefect, of the provinces by the governors; and they were very possibly required to take out some kind of a state license. Their original business was the exchange of foreign moneys, and until the imperial coinage had practically superseded every other in the Empire, there must have been good profit in exchanging Macedonian gold pieces for Roman denarii and the like. Close, however, on the heels of mere money-changing, came the writing of bills of exchange—a custom again borrowed from Greece; e.g., a banker in Rome would receive a sum to be paid in Athens, and would issue a bill to be paid by some Athenian banking correspondent—a process involving, of

[1] A remark in Livy (ix, 40, 16) would put bankers in Rome as early as 309 B.C.

course, the changing into foreign money as well as the mere transfer of the sum.

The *argentarius* also served as a general receiver of deposits. Sometimes without interest merely for the convenience and security of the owner, and payable against check, or, as was common, against interest, in which case the banker was permitted to invest it for his own advantage and make what profit he could. If he failed, the law protected the depositor, whose claims had to be satisfied before the other creditors of the bankrupt. In addition to these deposits and payments against check (*perscriptio*), bankers also did a general lending business, to whomsoever they thought solvent, and here, no doubt, came in the major part of their profits.

But their transactions did not end here. One of the most ancient and important of their activities was in connection with commerce and public auctions. At private sales they acted often as agents for one of the parties; they might even undertake to dispose of a person's whole estate. At public auctions the *argentarius* was always in evidence, registering the prices at which each article was sold, exacting payment from the purchasers, and keeping watch over the not always honest auctioneer. Of course, such petty work would not fall to the important head of the firm, but to their numerous clerks, their *coäctores*,[1] who were their collectors and general underlings.

A large banking establishment naturally had several partners, and the law made each partner liable for the firm's debts. On the other hand we find slaves conducting banks, being set up by their masters who allowed them to conduct the business, at least while all went well. A case to the point is that of Callistus, Bishop of Rome,

---

[1] Horace's father and Vespasian's grandfath*r were thus bankers' clerks.

from 219 to 223 A.D. His enemies charged that he was the slave of a rich Christian, one Carpophorus, a member of the Emperor's household. Carpophorus placed him in charge of a bank in the quarter called Piscina Publica. The Christian brethren and widows, trusting in his master's name, deposited their savings in Callistus' bank. He embezzled the funds and fled by sea, only to be recaptured, and sentenced to hard labor in the public workhouse. Carpophorus declared himself distressed, not for his own losses, but for those of the widows. Callistus ultimately got clear of prison, and became, perhaps, the first Pope to be blown upon by scandal. That the money transactions and deposits of the Roman bankers were on a comparatively large scale is attested by the chance remark of Cicero—by no means an extraordinarily rich man—that he had about 600,000 ses. on deposit with the *argentarii* as well as an equal sum of cash in hand.

The *argentarii* also appear to have been to a certain extent gold and silversmiths, like the bankers of the Middle Ages. This was inevitable in a society where, after all, money meant not banknotes but metal. The *argentarii* did not indeed manufacture articles themselves, but they seem to have sometimes handled old coins, sculptured vessels of valuable metals, gems, precious stones and the like. As banking became more extensive, however, this part of their business dropped doubtless in importance; and we can think of an *argentarius* in the best imperial age as practically a modern banker, only he did not have to handle vast sums in paper money and securities.

An elaborate banking system presupposes an equally elaborate system of bookkeeping, and this the Romans possessed. Unfortunately the details are largely lost, despite the laborious reconstructions of modern savants.

Not merely every banker, but every man of affairs, appears to have kept at least two account books. The first of these, the *adversaria,* was a kind of day book in which every transaction would be jotted down in no regular order, though presumably pains were taken to keep the entries of each day by themselves. More complicated, and for a banker more important, was his *codex accepti et expensi* into which the entries of the *adversaria* would be posted every month. The elder Pliny makes it plain that it consisted of a series of double pages, one debit, one credit. The entries had to be made in a certain order, on which much stress was laid. The *codex* was presumably a good deal like a modern journal (except that it had two pages), in which were various heads of accounts with individuals, or with the different departments of a large business. There was a "profit and loss" account, and Atticus kept a separate account for presents made to him. Great care had to be used in posting the *codex,* for it often figured in litigation, and erasures and corrections could not appear; also sufficient details of every transaction had to be given to make the entries intelligible to an outsider. Money repaid by debtors, legacies received, interest received, the rent of leased land or buildings, price of articles sold, loans received, all had to be entered on the debit side; on the credit side the price of goods bought, presents given, capital loaned out, and, no doubt, repayment of loans and interest thereon. Both actual transactions in cash, and also transactions in credit had to go into the *codex,* the book being supposed to show the entire state of a man's financial affairs at any given moment.[1]

The books of the *argentarius* were naturally kept

[1] See the excellent article on *Codex Accepti et Expensi,* by Mr. L. C. Purser in Smith's Dictionary of Antiquities: Vol. I, p. 465.

more exactly and elaborately than those of private individuals, and possessed high authority as evidence in the courts. It was rare for any civil suit involving money to be concluded without the *argentarius* having a part therein, and no doubt they seldom left the court the poorer for their intervention. They could not, however, legally withhold their books from anybody who desired them in court to maintain his cause.

As to the social standing of bankers, here again the question of magnitude made the difference between gentility and vulgarity. Such a person as Atticus might aspire to almost any honor in the gift of the state, if he cared to mingle in politics; but far below this lordly friend of the premier orator were the petty money-handlers whose offices lined the fora, who loaned money at extortionate interest to needy farmers and spendthrift young aristocrats, and who were so unrelenting in exacting their pounds of flesh that they earned the name of *sectores,* a word meaning at once cut-throat and money-lender.

The profits of the *argentarius,* of course, depended greatly on the current rates of interest, and the prosperity and stability of ancient society can to a slight extent be gauged by the usury the bankers could exact at any given period. The fall of rates on loans which immediately followed Octavius' return from the East after Actium, is commonly referred to the Egyptian treasures he released in Italy; but probably the certainty his victory brought that hereafter commerce and property would be secure, had about as much to do with it. At the best period of the Empire the old prejudice against "making money breed money"—which lingered almost down to modern times—had sunk to a minimum. The Roman Republic certainly had its share of unhappy wrestlings with the usury problem, a problem unavoidable when a primitive society is rising from a natural to a money economy, and ready coin is scarce. The amount of interest made legal by the Twelve Tables is still under debate and probably can never be disposed of with the present evidence. Perhaps it was not more than $8\frac{1}{3}$ % per annum.[1] In 343 B.C. the usury question had become so serious that the Genucian Law forbade the taking of any interest at all—an enactment which, it is needless to say, soon became a dead letter. Finally after vain attempts to regulate the evil in 193 B.C., the *centesima* or 12% rate became established as the legal interest, and thus it remained through the later Republic and under the Empire, although a higher rate was permissible in cases of bottomry so long as the vessel on which money was loaned was at sea; if she had reached harbor, nothing more than the 12% could be demanded. Justinian, late in the life of the Empire, reduced the legal rate to 6%, and on bottomry to 12%. But for practical purposes the *centesima,* the one per cent per month, remained the regular rate of ancient interest.

Of course no such rate could be obtained on standard investments around Rome, any more than 6% can be depended on, in the case of conservative loans in Massachusetts. Cicero mentions a sudden rise from 4% to 8%. Under the early Empire we hear of "a modest 5%" on an investment, while 11% is considered extortionate. A benevolent institution in Veleia received on a mortgage 5%, another in Liguria only 2½%. On the other hand the *negotiatores* who had the provinces in their clutch devoured a vastly greater usury till the Empire drew their teeth. Verres wrung out of the luckless Sicilians 24%. Brutus in the extreme case of his loan to the

---

[1] The other view is that it was 10% per annum. The question is unfortunately involved with another question about the old Roman Calendar.

Cyprians demanded 48%. The young spendthrifts of the capital fell early into the hands of the money-lenders who knew neither conscience nor law. Horace hints that as much as 60% was sometimes demanded; Juvenal tells of a Crepereius Pollio who wanted to lend at 36%, but could find no one foolish enough to borrow. Many a debtor, unable to discharge his first obligation readily, had to borrow the sum elsewhere at a higher interest; and so passing from one creditor to another, always on harder terms, at last ended in ruin. But these are mere incidents to any complex society with its due proportion of fools and unfortunates.

Generally speaking, the previous statement holds good, that about 6% could be expected on property and conservative loans in Rome and its neighborhood. In the provinces, rates were higher. Pliny the Younger, however, writes from Bithynia to Trajan that he is unable to loan out the public money (as the custom was) at the legal 12%, and asks if he should reduce the rate to find borrowers. Trajan directs him to do so. In Egypt—the only province from which we have any considerable data—we can see a steady fall in the rate as the prosperity under the Empire rises. At first it was apparently 18%, indicating a lack of confidence and of loanable capital. By Nero's time it had sunk to the ordinary 12%; and thanks to the expanding Indian trade and general prosperity under the Flavian and Antonine Caesars, it fell in some cases to 10%.

The Roman world, then, had its capitalists, its bankers, its credit system. The next step for us is naturally an examination of its commerce.[1]

[1] A typical business document, preserved at Pompeii may have some interest.

"*Entry of account of Umbricia Jannaria.*

"Umbricia Jannaria declared that she had received from Lucius

5. *Sea Traffic and Foreign Commerce.*

Never again till Columbus and Vasco da Gama found new worlds was the ocean so covered with ships bound on long voyages as during the palmy days of the Empire. A few papyri preserved, giving the port lists of Alexandria, Ephesus, or Puteoli, would be most enlightening reading. The information we have about Roman sea traffic and distant commerce is scattered, but gives us a high opinion of ancient mariners and their enterprise. Talmudic writings show frequent trading voyages of the Jews to Rome and to Spain. Horace speaks of merchants going three and four times per year to the Atlantic, especially to Gades, which was in such close relations with Rome. At Puteoli has been found the gravestone of a Gaius Octavius Agathopus, on which he says that after weary journeys from Orient to Occident here at last he finds rest. Juvenal speaks of the havens crowded with ships, and declares there were almost more men on the sea than on the land. Wherever gain calls them they go. They push out boldly beyond Calpe (Gibraltar) and "hear the sun hiss as he sinks into the western waves." Aristeides the rhetor speaks of voyages which "uncounted numbers of private people" (no doubt traders) make to Britain; and in Domitian's day the havens of Ireland—an island never invaded by the legions—were known to the sea traders. The merchants indeed, whether by land or sea, did not wait for the shelter of the eagles. They had penetrated deeply into Gaul before

Caecilius Jucundus 11,039 sesterces, which sum came into the hands of Lucius Caecilius Jucundus by agreement, as the proceeds of an auction sale, the commission due him having been deducted.

"Done at Pompeii on the 12th day of December in the consulship of Lucius Durius and Publius Clodius." [Nine witnesses put their hands to this document and in a memorandum one Dec. Volcius Thallus adds his special attest.]

Caesar's conquest; they had crossed the Alps by the Great St. Bernard, paying toll to the local tribes before either end of the pass was held by the Roman troops.

The trader in short was ubiquitous. Juvenal speaks of voyages to Crete and Cilicia to buy saffron and raisin wine. Persius urges, "Bestir yourself: get the salted fish, oakum, ebony, incense, silken gauze from the Euxine; and be the first to lift the sacks of pepper from the backs of the thirsty camels;" while Horace admonishes his merchant to "hasten, that no one gets before you to the haven, and that you do not lose the Cibyratian and Bithynian business (with its iron wares and smoked products.)"

The commercial pace was furious, almost as furious—if the thing can be possible—as in the twentieth century. Distant commerce indeed had grave disadvantages, some of which have been done away with. The modern merchant is confident that the "tramp" or "liner" which carries his venture will ride through the fiercest hurricane. Not so, his predecessor of Gades or Alexandria. It was held that persons born under the sign of the Crab[1] would especially prosper in distant commerce; and the mere fact that a lad had been born under such governance often determined that he become a sea trader.[2] The dangers were many, the chance of total loss large; but the profits of a successful venture corresponded. That some merchants spent as much of their lives *en route*, as a "traveling man" of to-day, is shown by the tomb of a manufacturer of Hierapolis in Phrygia, which says that he had sailed seventy-two times around Cape Malea to Italy.

The distant trade of course was by no means con-

[1] Cancer: the fourth sign of the zodiac.

[2] Petronius' Trimalchio boasts that he was born under the sign of the crab.

6

fined to Romans, or to any other one nationality which was fused into the Empire. The descendants of the old Phoenician stock were everywhere. They are even more frequently reported as traveling than the Alexandrians. We have the inscription of the agent of a society of Syrians in Malaga, Spain. A certain Teym-ibn-Saad of Kanawat, Syria, is discovered as trading between Aquitania and Lyons. Traces of Syrian merchants are met in Dacia; their inscriptions are found in Trier on the Moselle. Even after the Empire was dissolving, the Syrian continued to live up to St. Jerome's word that he had an inborn passion for trade. In the fifth century in Gaul, "Syrian" was the name for banker, just as "Lombard" was in the Middle Ages. There were large colonies of them in the Gallic cities; and when on July 4th, 585 A.D., King Guntram the Frank entered Orleans, he was greeted by songs of welcome from the multitude, sung in the speech of the Latins, the Syrians and the Jews.

That Roman commerce was on more primitive lines than our own is sufficiently proven by the fact that a merchant had to do his business, not by correspondence, but by travel. "Merchant" and "traveler" are almost synonymous. The trader usually owned or at least managed a ship, whereof he would be either master or supercargo. He would go direct to the port where seemed to be the most advantageous wares, buy them, and voyage away to the most profitable market. Our geographical knowledge of antiquity is almost entirely due to these commercial wanderers. The Oriental trade was wholly in such hands, and the bulk of the grain trade to Italy. By land the trader had an equally varied life; and again inscriptions and tombstones tell that it was not Syrians only who wandered far in search of gain. Inscriptions at Augsburg name merchants from Lyons,

Trier and Bourges. Aquileia (the precursor of Venice in northern Italy) was particularly a meeting place of the nations, from the barbarian North and from Italy and even from Africa. Tradesmen of every clime flocked thither; and we find there the grave-stone of a citizen of Cologne who had also trafficked in Dacia.

But the emporium of antiquity was, beyond doubt, Alexandria. The great Hellenistic city had a commercial preëminence not possessed by even London or New York to-day, not to mention Hamburg or the European capitals. Noble havens, protected by every known means, received the ships from the entire civilized world. Jews, Egyptians, Greeks, Italians competed here with Persians, Arabs and Phoenicians. The products of Egypt were important, but not so important as the imports from the interior of Africa and from the Indies. Nowhere else in the Roman world was honest labor more highly esteemed; nowhere else was so little social prejudice against commerce. The municipality itself was granted privileges which gave its citizens high advantages over those of the Egyptian back country. No Egyptian who was not first a citizen of Alexandria was allowed to become a "Roman." An Alexandrian again was exempt from the provincial poll tax and liturgies; was entitled to a free distribution of corn, and to the privilege (in case of condemnation) of being beaten with rods and not with whips. However unimportant this last honor may appear, there was no disputing the commercial preëminence of the great city. The business was enormous, apart from the regular export of corn to Italy. At Perinthus on the Propontis, at Tomis on the Euxine, not to name many nearer shipping centers, were societies of Alexandrian merchants, and their vessels were in every haven. It will not be forgotten how the Apostle

Paul took passage on a Alexandrian ship at the road-stead of Myra in Lycia.

Alexandria boasted that she supplied all the world with paper and every manner of manufactured wares, spices, and incense. Alexandrian vessels visited the harbors of Spain, western Gaul, the Scilly Isles and Cornwall, seeking the tin which was absolutely needed in the city's extensive bronze factories. In a moment we shall speak of her connections with the Far East; but while she was undoubtedly first in this Orient trade, she had to face considerable competition, especially after the conquest and opening of Arabia Petra in 105 A.D. The Arabian commerce in particular probably found the caravan route to Damascus via Petra more convenient. Thither passed the dates of Hedjaz, the perfumes of Yemen; and into Arabia went the corn and raisins of the Jordan district, and the cloth stuffs of Asia Minor; while through Damascus wound long caravans from the far East seeking the Syrian port towns.

The exports from the eastern provinces to the western were in large proportion textile products. The Italians had been originally limited to purely woolen garments, and these spun and woven almost entirely on the home estate. "She spun wool" is recorded on the tomb of many a Roman matron; and the occupation was not despised even by ladies of the palace. However in the last republican days, women wore linen, and men used linen handkerchiefs. By the third century linen tunics were very largely worn by men, and generally speaking the advance of the Empire involved a general decline in the supremacy of woolens. The best linen came from Egypt, Syria and Cilicia. Cotton goods only came to Rome after the first war in Asia (191 B.C.). Chinese silk passed into the Roman world scantily and slowly, though in gradually increasing volume. In the first century A.D. it was worn mixed with linen or cotton by women and by effeminate dandies. But it was Elagabalus in the degenerate third century who was the first to wear heavy all-silk garments (thanks, possibly, to increasingly better communications with the far East).

Other costly fabrics, of course, existed, and gave employment to prosperous industries in Egypt, Asia, and elsewhere. The use of gold and silver embroideries increased as silk became more common, and as manners changed for the worse; but gold was not greatly used for purposes of dress ornament, except on carpets, triumphal robes and the like, and we must not imagine the Romans having those mantles of gold and silver stuff common in the Middle Ages.

A long catalogue could be made of imports into the Empire from the South and East, though in the absence of enlightening details such a list does not mean much. From Persia were imported slave-eunuchs, carpets, and morocco leather; from East Africa and Ethiopia the fashionable negro slaves, apes, ivory, and rare marbles; from Central Africa came the highly prized wild beasts for the arena; from Arabia and India (as well as from the highlands of Eran), spices and medicines; from India in particular indigo, various steel and iron manufactures, also all kinds of precious stones, sapphire, topaz, sardonyx, onyx, amethyst, carbuncle, and pearls. Emeralds came from Bactria. The African coast of the Indian ocean sent tortoise shell, and above all, from that dim world beyond India came the precious silk and silken yarn.

The eastern trade was thus of considerable magnitude, and the imperial government endeavored to make it as profitable to subjects of the Empire as possible, especially to reduce the number of foreign middlemen. To put a stop to transhipments at Arabian ports, in

Claudius' day, a duty of 25% was laid on all wares coming from such harbors to Egypt, to compel the merchants to make the voyage straight up the Red Sea. The usual route for the Far Eastern merchants was from India and up the Red Sea to the ports on its western shores of Berenice-Troglodytice, or Myoshormos, whence routes across the desert took them to the Nile, and then easy river transport led to Alexandria. The Upper-Egyptian deserts through which these routes led must have been threaded by incessant caravans, when this trade was at its height. During the summer heats the merchants went along only in the night, "guided by the stars," as says Strabo. Already in Augustus' time springs and cisterns had been arranged along the route by the Roman army at convenient stopping places.

Of the many pages of ancient history that seem lost, none are much more to be regretted than those which described the ancient exploration of India and of the East African coast. We only know that by the time of Vespasian the Alexandrian merchants seem to have penetrated as far south as Zanzibar. The Arabian Sea appears to have been explored thoroughly. Many voyages had been made direct to India. Dionysius, the author of a poetical description of the world, who lived under Hadrian, said that "he was no merchant or voyager, and had never been over the Indian Sea to the Ganges, as so many had done who set their life at stake in order to gain immeasurable riches."

The merchants of ancient India were surely handicapped by their very imperfect shipping. The ancient man-of-war was beyond doubt a very formidable fighting instrument, but we get a poor opinion of the seaworthiness of Greek and Roman fleets—witness the fearful losses by storm in the First Punic War, and in Octavius' war against Sextus Pompeius. Of the ancient merchant ships we are very imperfectly informed. We know they were built on different lines from the war-ships, and probably were far more seaworthy. They were driven by sails, yet had a few oars, usually twenty, and from their build were called "round" ships, as against the "long" war-ships. Their tonnage was reckoned by talents or amphorae.[1] We thus read of vessels of 300, 2,000, 3,000 talents burden and the like; and the largest merchantmen were of 10,000 talents. Lucian describes an Egyptian corn ship as of more than average size, and makes it 180 feet long, 45 feet wide, and of about as much depth. Some of these large ships had three decks. But it is very unsafe to generalize about their capabilities. We know that Saint Paul's Alexandrian corn ship had on board two hundred and seventy-six souls, yet was not capable of risking a winter voyage from Crete to Italy.[2] Indeed, the general impression one gets about ancient ships is that they did not differ much, save in size, from the picturesque little *fulcennas* that to-day dot the Mediterranean—excellent, handy vessels in a calm, but none too staunch in a tempest.

However, with such shipping the mariners of Roman Egypt succeeded in penetrating well into the Far East. We can trace their progress in geographical knowledge by scattered hints. For example, in Augustus' time the expedition of Aelius Gallus against southwestern Arabia came to grief through ignorance of the proper route to the region, so that the army wasted away through mere disease and thirst. But in that same age the route to

[1] A talent was equal to a cubic foot of water, or about 57 lbs.

[2] A monster Alexandrian ship, used in Augustus' time to bring an obelisk from Egypt to Rome, carried, besides the monument, 200 sailors, 1,200 passengers, 400,000 Roman bushels of wheat and a cargo of linen, glass, paper and pepper. A liner surely of unusual size, and not many could have been like her. We do not know her tonnage.

India was well understood. "Not twenty Egyptian ships in the year," says a writer of the period, "sailed forth, while the Ptolemies reigned, from the Arabian gulf; now one hundred and twenty merchantmen annually sail to India from the port of Myoshermos alone." Probably the policy of the government in favoring direct voyages had something to do with this. In the elder Pliny's time the favorite route was from Berenice to Ocelis in Arabia,—a voyage of thirty days—thence forty days more to Muziris on the Malabar coast (probably the modern Mangalore); but no halt was commonly made here. The voyage finally ended in Barace (Barygaza). All haste was made at this emporium to disembark the outward cargo and reload, to catch the returning monsoon back to Berenice. All in all, it took ninety-four days to get from Alexandria to Malabar, and the entire voyage would consume six to seven months.

The eastern commerce was of course open to serious danger from pirates. Freebooters were almost unremovable from the ocean so long as commerce hugged the shore, and thus was liable to attack from small, swift boats; and even until steamers and heavy cannon made the work of governments easy. The Roman merchantmen carried archers in their crews to beat off pirates, and probably sailed in squadrons; still this risk was always to be added to the ordinary perils of wave and weather.

That the Indian and Arabian trade was of no small magnitude is shown by the elder Pliny's lament that the Orientals had much to sell, and would take little save gold in return, consequently the Empire lost every year 50,000,000 ses. in metallic money to India, and as much more in value was bought in Arabia, where indeed the countervailing imports were greater. But this serious drain on the precious metals of the Empire was hardly realized by the Roman world in the first century of its prosperity, and for a while the boundary of Oriental commerce was steadily pushed eastward by private enterprise. To Claudius came an embassy from Ceylon conducted by the freedmen of Annius Plocanus, the farmer of customs on the Red Sea. The barbarian prince of the island was very anxious to have friendly relations with the monarch whose head he saw on so many coins, and expressed great admiration for the standard weight and value of the Roman money, an admiration that doubtless vanished after the debasing of the silver by Nero.

When Ptolemy the geographer undertook to write in the middle of the second century, he shows the extension of geographical knowledge, thanks undoubtedly to the extension of trade. Besides Ceylon (Taprobane), of which he knows a good deal, he can tell about the mouths of the Ganges, the Malay Peninsula (the Golden Chersonesus) and apparently something of the Malaccas and possibly of Tongking.

The eastern trade assumed such magnitude that it even seems to have been profitable to prepare a regular "trade-money" for deceiving the unsuspecting Hindoos. Many finds of Roman denarii have been made in the Punjab, usually of the coinage of Augustus—but debased and plated to pass at full value. In Ceylon and the Cape Comorin region too, considerable Roman money has been found, and near Calcutta a great treasure of gold pieces from the later imperial period, although the mere finding of coins does not prove the presence of Roman traders; money can travel rapidly and through many hands.

In the fourth century A.D., there was still considerable India trade through Egypt, but in the wars and confusions the Roman merchants were letting it slip by

them. The rise of the strong Persian monarchy, able to
control and protect the through caravan routes, probably
had something to do with it; and commerce was seeking
the Red Sea less. Again, the Axumites of Abyssinia
and the Homerites of Southwest Arabia were asserting
themselves, and the emperors were too weak or too
preoccupied to check them. The trade was drifting back
to foreign middlemen, and we discover the praefects of
Constantine I negotiating treaties with the desert tribes
for the expediting of commerce.[1]

Passing from the Indian trade, the question as to
intercourse with China arises most naturally. The
means for answer are painfully scanty. The envoys
from Ceylon and the India merchants—Pliny relates—
described the "Seres" as carrying on a barter at a river
bank with traders who came for their silk. In the second
century A.D. Marinus of Tyre speaks of a caravan path
leading across Turkestan, and through the deserts of
Central Asia to the Chinese city of Issedon. But the
route, as he describes it, is most hard to trace. Beyond
Issedon the way is declared to have gone on to the capital of the Seres, seemingly Si-ngan-fu.

The intercourse between the great eastern and western Empires was thus probably extremely limited, though
by no means non-existent. The Chinese annalists can
perhaps tell more about it than the Roman. In the
reign of Chang-tí, whose armies penetrated almost to the
Caspian, the Celestials began to hear of the great power
whose civilization was so different from their own. The
Chinese authors of the age speak of the Romans with
great respect. "Everything admirable in other coun-

---

[1] Yet even in this reign direct communication existed with India.
Constantine received an embassy of Hindoos, and the Byzantine historian,
Cedranus, makes him send the philosopher Metrodorus as his agent on a
trip to India.

tries comes from this land [of Rome.] Gold and silver
money is coined there; ten of silver is worth one of gold.
Their merchants trade by sea with Persia and India, and
gain ten for one in their traffic. They are simple and
upright, and never have two prices for their goods.
Grain is sold among them very cheap, and large sums
are embarked in trade;" remarks which prove that the
shop-keeping Chinese were mainly interested in the
opportunities Rome might give for commerce, and that
"the white man's bond" was already valued in the Orient. All the above however might have been written
with only hearsay evidence from Persian and Indian
merchants. Nevertheless a direct embassy, the Chinese
say, from the Emperor "Antun" (Marcus Aurelius
Antoninus) entered South China probably by Canton.
It is likely it was simply a band of western merchants
who tried to give themselves importance by posing as
envoys from their master; just as in Augustus' time,
Florus says "ambassadors" came from the Seres and the
Indians with gifts of elephants, gems and spices. Nevertheless the intercourse with China and the West, if slow
and indirect, was presumably of some commercial
importance. In the province of Shansi there have been
found sixteen Roman coins from the time of Tiberius
down to Aurelian. A Chinese work written about 350
A.D. concerning plants imported from over seas, represents the port of Canton as open to foreign commerce,
and native writers represent their country as receiving
from the Romans, glass and metal manufactures, dye-
stuffs, amber, jewels, drugs and coral. Some of these
last named articles surely came from regions outside the
Empire, possibly from the East African coast, and the
amber may be imagined as coming clear from the Baltic,
albeit through Roman hands. When this little has been
said—and it is surely little—we are forced to turn away

from the Far East, conscious that a most interesting page in the history of commercial exploration and enterprise has been forever lost to us. How many of those verbose treatises on the degenerate Epicurean philosophy, preserved at Herculaneum, would we not gladly exchange for the journal of the envoys of "Antun" to the Seres!

Whatever else we know of the Oriental trade, we know its gains were enormous. The profit was first and last 5,000%. The retail handler according to Juvenal, only made 50% on his sales; but the gain, considering the distance, risk, expense and time of journey was not excessive. Florus speaks—perhaps with exaggeration—of the land caravans from China taking four years. Nearchus, Alexander's admiral, took eighty days on his voyage of discovery from the Indus delta to the mouth of the Persian Gulf. The figures given above for the time of the India voyages would often have been exceeded. Wages and bonuses to shipmen in such dangerous waters must have been high; and we know that transport by land caravan was very expensive. The main means of communication was by camel; the ass could only bear half as much; the wagon four times as much—if the roads in the wilderness would permit its use. A camel could carry four hundred pounds[1] or more. For an Arabian caravan from Sabota in south Central Arabia to Rhinocolura on the Mediterranean between Pelusium and Gaza, the elder Pliny says the charge per camel-load was fully 688 denarii. Besides the freightage, the importer had to face all kinds of customs, tolls, fees and petty exactions. The Oriental trader then was not seeking an unreasonable profit.

That sea communication was sometimes painfully

[1] That was the legal load as fixed by the Edict of Diocletian; but probably this was merely a minimum.

slow, is shown by the dating of a number of official documents in Egypt in 193 A.D. The Emperor Pertinax was proclaimed in Rome on January 1st of that year. On March 6th, the Praefect of Egypt proclaimed him also—naturally the first thing for a provincial governor to do after getting news of a new accession, unless he wished to pose as a rebel. Pertinax was murdered on March 28th. Yet on May 19th, the news had not reached the Egyptian Fayum, for official papers drawn on that day were dated with his name.

However, notwithstanding these drawbacks, the gains of the Roman captains of commerce were sufficiently large. Fortunes were put on a more solid basis than under the Republic even if the enormously profitable syndicates of *publicani* were no longer possible. Pliny speaks of the period of the later Republic as a time of comparative poverty as measured with his own; and the prosperity must have maintained itself until the great plague and the barbarian invasions began to make themselves felt in the age of Marcus Aurelius.

The exports of the Empire were far less important than the imports. To southeast Africa there were sent considerable quantities of grain, wine, oil, iron, copper, and tin; also all kinds of wearing apparel, glassware, pottery, tools, and weapons. But the negro tribes of the south could not have been extensive customers, and the relations of Rome with Abyssinia were never very cordial.

It is a mistake however to imagine all the foreign trade centered in Alexandria and the Syrian cities. Carthage was the head of caravan routes to and from the Soudan; Olbia on the Euxine was the center of a lively Northern trade, and the terminus for important caravan routes from Persia and China by way of the Caspian. But perhaps the greatest interest apart from the Oriental commerce, centers in the commerce between Rome and the Germanic North; for here the future masters of the world were gaining their first lessons in civilization. The indomitable Roman trader probably penetrated to the Baltic, in the quest of amber; although the middleman must have had a large part in the traffic. The amber trade appears to have gone across Silesia through Bohemia into the Empire, the trade routes usually following the basins of the great rivers. Discoveries of Roman coins have been met with in Germany from Hanover to East Prussia, in Denmark and even in the south of Norway and of Sweden;[1] though here, as in India, it is dangerous to conclude that Roman hands actually buried them in their destinations. Pliny the Elder tells how Nero sent an *eques* with a large sum of money to the Baltic to buy up all the amber to be had. Roman ladies admired blonde German hair, and the trade in flaxen tresses from the North was very extensive. Not merely coins have been found in the Baltic region, but on the Island of Fünen on the east coast of Jutland, and also near Königsberg have been unearthed arms and utensils of Roman make—imports from the Empire and very useful to the barbarian. At the other end of the northern frontier, at Dioscurias on the eastern extremity of the Euxine so many nations came together to trade that the elder Pliny says one hundred and thirty interpreters were needed. But here again may be recognized the terminus of an Eastern caravan route.

Generally speaking the North had not a great deal as yet to offer the more cultured South. Amber and flaxen hair paid for the bulk of the Italian wine and Gallic iron manufactures that the Germans welcomed eagerly. Still they could send the Empire quantities of the highly

---

[1] A find in Scania in Scandinavia amounts to 550 silver denarii dating from Nero to Septimius Severus.

prized German goose feathers; and last but not least a goodly number of stout slaves to work the great capitalists' plantations. Britain, the least Romanized of all the provinces, could buy her manufactured imports with pig lead, tin, hides, and valuable dogs, not forgetting many slaves also; a contribution, however, that dwindled from decade to decade, as the conquest advanced, and British society became more obedient, settled and hence less exposed to kidnapping.

The foreign trade then of the Empire was great, but compared with the internal trade it was almost insignificant. The remark is worth repeating that the Empire was economically self sufficient, even beyond the United States of to-day. The barrier between race and race, between man and man seemed cast down. Every year for decades the force of local prejudice and local tradition became less. Every year the financial returns of the government must have reflected the general and rising prosperity; and it was still more decades before men began to realize that the great age of material well-being was slowly but surely on the wane.

6. *Roman Roads and Land Travel.*

Highly as one may rate the sea-borne commerce of the Empire, the "Indian" fleet, the "Egyptian" fleet, the "African" fleet, the argosies that bound Gades with Rome, Gaul with Britain, Corinth with the Euxine; the land traffic of the Empire no doubt exceeded this ocean traffic many times. In the greater part of the imperial dominions the opportunity for safety, ease, and rapidity of travel was never equaled till the period of Napoleon; perhaps not till the introduction of railways. A world-wide empire almost implied that at least the upper classes must change their residences frequently, and journey often; and landways and waterways were ready to make this travel easy—if needs be, luxurious. The deeply cut wagon tracks in the hard basalt of the streets and roads near Rome testify even now to the departed roar and bustle of a great traffic. And if we say that at present the commerce of the northern and western parts of the Empire is far greater than of old, the southern and eastern parts enjoy a great deal less.

Even rather obscure people traveled in Cicero's time, accompanied by that swarm of retainers with which a Roman gentleman could never dispense. Cicero himself met in the depths of Asia Minor a certain Publius Vedius, a man of no great consequence, with two chariots, a carriage, a litter, horses, many slaves, besides a monkey on a little car and numerous wild asses. More humble personages of course tramped the dusty miles on foot, as did Saint Paul and his companions, accepting the dubious hospitalities of the wayside inns, and following in the wake of a merchant's caravan or a nobleman's retinue when passing through a region infested by robbers.

Traveling by sea was practically at an end in winter save in pressing emergencies.[1] Even in summer time the younger Pliny found disagreeable the getting from Ephesus up to his Bithynian province. He wrote to Trajan that he was greatly troubled by heat and some attacks of fever while going by carriage to Pergamus. Then he tried a coaster through the Hellespont, and contrary winds detained him so that he reached Bithynia much later than he had expected. Pliny, however, was a somewhat delicate person, and most travelers would have made less of the "etesian winds and summer heats."

[1] For example, Cassius Dio mentions it as something unusual that Octavius while pursuing Antonius after Actium, went from Italy to Asia in mid-winter, dragging his ships across the Isthmus of Corinth to avoid the perilous Laconian capes.

A proconsul did not have to contend with one drawback to ancient travel—the absence of good hotels. Persons of consequence could always find some friend or some friend's friend along the way, whom the old time notions of hospitality would compel to keep them over night. The Greek and Roman inns to which the plebeian travelers resorted had a very ill name, and perhaps deserved it. They were usually low drinking houses with brothels annexed; and if in the open country, might be dens of thieves. Two inns have been found in Pompeii that give us an idea of their arrangements; although hostleries in such a refined little city were doubtless better than the road houses in the country. One structure is called the "Elephant Inn," otherwise "The *Hospitium* of Hyginius Firmus." It had a large room in front, opening directly upon the street. This room was probably the dining room. At one side, apart from the main room, was a wine shop also opening upon the thoroughfare. The kitchen was behind the wine room, and at one side of the main room. On the other side of the great room were six bedrooms. In the extreme rear were stalls for cattle. "The Elephant Inn" was clearly not prospering at the time Pompeii was destroyed, for the "To let" sign was upon it. We do not know whether the other inn, "The Inn of Hermes," was more successful. It had only three bedrooms below; but there were rooms in the second story, an arrangement which gave more space for the stables.[1]

But if the inns were bad, only praise can be given to the Roman road system. Primarily indeed this great network had been laid out for military purposes, but it

---

[1] The landlord was legally responsible for injuries to his guests.

An inn at Lyons bore this inscription: "Here Mercury promises profit, Apollo health, Septumanus good bed and board. He who will stop here will find himself well off. Traveler, take heed where you stay!"

served the ends of commerce almost equally well. A
system of great "Trunk Lines" running out of Rome
placed the Mistress of the World in close connection with
all her subjects. The Via Appia, "The Queen of Roads,"
led to Capua and to the ferry at Messana, where a road
along the north coast of Sicily, by way of the modern
Palermo, brought the traveler to the brisk haven of
Lilybaeum. Thence an easy run by water of about
twenty-four hours carried him to Carthage. From Carthage a good road ran clear along the northern shore of
Africa to Tingis (Tangiers), giving ready entrance to
Spain.

If the traveler was going east from Rome he would
again follow the Via Appia to Capua, after which he had
the choice of two roads to Brundusium. It took only a
day and a night to make the other end of the Adriatic
ferry at Dyrrhachium. From this point the great Via
Egnatia took him through Macedonia and Thrace to
Byzantium. It was tapped by cross roads leading to
southern Greece, especially to Athens. Another branch
led to Lampsacus on the Hellespont, whence a ferry of
one hour set the wayfarer down in Asia Minor. Direct
roads through the thriving industrial district of the great
peninsula brought him to Antioch, whence a network of
pre-Roman highways could take him to the Euphrates,
or through Syria to Egypt.

If the journey from Rome was northward, three routes
were open. The first was the Via Flaminia which led to
Ariminum, and thence continued by the Via Aemilia to
Milan. On the way at Modena a road branched off
toward the north to Verona, thence to Aquileia, a very
commanding point. From Aquileia a road system led
into Istria, through Dalmatia and to Dyrrhachium; likewise another one across the Cornican Alps to the Danube
region and to the series of frontier towns and legionary

camps in that vast territory. A second northern highway ran along the west coast of Etruria to Pisa and
Genoa; thence along the Riviera and across the Alps to
Massilia and the Arlate region, to be continued through
the important city of Narbo into Spain, where it ter-
minated at Gades. A third northern route passed over
the above mentioned ways to Milan, then into Gaul by
the greater and lesser St. Bernard passes, and finally up
to the Rhone, Rhine and Loire country by the great network of the Gallic road system.

The actual processes of Roman road building are of
course of a technical nature, and therefore of little
interest to the average reader. From the numerous
remains of highways that have defied time and from the
remarks of Vitruvius and Strabo, we can gather a sufficient idea both of the details of the work and the excellence of the production. The usual method was to dig
two ditches marking the limits of the road on either side,
which might vary in breadth from eleven to fifteen feet.
The whole of the loose surface earth was removed, and
excavation was continued until a firm subsoil or, better
still, a bed of rock was obtained. If the ground was
swampy the indefatigable workers would drive piles to
secure a solid foundation. On such an unyielding basis
the Roman would proceed to build his road in several
strata, first one of large stones, a second one nine inches
thick of smaller stones cemented with lime, next a stratum
six inches thick of still smaller stones, pieces of broken
brick and pottery, the whole bound together by the
admirable Roman cement, and smoothed and flattened on
the top. Above all were laid large, flat blocks of the
hardest stone readily procurable, irregular in shape, but
fitted with extreme nicety one to another, so as to present
a perfectly smooth surface to the marching legions, or
the wheels of incessant commerce.

The amount of money sunk first and last on the roads was enormous. Of course the price per mile of road-building varied with place and climate; it was far higher near the confines of unsettled Germany than on the teeming plains by the Po. A mile of road built in Hadrian's time from Beneventum to Aeclanum cost 100,000 ses., and this perhaps is a fair average for work in a peaceful, long civilized province, with labor and material at normal value.

That the Roman builders wrought not for their own age only is testified to by the many cases where their unerring instinct seized upon lines of travel well beaten to-day. For example, the Via Egnatia across the lower Balkan peninsula is still the main avenue of communication in that Turk-infested region. Hardly any province had a finer road system than Gaul; 13,200 miles of Gallo-Roman roads have been counted in its confines, and by no means all have been identified. The construction began in the southern province as soon as the Republic established its hold; Augustus's age saw a great exten-tion northward, especially under the fostering direction of Agrippa, who designed the vast network that is to-day the basis for communication in France. Compared with the modern French chaussées, the Roman roads are declared more solid, better paved and adjusted. They do not strive to circumvent natural obstacles, but to sur-mount them, going boldly over hill and dale, cutting through hewn defiles and lining precipices, and going straight to their mark. "More than any other monu-ment," declares a present day Frenchman, "these mag-nificent roads spoke to the peoples of the majesty of the Empire, visible still across so many ages in their ruin, in every part of Gaul and in the most distant provinces. And the emperors knew well that they maintained the life of the great body by them, for they did not cease to maintain them with unabated vigor up to the last days [of the Empire]."[1]

The number of ancient mile-stones in Spain, however, leads to the conjecture that the road system there was even finer than in Gaul. The emperors, however, seem largely to have contented themselves with building one great government highway from the north to the south of the peninsula, and trusting to the local communities to supply the rest; for since Spain was accounted a highly peaceful province, the military motive for building roads was lacking.

In Sicily the Romans had more than one thousand miles of roads, giving an easy communication with all parts of the island such as it never again enjoyed till the coming of steam. In Sardinia were another thousand miles, many stretches leading through what is now sheer wilderness.

Almost every emperor found time and money for this beneficent work. It is difficult here to distinguish. Trajan built his highly difficult coast roads on the lower Danube more for military than for commercial ends; but no warlike impulse prompted him when he built the magnificent bridge of Alcantara in Spain, or caused the water-road, the old canal between the Red Sea and the Mediterranean, again to be made practical. Septimius Severus was a mighty road-builder; no other reign presents so many inscriptions of highways built or renewed. His activity was known to have been marked in Spain, Phoenicia, Pannonia, Noricum, Raetia, southern Italy, Africa, Sardinia, and Germany; and we cannot doubt in all the other provinces. A fairer monument thus to his stern, strenuous reign than his monstrous seven-belted Septizonium façade on the Palatine!

The superintendence of the road system was naturally

[1] Bloch: in his *Gaule romaine*, p. 426.

an important matter with the government, and its details would be an important matter in Roman administrative history. It is enough to remark that Augustus set up a regular department of highways—of which Dio Cassius the historian was two hundred years later the superintendent. Under him were "road-makers" of praetorian rank. But Augustus gave each of the great highways its special curator, who held office as a perpetual magistrate; and as consul he took pains himself to repair the great Via Flaminia, and compelled various senators to assume the expense of renewing other highways. In the country districts the greater part of the expense and care of the roads fell on the rural communities and their magistrates, all working however under the watch of the imperial curator whose power sometimes might be very great. Thus Corbulo, as curator in Tiberius' and Caligula's times, followed up the shortcomings of the local officers with great severity, and visited fines and imprisonments on not a few. The road system in short was a heavy drain on the communities, but one for which they gained fair return in commerce and military protection so long as the Empire prospered. When the Empire declined, the provincials saw their commerce wane, and the legions unable to hold back the enemy; but still the expensive up-keep of the roads continued to be one of the many burdens that afflicted the dying Empire.

The construction of the Roman road system ought then to be compared somewhat to the construction period of railways in 1830 to 1850. A great leap was taken in human development. It is surprising that the Romans did not go a step further and organize a postal system somewhat as known to-day. They never went further than forming a governmental post service, that forwarded only officials and official despatches, and which—even after Hadrian reorganized it—was a heavy financial

burden on the communities with no corresponding gain.
Private enterprises existed indeed, which at most post
houses provided teams and carriages by which one could
travel forty to fifty miles per day. The forwarding of
private letters was uncertain business, and this must
have been a decided hindrance to commerce. Pliny
the Younger writes to a certain Julius Servianus com-
plaining that he has had no letter from him, and urging
him to write at once, "and do so *even if you have to send
a special messenger*. I will pay the traveling expenses,
and give him a present, if only he brings me the news I
wish to hear." Pliny was however a consular and could
afford special messengers; but such luxuries were beyond
many an honest merchant.

Besides sea and road communications, the Romans
made considerable use of rivers. There were flotillas
on the Rhine and the Danube, but these ships of course
were primarily men-of-war to aid the frontier guard.
In Gaul, however, Strabo notices how the rivers were
notable arteries of commerce, and we can imagine the
Loire, the Garonne, the Seine, the Moselle, and the Rhone
covered with ships, boats and barges; but Gaul lacked
the extensive canal system so useful in modern France.
In the later days of the Empire this water communication grew in favor, because a boat in midstream was less
exposed to sudden attack from the barbarians than a
caravan on the highway.

If travel was slow and precarious in winter, in summer, both by land and water, it was decidedly rapid.
One could travel fifteen or twenty leagues per day on
the roads, or faster using the imperial post. The journey from Antioch to Byzantium (nearly 700 miles) could
be accomplished in less than six days. By sea one could
get from Ostia to Fréjus in three days, to Gades in seven,
to Carthage in two, from Messana to Alexandria in six

or seven. But these were indeed "summer voyages," and from the eleventh of November to the fifth of March navigation was at an absolute standstill; all vessels were drawn up on shore, and probably the roads were not a little deserted.

Among the rich, travel was popular and frequent. For a Roman it was almost as fashionable to visit Athens, Alexandria, and the Nile, as for an American to "do" Paris and the Italian art cities. The desire of seeing new sights is strong in every race, and they grasp eagerly at the means to satisfy it. Besides it was an unsettled age, when men changed their home and their calling easily. Seneca says that less than half of the inhabitants of Rome and of the free cities were natives of the place. The supreme type of a traveler is the unwearied Hadrian, whose biography is, in one sense, a continuous round of sight-seeing.

Whole families appear to have gone on long pleasure trips together, if not to "Europe" at least to "Egypt." On the so-called "Vocal Memnon" in Egypt is the inscription of a certain Gemellus who visited it with "his dear wife Rufilla" and his children. On the pyramids a Roman lady has written "I have seen them without you, dearest of brothers. Remembering you, I have shed my tears and I write here my lament." As for the journey to Greece, it is needless to expand upon the fact how every young Roman of parts aspired to visit and perhaps study at Athens, and how all the decaying Greek cities were overrun with gaping travelers, and ignorant, knavish ciceroni exhibiting the local art treasures and pattering off the ancient legends of every rock and temple.

How the Roman wheeled carriages compared in comfort with ours, it is hard to say. Surely the litters in which the wealthy went on short journeys were easy and luxurious, while four or eight tall, even-paced Liburnian or Cappadocian slaves swung them along. Juvenal tells how one could pull down the shutters and sleep in such litters, or even read and write in them, the last feat surely being one difficult in any modern vehicle short of a "Pullman."

There was one bane to ancient traveling which seems never to have been fully eliminated—banditti. The Taurus region, Corsica and Sardinia were always full of them. In Italy the Pontine marshes, the Gallinarian forest on the Campanian coast and lower Italy generally had a very bad name for safety. Under the abler emperors the ill-doers were kept within bounds. In times of confusion they rose to a fearful plague. A certain Bullas, profiting by Commodus' feeble rule, became the leader of 600 men, and committed wide depredations before he was captured and flung to the lions by the officers of Septimius Severus. On the Mediterranean an occasional pirate—after Pompeius's great raid on the freebooters—preyed on commerce. When all is said, however, comparing the imperial age not with the present, but with the centuries before the coming of Rome, the merchant and traveler had little of which to complain.

7. *Internal Commerce and Industry.*

It was inevitable that very few of the exports and imports of ancient times should go from producer to consumer direct. Even within the Empire, in purely internal commerce the importance of the middleman was hardly less than it is to-day. Great emporia for the transfer of goods sprang up. Alexandria was, of course, a chief case to the point. But Alexandria was a little too far east to be the convenient dividing point for all lines of traffic. In Hellenistic times Rhodes had been the chief emporium. After 146 B.C Delos, under Roman fostering, became a successful rival, and a most convenient station on the highway from Italy and Greece to Asia. At its free port 10,000 slaves are said by Strabo to have changed hands in a single day. The Mithridatic war, however, inflicted on Delos a blow from which it never recovered. The generals of the King thoroughly devastated it, and Pausanias speaks of it as almost deserted in his time. Its successor was mainly Corinth which, thanks to its commanding position, grew rapidly after 46 B.C., when Julius Caesar refounded and settled it, with a colony of discharged veterans and freedmen. It was flourishing in Saint Paul's day; and continued to flourish in an age when the rest of Greece was in great decline. Apuleius tells of "the vast number of citizens that came out to meet us," Pausanias of its magnificent public buildings, while to its general prosperity the recent excavations on the site by the American School in Greece are sufficient witness.

A good share of the trade of the Greek emporia nevertheless drifted on to Italy, where Puteoli was the largest "clearing house." As early as 212 B.C. this town was an important harbor for the import of corn. It was the first really good port to the south of Rome, and became in a manner the haven of the imperial city, though a good hundred and fifty miles distant.[1] Strabo declares it was one of the chief trading cities of his time. Seneca indicates that its prestige had nowise declined. The Alexandrian corn trade—important as it was—represented only one branch of its teeming commerce. It had elaborate moles on which we are told the eager population would gather to watch the coming of the precious grain ships; it had close relations with Spain and the Syrian cities. It had important iron manufactories, and sold

[1] Antium, though nearer, could not compare with it as a haven, and Ostia was useful only to rather small ships.

an excellent cement—famous to this day for its remarkable hardness, durability and power to resist sea-water. In Antoninus Pius' time its mole and port were repaired, and many inscriptions testify to its importance down to the disastrous reign of Honorius, when its capture by Alaric (410 B.C.) was a rude blow to its prosperity. From Puteoli the Via Campana to Capua, thence the Via Appia to Rome, must have been covered with an incessant wheeled traffic; though not a little of the transport to Rome was by ships of light draught and special build, coasting up to Ostia, or even threading the Tiber to the Capital.

As an actual market to consume foreign wares, Rome was beyond peradventure the first; here were the largest shops, and, as Pliny remarks, all the goods of the world close at hand for purchase. Aristeides the rhetor asserts, however, that at Corinth every thing on sea or land was ready on sale; and that in Alexandria one could buy everything except snow. The same could be said of Antioch. As for the Arlate it was boasted as late as 418 A.D. that here could be bought the products of the Orient, Gaul, Spain and Africa in all their fullness; and presumably the like was true of the shops of Carthage.

It is a matter of grievous regret that we have by no means the same full information about ancient commercial methods that we possess about ancient agriculture. The "factory" system, somewhat on the medieval plan, seems to have been widely developed. Berytus and, it would appear, Damascus as well as the other Phoenician and Syrian trading cities had their "factories" at Puteoli, for which the modern "commercial correspondents" are substitutes. Tyre (which barring Alexandria was still the greatest trading spot in the Levant) had a factory at Rome as well as at Puteoli, and in 174 A.D. we find the Tyrian senate voting 10,000 denarii as annual rent for the buildings.

On examining the nature and volume of the internal trade it becomes at once plain that the East gave the West far more than it took in return. Italy especially had rather insignificant exports. Only wine, oil, crockery, wool, linen and hardware were sent away in any quantity.[1] Many of the old trading centers were deserted in favor of Rome, Ostia and Puteoli. Brundusium still remained important only because it was the head of the ferry to Greece. The wines of Italy to be sure were valuable and profitable, and Italian wool was exported as being the best in the world, while Italian rams were sent frequently to Spain for breeding purposes. The Puteoli iron works, afore mentioned, had also significance. The iron came from Ilva (Elba), wherein Strabo praises the abundant mines; was worked over in the busy foundries of the emporium, which almost as having a monopoly, seems to have supplied iron wares to all the world. It is not unreasonable to assume that the Roman weapons found in the graves of Silesia, Jutland and Scandinavia, are products of these foundries, though we know that Roman models were more or less imitated.

Dalmatia (Bosina) was, however, the seat of rich iron mines, as also of a textile industry that has immortalized itself in the name of the priestly *"Dalmatic."* The mining interests of the Empire were widely distributed. Greece still could send her marbles; Spain sent copper and lead, as well as the precious metals; from Britain came silver, lead and iron; from Gaul copper and iron;

[1] As an example of how ancient commerce spread itself, may be noted how bronze vessels stamped with the name of P. Cipius Polybius (an Italian manufacturer) have been found in Switzerland, Hanover, Pomerania, England and Scotland.

from the Danubian provinces besides the iron were supplied gold and salt. The tendency to regard mines and
mining as a state monopoly, however, paralyzed private
enterprise in the taking out of mineral wealth, and prevented the mining industry from becoming a great feature of the imperial age.

But all the provinces except the newest and rudest
were teeming with an intense industrial life. We would
give much for a view into one of the busy factories of
Alexandria, that great city which was given up to man-
ufacturing almost as much as to commerce. A letter
attributed to Hadrian, but more probably written in the
third century, says that in Alexandria "no one is idle,
some work glass, some make paper, some weave linen.
The only god is money." Glass, paper, and linen were
indeed the bulk of the Egyptian exports of manufactured
goods. The glass and paper industries seem concentrated within the provincial capital; but linen weaving
appears to have been carried on all over Egypt, and
there was many an active loom between the Delta and
Syene. The Egyptians had indeed to compete in these
staples with the Syrian product. The Egyptian linen
was not considered as fine as that made in Phoenicia.
On the other hand the Egyptian glass was counted superior, and the papyrus plant gave the Nile country practically a monopoly in making paper, also in ropes and
baskets. Egypt, too, could export an abundance of
beautiful building stone—the red granite of Syene, the
green breccia of the Kosêr region, basalt, alabaster, gray
granite and porphyry from the mountains above Myoshormos.

Syria was a dangerously close rival to Egypt in many
avenues of commerce; besides the trans-Asiatic trade, she
boasted scores of prosperous industrial cities. "In the
district [along the Orontes from Apamea going down to

the sea]," remarks Mommsen, "there still stand the ruins of nearly an hundred townships, with whole streets still recognizable," the relics of thriving life. Syria enjoyed prosperity longer than most other parts of the Empire during the period of decline; and in the best centuries she was a continuous garden interspersed with busy factories. We have mentioned the Syrian linen and glass. In Syria also the precious Eastern silk was made into dress goods, and morocco leather was prepared. In Antioch, Apamea, and hardly less in the cities of lesser Asia —Ephesus, Miletus, Smyrna, Laodicea, Cibyra and Rhodes—were thriving woolen industries. Tyre and Sidon still continued their famous purple manufactures. The whole eastern coast of the Aegean far into the peninsula of Asia Minor was then at the height of its prosperity, a prosperity in marked contrast to the dwindling fortunes of the western coast of Greece. Between the cities on the Euxine and the ruder northern shore there was a brisk trade in wine, clothing, and all kinds of trinkets and toys so dear to the barbarians, in return for furs and salt fish from the Russian steppes and rivers.

Greece itself was in an evil way. Only Corinth, Athens and Patrae—of some importance on the western coast—were prospering. The decline in population and wealth had begun long before the Roman conquest. The Mithridatic wars and Roman civil wars had heaped up the disasters. Towns were decaying; farms were empty. The grazing interests and the increase of great plantations were ruining the relics of the free peasantry. There were not a few robber bands. The only important exports were the famous marbles, Hymettus honey, and probably olive oil from Attica. Corinth was flourishing; Athens preserved a genteel, quiet existence, trading on her great past. But generally speaking, Greece proper had no large part in the vast commercial activity of the Empire.

Sicily, too, was not flourishing. It had never been famous for industries or commerce. Strabo makes it clear that in the age of Augustus even its agricultural prosperity—its mainstay—was deserting it. African and Egyptian competition made it hard for it to sell its corn. The old cities in the interior were decaying; the population was greatly reduced. Only the coast towns preserved something of their ancient prosperity, though here was decline also. "The Romans," we are told, "have given the hills and most of the plains over to horse-breeders, herdsmen and shepherds who [by their brigandage and revolts] have brought on the island great perils." The country itself, thought Strabo, was marvelously fertile; it surpassed Italy, producing great quantities of wheat, honey, cattle, saffron, hides and wool. Rome was almost the sole market of the island. Everything Sicily produced was shipped thither; only just enough being kept for home consumption.

That Italy was mainly a receiver, not a giver, has already been explained. Gaul and Spain were in a better position. Their wide tracts of untilled land supplied hides, fur and timber. The West also could export quantities of cheese, pork, salt meat, and among the luxuries those oysters so prized by the city gourmands. If the wines of Gaul took some time ere winning the largest market, this was mainly due to the unwise attempts of the government to encourage the vineyards of Italy by discouraging, nay, often prohibiting, wine culture elsewhere; futile legislation that was a dead letter long before Probus in the third century formally abolished it. From the northern Gallic province, Belgica, came a supply of excellent horses for the army. Much wool was raised. The manufactures in Gaul were not contemptible. There was a good deal of metal work made. The sail-cloth of Cahors was the best to be had in the West. The cloths of Saintes, Arras and Tournay were in wide demand, while ready made cloaks and capes in the Gallic style were sold for export into Italy. Italian pottery and Alexandrian glassware found a ready sale in Gaul, and one cannot imagine the finer and more artistic products of the age manufactured in the western provinces; but the recent finds of the German excavators along the Rhine prove that the West had workshops of its own, made most of the staple necessities, imitated Eastern models more or less successfully; and we can imagine Lyons, Paris, Trier, not to mention Mainz and the other Rhine towns, centers of busy industry as well as of mere trade.

Britain could contribute raw metals, hides, furs, fish, smoked meats, and highly desirable dogs; but Britain was too remote from the Mediterranean—with the stormy channel and the roads of broad Gaul to traverse—to hold a very large place in ancient economy.

Spain was vastly more important. Besides her precious mines and her agricultural products—in the main like Gaul—the peninsula was famous for the excellent weapons produced on Spanish forges. The fiery Spanish wine was exported both to Rome and to the North. But considering the long period that Spain formed a part of the Roman world, we have surprisingly little information of her economic life and internal development, and can only remark that probably during the first part of the Empire she was both more populous and more civilized than her great neighbors north of the Pyrenees.

Except for crude natural products, the Danubian region had no great place in Roman commerce. By 100 A.D. the cultivation of grain was so general in large tracts of Moesia that the province could export considerable amounts to Italy; but as a wheat-producing land the Danubian provinces surely never competed with Egypt and Africa.

In the last sentence, however, the most important single trade of the Empire has been mentioned—the export of grain from North Africa and the Nile valley to Italy, especially to Rome.

What this vast import of foreign foodstuffs meant for Italian agriculture will be considered in another place. At present one need only observe that among the most pressing duties confronting the early emperors was that of saving the "Lords of the World, the Toga-wearing Race," in other words, the Roman proletariat, from a bread famine. To this end the entire province of Egypt—which was accounted the emperor's special property—was laid under a peculiar tax in grain, levied in every village,[1] which was by far the most important of all the taxes paid by this wealthy province. The tax was carefully apportioned, pains being taken to lighten the burden on lands insufficiently fertilized for the season by the Nile. A board of *sitologoi* and assistants attended to the collection from every farm and community, and had charge of the numerous public granaries. Every month they made report to the district *strategos* of the amount of corn in store. A force of special carriers with camels and asses delivered the grain at the river, whence it made its first voyage to Alexandria. In this way 144,000,000 bushels of grain were dispatched to Rome as annual tribute. The coming of the "Egyptian fleet" was an event of great importance to the capital. Of the two hundred and ninety great *horreae*—the warehouses of Rome—the largest were for the grain.

---

[1] Alexandria and the "Melenaite nome" were alone exempt. If a farmer desired, he was, however, allowed to pay an equivalent tax in cash and keep all his grain.

8

The "*Horrea Publica Populi Romani*" extended around the docks of Trajan for two and a half miles. At Ostia such warehouses covered one third of the city. In Rome the *Horrea Galbana* alone covered a space of two hundred by one hundred and fifty-five meters.

On this grain supply the capital depended so absolutely for its existence that Vespasian, in order to bring his enemies in Italy to terms, made every effort to seize Egypt, and stop the corn fleets. More than an hundred year later, Septimius Severus, however, with the same object seized Africa. The alteration is significant. Africa and Numidia had been undergoing a great development, and gradually supplanting Egypt as the chief granary of Italy.

The African region of the Byzacium (the heart·of modern Tunis) had indeed become in the second century a land of proverbial richness. Corn was returned a hundred fold. Africa was allegorically represented as a girl with her two hands laden with heavy corn ears. Remote from the northern frontiers, the movement of legions and the inroads of barbarians, remote even from most of the wars between pretenders to the purple, North Africa was exposed only to the petty raids of Moorish tribes, and as possibly no other province enjoyed the fruits of the *Pax Romana*. The natives had already been accustomed to foreign domination by the Semites of Carthage; the Berbers now readily submitted to the juster guardianship of Rome. The magnificent irrigation and husbandry which made the African waste to blossom has been already mentioned. One third of all the grain used in Rome was, even in Augustus' time, appointed to come from North Africa. Later the proportion was no doubt greater. Oil also was produced in very great quantities. The community of Little Leptis alone was taxed by Caesar 3,000,000 pounds of oil per annum for the Roman baths. In the fourth century African oil was preferred above all others. The wine of the region was of little importance, but horse and cattle rearing flourished particularly in Numidia and Mauretania. Industry indeed did not keep pace with agriculture, although there were purple factories at the island of Gerba (Jerba), where the descendants of the colonists from Phoenicia were to some extent rivals to the purple-makers of old Tyre. Cheap woolen stuffs and leather goods also were made in Mauretania largely for home consumption. On the unsettled Moorish frontiers the kidnapping of slaves was a profitable and common, if utterly nefarious, pursuit. Likewise in North Africa were still to be found elephants,[1] and their ivory occasionally drifted into commerce.

Such is a very scant picture of the commerce and industry of the Empire. Scanty it certainly is, though eked out with conjecture and inference; yet unless every sign belies the investigator he is hardly rash in asserting that a greater commerce was hardly to be seen by the civilized world before the nineteenth century.

8. *Local Trading, Especially in Rome.*

The commerce of the Empire then was so extensive that women of the Bernese Oberland bought jewelry ornaments made in Asia Minor; that merchants of Carthage and Arabia lived in Lyons; that a Greek, a Thracian woman and a citizen of Nicomedia lie buried in Bordeaux, trade compelling them all thitherward. Still when everything is said, it is idle to pretend that foreign manufactures and products were then as widely diffused as in the twentieth century. Even Roman roads were no perfect substitute for railways. An ocean commerce that must be suspended from November to March

[1] Now extinct in the whole region.

suffered thereby a grievous handicap. Certain localities, to be sure, by chance or circumstance, would establish a monopoly in producing a given line of articles. Thus Brundusium was the center of the manufacture of mirrors, not to name Alexandria, the Syrian and Asiatic cities, Puteoli and many more. Yet the great bulk of all articles needed in a Roman household were undoubtedly made in the same region or city where they were purchased. An ancient town was not unlike a semi-oriental city, such as Palermo of to-day, where the average shops are very small, sell only a narrow line of goods, and in many cases—except where valuable imported wares are handled—selling articles made in the shop itself; the potter retailing his own pots, the shoemaker his own shoes.

How small these shops might be, how limited their traffic is shown clearly enough at Pompeii. But undoubtedly the larger cities had correspondingly larger stores, though nothing approaching the overgrown establishments of present day capitals. Especially in the city of Rome was the ancient wholesale and retail trade brought to its highest development. Here the demand was greatest, here was the most money to spend, and, as usually corresponds, here were the most objects to spend money upon. If we could have entered the shops of Antioch, Alexandria, Carthage or Lyons we would probably have found *mutatis mutandis* similar conditions; but our information is mainly of the metropolis, and what follows applies primarily to Rome.

The merchandise trafficked for in the imperial capital is concisely summed up in the Apocalypse.[1] It consisted of "gold and silver and precious stones, and of pearls, and fine linen, and purple, and silk, and scarlet, and all thyine wood, and all manner of vessels of ivory, and all

[1] Revelation 18: 12-13.

manner of vessels of most precious wood, and of brass and iron and marble, and cinnamon, and odors, and ointments, and frankincense, and wine, and oil, and fine flour, and wheat, and beasts, and sheep, and horses, and chariots, and slaves, and the souls of men."

The mere importation of foreign wares into Rome gave employment to myriads. The Tiber, "the mildest trades-master in the world," as Pliny says, was covered with coasters and barges from Puteoli and Ostia, and they and their lading employed a vast number of wholesale and retail traders, porters, stevedores, clerks and commission brokers. As has been hinted, not a little of the traffic really was to the gain of wealthy gentlemen who committed the vulgar management and money-handling to freedmen and slaves. Many of the small shops and workrooms that lined the streets running into the Forum, and of those in the roaring *Subura* quarter, were thus no doubt owned by Senators of long pedigree. However, the servile classes were always getting clear of the master or patron, and setting up for themselves; and since they were usually sharper and abler in trade than the poor freeman, these ex-slaves gradually crowded him to the wall, and got the bulk of the retailing and of the petty industries into their hands.

The magnitude of the Roman retail trade can be judged by the fact that early in the fourth century A.D. there were listed 254 bakeries and 2,300 places where oil could be purchased in the capital. Besides there were special markets for the sale of cattle, wine, vegetables, fish, and various delicacies, as well as for all the necessities of house furnishing, dress and the toilet. Very early, trades became quite differentiated; for example, the old guild of shoemakers dated back to Numa. Under the Empire this guild broke up into special guilds of boot-makers, sandal-makers, slipper-makers, ladies' shoemakers, etc. When Trajan reorganized the baking industry, he differentiated fine bread and cake-makers. The coppersmiths were divided into candelabra-makers, lantern-makers, shield-makers, and the like; and thus the perfumers, iron-workers, carpenters, and all engaged in the artistic industries, such as modelers, polishers, casters, gilders, workers of marble, etc. Every trade had its own street or even quarter; we hear therefore of the scythe-makers' street, the sandal-makers', the corn-sellers', wood-dealers', glaziers', or salve-sellers' streets in Rome.

The grain warehouses in or near the imperial city have been mentioned; but they were only the most important out of many similar *horrea* along the Tiber front for the storage of salt, lead, brick, and a great number of other commodities. There was a special guild of porters (*saccarii*) for disembarking these staples. The trade in marbles was extraordinarily brisk in Rome. The amount, both of local Italian marbles and foreign marbles, needed for the huge public buildings, the palaces, the baths, the basilicas and the fora, as well as for the luxurious private residences, can hardly be computed. It was a commerce in itself. Tibullus speaks of the streets of the city being always obstructed by the carts bearing imported marbles. At an earlier day, when Marcus Scaurus in 84 B.C. was collecting the 360 marble columns for his theater, the contractor attending to the sewers sued him for the damage their transport would do the drains. There were special wharves for the disembarking of these veritable mineral treasures, and many a fat fortune must have been amassed while procuring or preparing the stately piers and capitals that became the glory of the city.

The marble-sellers, of course, stood at one extreme of the metropolitan traffic, while the wretched Jew pedlars from Janiculum, hawking sulphur matches, stood at the other. Between were the vast majority of the trades and shops. The shops opened upon the street, closed only with linen curtains which might be covered with notices or pictures. Outside was a signboard which indicated the trade within. Thus the sign of a ham-seller showed five hams hanging in a row. The larger shops might be divided into "departments;" e.g., a cloth-ing store into men's and women's divisions with male and female clerks respectively. A good deal of the business was done by means of special fairs, as on the seven days following the Saturnalia festival a fair was held on the street called the *Sigillaria*. Here were sold little toys, images and dolls (hence the name of the street and the festival), and also elegant vases of bronze and silver. Here also were booksellers' shops, where we hear of the several books of the Aeneid being on sale separately; though the booklovers of Rome surely did not allow an annual fair to be the only time when the latest editions of Vergil, Horace and Martial were purchasable.

The shopkeepers of Rome formed a class proverbial for their conservatism. The least public disturbance they feared and justly. "By far the greater number of the shopkeepers," says Cicero, "or rather, the whole class, are devoted to peace and order. All their liveli-hood, labor and gain depends on the briskness of traffic. Every closing of the shops invades their profits." The shopkeepers were therefore very unwilling to see any revolution prosper; but, after it had conquered, they were equally opposed to a reaction. The quiet pros-perity brought by the emperors was entirely to their heart. They were ever loyal to the ruling Caesar. On his birthday and festival days their booths and shops would be covered with laurel boughs, and at night be illuminated; on days of mourning in the imperial house, every shop was closed. They were a superstitious class withal, scanning the heavens for every sign, and small dealers—says the elder Pliny—believed that if the day of the setting of the Pleiades (early in November) was cloudy, the winter would be a rainy one; if the heavens were clear, then it would be rigorous. In the first case they advanced the price of cloaks; in the second that of divers other garments, anticipating the probable demand.

The regulation of so great trafficking was enough to give full employment to all the aediles, curators, praefects and "neighborhood magistrates"[1] who had oversight of the good order of the metropolis. As was usually the case in ancient communities, extreme stringency in certain instances was compatible with equal laxity in others.[2] How truly "Prussian" local authorities might show themselves under the Empire is indicated by a case, not indeed from Rome, but from Oxyrhynchos, Egypt, though we can hardly call it exceptional—a certain Aurelius, "an egg-seller by trade," there takes oath by the emperor that he will only sell his eggs publicly in the market-place, never secretly or in his house (where his doings could not be watched) and if he did otherwise he invoked on himself the harsh penalties of the law.

The Roman fora and business streets were certainly scenes of extraordinary bustle and prosperous confusion, though hardly of a modern kind. Since driving was practically forbidden inside the capital, the place of fine equipages was taken by the gorgeous litters of rich shoppers; and Juvenal pictures a pompous lawyer—who

---

[1] *Vicomagistri.*

[2] Just as in police-ruled Berlin to-day a painful supervision of many household minutiae is quite compatable with the toleration of dangerously primitive plumbing.

wishes to be thought richer than he really is—so fat that his Oriental bearers can hardly stagger under the sedan, passing ostentatiously to the Forum to bid for slaves or for plate or for myrrhine vases, or even for a villa.

Fixed prices were even less known in ancient Italy than in modern. Everything had to be bargained for; the smallest transactions demanded much time, gesticulation and wind. A book for the study of the Greek and Latin languages in parallel, gives this dialogue relating to trade. "I go to the clothing dealer. 'How much costs this pair?' 'A hundred denarii.' 'How much this raincoat?' 'Two hundred.' 'Too much; take an hundred.' 'Impossible; it cost me that sum from the wholesaler.' 'What shall I give then?' 'Whatever you fancy' (a clear sign the first price named was a mere 'talking price,' and that now the dealer appealed to the buyer's generosity). 'Give him one hundred and twenty-five denarii,' says the buyer to his slave; 'now we'll go on to the linen seller.'" If we may believe Juvenal, the schoolmaster even had to haggle long as to his honorarium—and so through all the weary course of traffic.

The finest shops in Rome were in the great market-buildings by the Septa Julia on the Campus Martius.[1] Here could be had valuable slaves, citrus-wood tables, ivory inlaid furniture, crystal and myrrhine cups, and all kinds of jewelry. Under the arcades by the Circus Maximus and in the "Tuscan Quarter," between the Palatine and the Capitoline, were also very good stores. Along the Via Sacra again the trade was especially in luxuries. Besides the innumerable bankers who almost monopolized the old Forum with their offices—inscriptions

[1] Perhaps to be compared with the modern "Passages" and "Arcades."

along this street show jewelers, dealers in pearls and precious stones, in chased metal ware, in colors, in ivory, crystal vessels, fans, peacocks' plumes, and all kinds of oddities for women; also in fine fruit, honey and flowers for dinner parties.

But trade was by no means confined to this one quarter. The fact that Rome had no system of rapid transit must have caused the shops to spread themselves over the entire city; for it would have been grievously inconvenient to have gone down from, say, the quarter around the Praetorian camp to the Forum for every petty purchase. In Domitian's time the multifarious traffic filled all the squares and streets; and the shops in the house fronts, the booths and the workshops made the ways nigh impassable. The Emperor enacted stern measures for repressing the evil. Martial declares that before this intervention wine-pedlars chained their flagons to every column, and barbers shaved their victims in the middle of the street. "Now," he concludes, praising Domitian, "the city is again Rome. Recently it was one great shop."

Such regulations, however, hardly reformed the habits of so vast a population. To trade, to chatter, to live in the highway is second nature to the South Italian; and the streets of Rome were probably crowded with booths and pedlars till Alaric, Geiseric and Totila brought the long silence.

9. *The Professional Careers as Means of Livelihood.*

Social prescriptions and actual public law had confined Romans of good family to the three spheres of activity: those of the forum, the battlefield, and the farm. How trade was in theory tabooed and in practice carried on indirectly by high as well as by low, has already been made clear. But between the usurer, sea-merchant or forum huckster and the lordly master of patrician acres there was naturally a class of what would be to-day styled "professional men," whose incomes indeed were far less than those of many rising freedmen, but whose social status was considerably better. The old Republican law indeed debarred any one who followed a profession as well as mere tradesmen from holding a public office, but a prosperous physician was not likely to be chagrined because he could not become consul. The severity of this prohibition was relaxed also in the case of one very notable profession—the advocate's; and as for the others we find the greatest variety of good report and remuneration.

That an advocate should gain his livelihood by his legal knowledge and oratory was contrary to the old Roman conception of right things. A litigant ought to plead his own case. If friends wished to help him, good; they ought not to demand fees of him because they chanced to be clever talkers. The law against the receipt of fees by advocates was as old as 204 B.C. In 17 B.C. Augustus—ever anxious to repress changes from the worthy old customs—renewed it; but it met the usual fate of legislation which is contrary to the entire spirit of an age. In 47 A.D. Claudius found it necessary to enact that an honorarium to an advocate was permissible, though the sum was never to exceed 10,000 ses., and that the advocate who took more was guilty of extortion. The occasion of this alteration had been the case of an *eques,* one Samius, who had given Suilius, the advocate and delator, 400,000 ses., and then found that he was playing him false. Samius in despair committed suicide. The affair caused a stir. The whole question of lawyer's fees was ventilated in the Senate. Suilius had plainly abused his opportunity; but it was argued that if all fees were forbidden no one would find it worth while to study eloquence, hence the permission of a moderate honorarium. In the beginning of Nero's reign, in the brief lease of power then afforded the Senate, it was enacted that "no advocate should defend a cause for fee or reward," seemingly a repeal of the Claudian legislation. However, in Trajan's time a *senatus consultum* more or less strictly enforced by the praetors, obliged all litigants, before their cases could be heard, to take oath that they had not given nor promised any sum to their advocates, nor even so much as contracted to pay them. Nevertheless, when the case was over, the litigant was *allowed* to make his advocate a present of not over 10,000 ses., a proviso which indicates that the Claudian law had again come into force.

In a well-known letter, Pliny the Younger makes his boast that he never took fees or gifts from his clients, nor even "friendly acknowledgments;" and we may believe that the high-minded consular from Comum had more grounds than some for his boast. But we also know that one hundred and fifty years earlier an equally high-minded consular, and a far greater orator—Cicero himself—had profited vastly from his eloquence. He boasted, to be sure, in the case of Verres that he got not an obol from the plaintiff Sicilians; but on other occasions he was none the poorer for his services, even if he never demanded a fee. For example, a Papius Poetus gave him valuable books. He "borrowed" money when he needed it from rich men he had defended. He bought the house of Crassus with the money of such friends. Publius Sulla, for whom he had pleaded, "loaned" him 2,000,000 ses., and Cicero had some trouble in excusing this affair in the Senate. Especially people he had defended remembered him handsomely in their wills, and here must have come not the least gain of a Roman advocate. Cicero himself (near the close of his own life) values the sum total of all legacies left him at full 20,000,000 ses., though some of this, of course, came from friends who had never been his clients.

But greater wealth than Cicero's came to truly successful advocates; advocates who could mingle a little successful "delation," i.e., private accusing and blackmailing with their formal oratory. In spite of every law against fee-taking, Eprius and Crispus (a famous advocate who flourished from Caligula's to Vespasian's time) heaped up fortunes of 300,000,000 ses., almost the maximum for personal riches in antiquity. These huge estates must have been amassed from much the same sources as was Cicero's, though the grasping and "borrowing" must have been far bolder, legacies more shamelessly sought, every advantage more ruthlessly pressed. And in Roman times as well as to-day it was doubtless true that the work done far from the Forum, the "Solicitor's" work as apart from the "Barrister's," was by far the more profitable; and on these pickings out of court the law could have had next to no hold.

The lawyer's profession then remained—for the happy mortals at its summit—highly profitable, highly honorable. A great advocate would be dreaded as an enemy; sought after as a friend; remembered in countless testaments and codicils; would receive multitudinous favors; and be sure of a respectful hearing when he harangued the Senate.

Unfortunately there was another side to the shield. The lot of the humble pettifogging advocate was worse in the first than in the twentieth century. Without previous riches, social prestige, a train of freedmen, a high-sounding ancestry, the road of a poor Roman lawyer was a stony one. And indeed the great incomes were so rare that Juvenal hardly exaggerates when he says that even the most eloquent of advocates got very little. "Put in one scale," cries the satirist, "the estate of one hundred lawyers, and you may balance it with the single fortune of Lucerna, the charioteer of the Reds." To be a successful lawyer, one must appear wealthy and live amid show and splendor. "It is the violet cloak that attracts the clients."[1] "If the old orators came to life again, no one would now give Cicero himself two hundred sesterces, unless a large ring sparkled on his finger." "The first point a would-be litigant looks at is whether his lawyer has eight slaves, ten attendants, a sedan to go behind and friends in the toga to go before." Consequently, asserts Juvenal, an orator would even hire a costly sardonyx ring to wear before he went to plead.

As usual, Juvenal is here overstating his case. All lawyers were not charlatans nor starvelings, even as all did not win the fortunes of a Crispus. We know that the lawyers followed the legions into the wilds of Germany; and the direct cause of the revolt against Varus was his ill-starred attempt to introduce the Roman legal system among the rude tribes of the North, and his delivering the unlettered Sygambri and Cherusci over to the arts and wiles of the "advocates" who found their pickings around his praetorium.

The legal profession, to conclude, had its grievous drawbacks and its great successes. But its chief advantage was that it carried no social stigma. The advocate could hold up his head with the best, and look for the best in the public gift; this, because his duties were in a manner a public service, therefore fully commendable to a "gentleman." The same could not be said of any other profession.

Turning to the teacher's profession, the eve naturally

---

[1] Just as to-day it is asserted that a young lawyer should line his office with numerous sheep-bound tomes, to give the impression of wide practice and prosperity.

runs up the long ladder which led from the miserable teachers of day scholars to the aristocratic professors of the Alexandrian museum. The elementary teachers— who commonly followed the business for need of bread rather than for any special call thereto—were to be pitied in their lot. The average honorarium in Rome for "grammatical" instruction during a school year of eight months was 500 ses. If there were as many as thirty pupils, this would make an income of 15,000 ses. The rent of a schoolroom, however, was always a heavy item. Many teachers had to struggle along with very few pupils. Martial ridicules a teacher who had only two. Diocletian, in his tariff of prices, set the legal charge for teaching a boy in reading and writing at only 50 denarii; in stenography and accounting, 75 denarii; in Greek, Latin and mathematics, 200 denarii; and these denarii were moreover fearfully depreciated at Diocletian's time. In addition to this actually low pay was the difficulty of collecting it. Parents often found it easy to raise money for many things before that for their children's tuition. When the teacher at last was satisfied, the poor pedant had to hand a liberal slice over to the child's pedagogue,[1] also to the steward who made the payment. The teacher in fine, remarks Juvenal, had to submit to this extortion just as if he were a pedlar.

The grammarian, the man of real learning, who taught with some love for his subject could, if fortunate, make a very fair income. In Augustus' day, Marcus Verrius Flaccus, who instructed the young people in the palace, received a round 100,000 ses. per year. Epaphroditus of Chaeronea, who taught in Rome from Nero's time down to Nerva's, died possessed of two houses in the capital, and of a library of 30,000 rare and valuable

[1] The slave or freedman who escorted a child to and from school, and generally attended to his education.

books. Rhetoric teaching paid still better. As high as 2,000 ses. is mentioned as the payment for tuition in a single course by a rhetor. Besides, they stood in closer touch with actual life, and many opportunities for fat perquisites came their way, especially large fees for the preparing of polished speeches for none too polished magistrates. Quintilian, the first occupant of the rhetoric chair founded by Vespasian, was not merely rich, but because he was a teacher in the palace received the consular insignia. The state professors of Latin and Greek oratory were paid in Rome 100,000 ses. per year (as much as a procurator of the third rank and a majority of the military tribunes); and in the third century when the sentiment against the trades and the professions had decidedly waned, they rose to be imperial secretaries, as earlier they had become senators.

Of course this prosperity was only relative. Compared with most of his fellow rhetoricians, Quintilian was exceptionally favored; yet we find Pliny the Younger offering to help him out with the dowry for his daughter, as if he were in decidedly modest circumstances. On the other hand, Juvenal says that he had enjoyed extraordinary good luck, for he was handsome, noble, wise, well-bred, a senator, and gifted with a magnificent voice and oratorical presence. "Quintilian was indeed fortunate, but he was a greater rarity than a white crow." Most rhetors (Juvenal again informs us), whether in Greece or Rome, practically starved; but again we meet plain exaggeration.

Professional philosophers, the clergy, if one may say so, of the Roman age, enjoyed exemption from jury duty, a distinction which caused very unworthy personages to assume the rough himation and long beard, and claim the honored title—as appeared in a case brought before Pliny in Bithynia. There were a vast number of "philosophers'' drifting over the Empire; some of the Cynic school little better than begging charlatans, the precursors of the begging friars of the Middle Ages; some eking out a precarious living as ''house philosophers'' of this or that wealthy dilettante or learned lady. Others, again, were the honored companions of proconsuls and Caesars, like those sophists whom Marcus Aurelius gathered at his court.

The age beginning with the Flavians saw the imperial government take an active hand in shaping the higher education—a policy entered upon by the practical Vespasian, more perhaps because he realized the influence of the professions and rhetoricians in controlling the political views of the upper classes, than because he was interested in spreading Stoical doctrines or ''Asiatic'' oratory. He created chairs of rhetoric for Greek and Latin professors, the salary being payable out of the *fiscus*.[1] Quintilian was the first to enjoy the benefits of this foundation. At the end of twenty years the professors could retire on a pension, just as if they were legionaries who had finished serving their time on the frontiers. Hadrian, besides sustaining the old Ptolemaic professorships at the Alexandrian museum, presented sinecure positions there to a number of sophists who do not seem to have been obliged to reside in Alexandria, but who simply ''held the benefice'' (to use a medievalism), and gave the museum the glory of their names. The best known of these were Polemon of Laodicea and Dionysius of Miletus.

Capitolinus tells how Antoninus Pius established ''rhetors and philosophers in all the provinces, and gave them honors and salaries;'' but we do not know the details. He also exempted teachers of sciences from all taxation. Marcus Aurelius—probably when he was in

The part of the treasury especially controlled by the emperor.

9

Athens, after the suppression of Avidius Cassius' rebellion in 176 A.D.—set up in that university city four professorships in philosophy—Stoic, Platonic, Peripatetic, and Epicurean—and set the salary at 10,000 denarii each.[1] In after days these chairs were so much sought after that there seems to have been violent canvassing in Athens of a regular political nature whenever one of these snug places became vacant, though which of the venerable organs of Athenian government—Areopagus, Boule, or some other body—did the electing does not appear. Finally, in Constantius Chlorus' time, we find him appointing a certain Eumenius—a man of noble birth—professor of rhetoric in Autun, at a salary of no less than 600,000 ses. per year.

A successful grammarian or rhetorician was not, of course, dependent solely on imperial bounty. The great cities maintained public lecturers, and the post was highly honorable and eagerly sought after. A famous teacher was likely to be given the *ornamenta* of a municipal decurion by his native town. Some received salaries from the cities they favored by their presence. A grammarian of Spanish Terraconensis tells on his gravestone how he received a salary from his city when he was only twenty-five years old; but most men of his calling had to wait weary years longer, and then receive very uncertain rewards.

Literature, pure and simple, hardly deserves to be ranked as a profession. A vast amount of bad verse was written by rich men with overmuch time. Much history of a better quality than the verse was also written, sometimes by noblemen of fairly active life—as for

[1] It is interesting to note that this would give a salary of about $1,600, modern money, and taking ancient money at thrice the purchasing power of modern, we have an income of $4,800. This is more than most large American universities pay their full professors. Living expenses in quiet Athens must have been a great deal lower than in Rome or Alexandria.

example Tacitus. But to undertake to live by one's pen was a frightfully hazardous venture. The only hope was in finding a rich patron, and genuine Maecenases were rare. We are told that even the most applauded poets of Trajan's time received little reward beyond the empty praise. Consequently they had to hunger or give up their profession unless they had wealth themselves. Statius had to sell a poem, his "Agave" (probably a pantomimic ballet), to Paris, the vulgar mime, at a time when all Rome was cheering his recitals of his "Thebais." Only a rich man could really afford to enjoy the glories of being a successful literateur. "Well plied with food and wine is Horace when he shouts his 'evoe'!" observes the oft-quoted Juvenal; and again, "Let Lucan recline at ease in his gardens amid his marble statues, and be satisfied with literary fame"—but fame would not feed poor men.

There was, of course, no copyright. Pliny the Younger writes to a friend that he is delighted to hear that his books were selling well in Lyons; but Pliny probably was none the richer, however huge the editions. Martial had a regular publisher in Rome, "Secundus, the freedman of the learned Lucensis, behind the Temple of Peace and the Forum of Pallas." Thanks to the large corps of expert slaves kept by Roman publishers,—many copying while one dictated—it was possible to duplicate manuscripts with considerable rapidity, and sell them at a fairly reasonable price. The publishing business in Rome was a moderately good one, but no author ever disputed with his publisher over the "advance payments" and "royalty."

From literature the next step is naturally to the fine arts. The attitude of Lucian is characteristic of antiquity, when he—gifted with a mind truly appreciative of art—deliberately says that while one can admire the works of Phidias and Praxiteles, no reasoning being could desire to be like their creators. A sculptor or painter—even the best of them—indeed had to work for a confessed money reward, and this put the taint of trade upon their whole calling. Besides, while the fine arts at their extreme are notoriously transmundane and unpractical, they readily taper down into a very plebeian handicraft indeed. The creator of the Athena Parthenos and the makers of those multifarious images left us from every seat of antiquity were alike sculptors; we do not give the same praise to the copyist, the slave laborer it may be, that we do to the friend of Pericles; but unfortunately in the intermediate stages the dividing line is decidedly hard to draw. This taint of vulgarity was a great misfortune, however, for art as art. Persons of the upper classes who inherited, no doubt, talent and taste were deterred from touching the brush or the chisel; the fine arts became more and more the vocation of plebeians and freedmen whose sole interest was in the patron's payments.

The income of a good sculptor in imperial times—whatever his social status—was truly considerable. In Nero's time the Greek Zenodorus in Gaul worked ten years on a colossal statue of Mercurius Arvernus, and received for this 400,000 ses., besides having time it would seem in the interval to fill a good many outside orders. But the great bulk of the sculpture of the imperial period was little more than the copying or varying of the unapproachable models of the great age of Greece. This was a mere handicraft, and in no patrician hands. Whatever the quality of the statuary in imperial times, the quantity was enormous. Only an examination of many different excavations and ruins will give a faint idea of the vast population of statues and

reliefs that filled the Empire.   There was a special business of making funereal monuments.   We hear of part-
nerships in the trade, where one man furnished the
capital, another the technical skill.   The preparing of
ready-made images in Rome was a great and highly
developed calling.   There were even special workshops
that supplied only the eyes, and set them in the heads.
The business was highly profitable.   The demand was
constant; and an ordinary portrait statue (whereof several at least would stand in the atrium of every gentleman) was worth 3,000 ses. and upwards.   Even in the
smaller towns there would be sculptors ready to execute
quick orders for statues, with certain staple figures or
busts always on hand—for example, of the more popular
gods, of the members of the imperial family, of Victory,
and of Augusta Fortuna.   Heads could be substituted
rapidly.   In the case of empresses or other great ladies
one could change the coiffures to suit the dictates of
fashion.   An aedile of Cirta, Africa, two months after
he had promised the citizens a statue of Concord, was
able to dedicate it—clearly a ready-made statue.   All
this—the profusion of statues in every village market-
place, in every country squire's atrium—tended infal-
libly to the devitalizing and commercializing of the
art; it sank to a mere handicraft long ere the downfall
of the Empire.   The wonder is that under such debasing
conditions the technique continued to maintain the high
average it long did.[1]

The statuary business was like every other, liable to
petty exactions and drawbacks.   Valentinian I had to

---

[1] How Roman art declined under commercializing influences can be
told at a glance by comparing those sculptures on the Arch of Constantine
at Rome, which have been stolen from the Arch of Trajan, and those
dating from Constantine's own time.   The first were the work of artists;
the second were the work of craftsmen.

enact a law forbidding magistrates to compel painters
and sculptors free of charge to make portraits of the imperial family or to decorate the public buildings; a law
that would have been unnecessary had there not been a
genuine grievance, presumably of long standing.

Of the architect's profession we can say little, for we
know little. It was in comparatively good repute. The
practical usefulness of the business appealed to the hard-
headed men of the Empire. The reward of the architects of the Flavian Amphitheater, of Nero's Golden
House, of Trajan's Forum and its buildings, of Hadrian's
villa at Tibur, of the Baths of Caracalla and Diocletian,
could have been nothing less than princely. The great
fires at Rome, the building activities of the government,
the ambitions of the great families to erect ever more
splendid palaces, put the profession at a premium;
although even in Augustus' time, when Rome was being
"changed from brick to marble," it was complained
there was an over supply of architects, and many a
skilful designer must have suffered want.

Musicians who really rose to a high excellence were
sure of recognition. The great public spectacles and
festivals gave them chances seldom afforded the wretched
poets and savants. At the rededication of the Theater
of Marcellus the sparing Vespasian gave two harpists—
Terpnus and Diodorus—200,000 ses. . Philosophers grew
jealous of famous singers and lyre-players; while Martial advises a father not to teach his son to be a poet or
to study serious things, but to make him a good harpist;
then he will make his fortune. Nero's reign was the
heyday of the musical profession; it continued to
thrive under Domitian, as well as did far meaner kin—
actors, dancers, fencers and jockeys. After the Flavian
emperors came the war-loving Trajan and the art-loving

Hadrian, and musicians probably ceased to command excessive rewards.

It was the misfortune of ancient medicine that the law afforded legitimate physicians no protection against the competition of quacks. Rascals and drones of all kinds gave up their work to turn to "doctoring." If luck favored them, all was well; if they failed, they could still become undertaker's assistants, or drift into the gladiator's business. Galen, writing towards the close of the second century, declared that most of the "doctors" of his time could not read, and warns his colleagues to beware of slips of grammar and pronunciation in talking with educated patients.

This contamination with ignorant charlatans put the really scientific and able physicians at great disadvantage in seeking social recognition and a polite practice. What could be said of a profession where a certain Thessalus—who started life as a weaver, but who in Nero's day won great prestige as a physician—could assert that half a year of study would give all necessary knowledge of medicines? Martial tells of the swarm of students who ran behind a "doctor" when he went to visit his patients; and laments that a certain Symmachus with "a hundred of his pupils" visited him when sick, and that "a hundred hands, frozen by the northern blast, felt for my pulse; [so that] I had not ague then, but I have it now!"

Worse still was the fact that in the richer families, which would naturally keep clear of the quacks, there was usually a slave kept as a house physician, just as the retinue included a barber and a groom. Many of the slave physicians would become freedmen in course of time, but they were legally bound to give treatment without charge to their patron and his friends. The free born physicians were nearly all foreigners. Pliny says that Romans became doctors only exceptionally. The profession was commonly in the hands of Greeks and Orientals, especially Egyptians. However, we do occasionally hear of prominent Italian doctors, as for example Scribonius Largus, the body physician of Claudius, and Vettius Valens (who was even an *eques*), employed by the same emperor. Augustus owed his life to Antonius Musa, a freedman, who saved him when all others gave up hope. Galen enumerates not a few Roman names when speaking of well-known physicians, especially of oculists. However, it cannot be denied that the physician's profession everywhere, and most of all in the provinces, was largely recruited from the humbler classes; and it never received due recognition.

The system of having state-salaried physicians that gave free treatment was very old in Greek cities,[1] and was extended so much under the Empire that Augustus had to protect the finances of the municipalities by a decree fixing the maximum number allowed in the large, lesser and small cities. Surgeons were also employed in the army, and if we can draw inferences from an inscription, there were about twenty-four of them to a legion, who ranked among the lowest of the under-officers. There does not appear to have been a medical staff and surgeon-general at Rome, and it is not likely that the army doctors boasted any great skill. They shared the disadvantages which weighed down the whole profession.

Nevertheless, despite the competition of quacks and slaves, a really able doctor could make his mark. The few lucky court physicians, and family doctors of the patriciate, enjoyed almost princely incomes. The usual way was for a great man to make a contract for so much per year for the medical care of his family. In this way

[1] Witness the famous case of Democedes, near the end of the sixth century B.C., as told in Herodotus (iii:131).

Quintus Stertinius, another physician in Claudius' time, reckoned he made 600,000 ses. per year, "by counting up," he said, "the houses in which he was family doctor." The annual stipend seems to have been payable on the first of January; but for especially difficult cases there was an extra charge. We hear of 200,000 ses. being paid in Gaul for the treatment of a single case. The great Galen received 400 gold pieces for healing a consular's wife. He indeed had such fame that people wrote to Rome to consult him,—particularly on eye diseases—from Asia, Gaul, Spain and Thrace; and after they had answered certain questions of his, he prescribed for them by letter. We hear of a Crinas, a physician of Massilia, who left a fortune of 10,000,000 ses. after he had rebuilt the walls of that city at his own charges.

As happens in every age, the profits of the pseudo-professions—the flatteries as against the sciences, as Plato would say—were often far greater than those of the more legitimate callings.

Despite the "infamy" of the actor's career, many a favorite comedian or mime must have heaped up a fortune. In Cicero's day, Clodius Asopus, the most famous actor of the period, and so able and cultivated a man that Cicero called him the "Summus Artifex," left a fortune of 20,000,000 ses. On the occasion mentioned above, when Vespasian rewarded the master harpists so bountifully, he was still more generous to Apollinaris, the tragedian, giving him 400,000 ses. And none of the performers at this reopening of the Theater of Marcellus received less than 40,000 ses., besides many golden crowns.

Moorish jockeys were in profitable demand, just as English jockeys are on the continent to-day. An inscription at Rome tells of one Cresceus who won 1,500,000 ses.

in a racing career of ten years. The gladiator's calling is usually thought of as reserved for convicts and condemned slaves; but notwithstanding the peril and the legal "infamy," the exciting life, the plaudits of the myriads, the great reward awaiting a preëminent *mirmillo* or *retiarius,* drew many men of good family into it; for men fighting under compulsion and mere fear of death would seldom show artistic skill. In Tiberius' reign two *equites* offered themselves, says Cassius Dio, in the games given by Drusus, the son of the Emperor. One of them was killed. Tiberius forbade the other to fight as gladiator again. Nevertheless, this same Emperor offered as much as 100,000 ses. to get really good arena "artists" to appear. And in the succeeding reign of the crazy Caligula, *equites* appeared once more in the open amphitheater. Nero gave large estates to some popular *mirmillones.* Hadrian and other good emperors favored the contests as increasing the military spirit; and finally in the third century a quondam gladiator, Macrinus, actually wore the purple.

Presumably the fortunes of these favorites of a day were as quickly spent as made. The amphitheater was no school for thrift. The best swordsman or netter seldom lived to enjoy his riches. However, honorable retirements occasionally took place, and one may hope that sometimes the winnings of a popular favorite were spent on a substantial farm rather than lost at dicing.

10. *Landed Property.*

From first to last, from Romulus to Romulus Augustulus, the chiefest as well as the most genteel means of livelihood continued to be agriculture. Rightly conducted in the right province it was as certain as the sea-trader's ventures or the *argentarius'* loans to yield a goodly income. The landed interest of Italy indeed was to suffer a great and widely important decline; but the Empire went far beyond Italy, though certain aristocrats were slow in learning it.   The loss of Italy was the gain of Africa, Egypt, Moesia and Gaul.   We are again at the disadvantage of knowing far less of conditions in the provinces than of those near the capital; but our scope will be kept as broad as possible, always remembering that circumstances near Rome were likely to reproduce themselves at a somewhat later date nearer the frontiers.

It is a pleasant picture which the younger Pliny draws of the peasant stock of Italy, even in the period of its marked decline.   He speaks of his Tuscan villa and the great number of old people who can be found around it, dwellers near the healthful Apennines.   "You can find the grandfathers and great-grandfathers of the young people, still living, . . . [and hear their old time stories] so that when you set foot there you may fancy you have been born in another century."   And beyond doubt it was a source of great content to a Roman gentleman to feel that his income rested not on fragile ships, or on the fluctuations of interest, but on a patient, honest peasantry, to whom—if he were a kindly man—they cheerfully yielded informal allegiance, as their lord of the manor.

In a later section we shall consider the farming interests of Italy from these peasants' standpoint, and see another side to the picture.   At present we have only to look at agriculture as a source of wealth to the upper classes.   In the main it had proved highly profitable to the rulers, whatever it was to the ruled.   There had been indeed rude interruptions.   Thus the government of the Second Triumvirate in assigning colonies to its veterans had given a rude shock to landed property by their wholesale confiscations of estates to give farms to the clamorous soldiery. The feeling that the Roman state, no less than the United States, was rich enough to give every man a farm, had obtained by the Tiber, as later by the Mississippi; but the great republic of antiquity ere its fall had found practically the entire *ager publicus* vanished into private hands.[1] The deadly strokes which ruined the bulk of the Italian small farmers had been given by the nobility before the coming of the Caesars. In the place of the numerous petty estates were a few very large ones, the ill-famed *latifundia,* and as time advanced the great estates gained over the small ones all over the Empire. In Gaul we can see this clearly in the degenerate days of Ausonius.[2] He speaks of huge landed properties, sometimes concentrated in one large territorial tract, sometimes dispersed. An estate is mentioned by him as decidedly modest in extent which consisted of one thousand and fifty acres, though it must be confessed only three hundred and fifty of these were under cultivation; the rest were wooded. The small proprietor was then being crowded to the wall in Gaul just as centuries earlier it had happened in Italy. The great Gallic estates, very probably like their Roman prototypes, were almost self-sufficing worlds to themselves —providing their own food, wool and fuel; with laborers, and the ordinary artisans, masons, carpenters, smiths, etc. In case of war these great properties could offer some slight defense against raiders. A small proprietor faced far greater risks, and greater proportionate outlays. If he had to borrow money, he had to pay much higher interest than his rich neighbor. Any sort of an accident ruined him. By the end of the third century

[1] For example Julius Caesar in 63 and 59 B.C. had much trouble in finding enough public land still left—even by expelling holders with uncertain titles—to carry out any elaborate scheme of land distributions.

[2] *Circum* 310 to 390 A.D.

A.D. the process had been completed in Gaul that had occurred three centuries earlier in Italy—the small farms had been practically devoured by the greater.

Africa, another great agricultural province, showed similar conditions. So powerful were the great land owners near Carthage that in 238 A.D., when they quarreled with the local procurator, they were able—by merely arming their tenants—to penetrate into Carthage, murder the imperial procurator, and initiate the movement that drove Maximinus from the throne.

Africa was indeed the home of scientific agriculture. Long before the Roman days, the Carthaginians had brought it to a very high degree. The great work on the subject by the Punic Mago was translated into Latin by order of the Senate—probably about 140 B.C. His twenty-eight books were supposed to be a golden key to agricultural success. This was perhaps an attempt to educate the farming classes; but the stupid peasants were no people to profit by learned treatises, and the bailiffs of the rich who managed the *latifundia* reaped the main profit. Africa, in fact, under the early Empire seems to have been in the clutches of a small number of plutocrats. Pliny the Elder says that in his time six men owned half the real estate in the province. This process was probably hastened by the harryings of Africa first in the Jugurthine war, then in that of Caesar against the Pompeians. Much devastated and confiscated land had fallen to the government, which doubtless found it simpler to hire or sell the vacant land to a few capitalists than to many irresponsible small farmers. In this way Caelius, an *eques* of Puteoli, accumulated the fortune which his son was to squander in Cicero's time. Under the Empire great noblemen, sent to Africa as commanders, were so impressed with the excellence of the country that they invested in it much of their fortunes. In this way the illustrious Roman families of the Lollii and Arii Antonini became settled in Africa with splendid estates.

The elder Pliny again gives a very high opinion of the fertility of Africa, telling of a case where the corn yielded four hundred fold; but, despite Mago's learned tomes, the richness of the soil barely made up for the wretched methods of the peasantry. They worked long and hard for their returns. "I have seen," says Pliny, "after the rains, the earth turned over by a plough to which were harnessed on one side a poor little ass, on the other a woman." It took a marvelously rich soil to compensate for this miserable labor, and make African lands so profitable.

But great properties existed also in the East. The devastations and depopulation of Greece had, as said before, caused *latifundia* to spring up in that declining country. Augustus bestowed on a Spartan Eurycles, who did great service in his naval wars, the whole island of Cythera as his property. And though Eurycles was later exiled by the emperor, his family preserved possessions and an influence almost princely in southern Greece, down to the time of Hadrian.

Egyptian agriculture stood in a highly prosperous condition during all the better Roman period. A great deal of the arable land belonged to the emperor, who leased it out at very high rents. But while the country throve, the small farmers could pay the rents and the heavy taxes in kind and still be contented. When, however, the decline set in, the small farmers were here also crowded to the wall. Land passed into fewer and fewer hands, and whole villages became dependent on a single rich man, the whole country drifting into the greatest poverty and misery, until the Arab conquests ended Roman conditions forever.

In Asia Minor—in some respects the most prosperous province in the early Empire—the Roman grandees rapidly acquired extensive holdings. This was true in the case of Seneca; also of Rubellius Plautus (that great-grandson of Tiberius who was put to death by Nero in 62 A.D.), who before his final ruin retired to his great estates in Asia Minor at the emperor's command. About one hundred and fifty years later we learn—from an inscription—that Ummidia Cornificia Faustina, the rich niece of Marcus Aurelius, owned a large estate in Phrygia, and we get some idea of its magnitude by noting that it was organized almost as were the imperial domain lands. It was under the general charge of a *procurator,* and leased to three *conductores,* each watched by an *actor*—an agent of the procurator—while the numerous tenants were known as the *demos,* i.e., the plebs.

An insight into the profits and disadvantages of Italian land-holding is gained from an interesting letter of Pliny the Younger to a friend, asking for an opinion about buying an estate. Pliny says he would like to buy it because it would round off his own property nicely; the place can be put under one steward, and not much extra will be needed for repairs, furniture, gardeners, smiths and gamekeepers. Still he hesitates. It is pleasant to be able to travel from estate to estate, changing one's air and place; nevertheless, though the land is fertile, the tenants lack capital; the last owner sold the whole stock, and the tenants have been unable to pay much and have fallen into arrears. "I must therefore set them up again, and it will cost me the more because I must pro-vide them with honest slaves, *for I have no slaves work-ing in chains in my possession, nor has any landowner in this part of the country.*"[1] The price of the estate is

[1] A very important statement, showing that by 100 A.D. the supply of prisoners of war was running down, and that Italian agriculture was shift-

3,000,000 ses. It once was 5,000,000 ses.; but through the lack of capital of the tenants, and the badness of the times, the rents had fallen, and the value of the property with it. Pliny says finally that his own fortune is nearly all tied up in land—as was no doubt the case with many senators—but that he can borrow the money for this purchase from his mother-in-law. He owned a property within one hundred and fifty miles of Rome, whence he drew an income of 40,000 ses. per year; but a fresh set of tenants kept moving in at every new pruning season, and he was obliged to attend in person to the letting of his farms. Pliny—we may presume—was by no means so wealthy as many of his class, who could hardly give to their vast properties much personal attention. A small army of procurators and accountants was needed on every estate, and the case of Faustina's property in Asia must have been typical. One of the charges against Torquatus Silanus, a victim of Nero, was that "he kept men of no mean rank with the style of secretaries, accountants, treasurers—names belonging to the imperial function—and made preparations for securing it." Vopiscus tells of a landed estate that had 500 slaves, 2,000 cattle, 1,000 horses, 10,000 sheep, and 15,000 goats; a good sized "*saltus*," as the phrase went; but not so large as the one mentioned by the elder Pliny of Caecilius Claudius Isidorus, who could almost be called a territorial prince from his possessions. He died about 8 A.D., and left 4,117 slaves, 3,600 yoke of oxen, and 257,000 head of other animals (probably sheep), as well as 60,000,000 ses. in funds.

Under the early Empire, Italian agriculture seems to have revived somewhat from the last days of the Republic, and was not in such a desperate state as is sometimes

ing to a free tenant basis, just as two centuries earlier the small peasant free holders were being driven out by slaves working in chain gangs.

represented. South Italy was indeed reverting to waste and wild, but in Middle Italy grain raising had not entirely ceased. North Italy, especially the Po valley, fared better still. The cultivation of millet there—in Strabo's judgment—made a famine impossible, and we have mentioned the great number of rich men in Patavium (Padua) where wealth must have been largely based on agriculture. Indeed the opinion has even been advanced that Northern Italy was never better cultivated than during this age of the early Empire.

The younger Pliny, a genial informant on so many things, draws a kindly picture of his life on his Tuscan estate, and how he was general arbitrator and adjustor of the grievances far and near for all the country people. He would ride on horseback around his wide property, "playing the paterfamilias" on tours of inspection; and one has no right to say that his case was exceptional among the great landowners. In another letter Pliny relates how his tenants had for five years been getting into arrears, despite great abatements, until at last many took not the slightest trouble to pay anything, despairing of ever getting clear. Pliny says, therefore, that he is thinking of giving up rents and taking instead a proportion of the produce in kind;[1] but complains to his correspondent that it is hard to get honest and vigilant superintendents to safeguard his interests.

The practice obtained, even on the large unencumbered estates, of selling off the produce to dealers, who bid against one another for the right to take the prospective crop;[2] and Pliny tells how on his estate the dealers once bid too much on one vintage, and he gen-

[1] An early example of the gaining of "natural economy" upon "money economy;" a process that especially marked the declining Empire.

[2] It is alleged that some such process is used in Russia to-day on the great estates of the nobility.

erously made remissions, one tenth in cases where over
10,000 ses. were at stake, one eighth in cases under.
From his letter it appears that not all the buyers paid
cash in advance, but some waited till they could realize
on the harvest.

The profits from agriculture on a large scale were
sufficient; though probably the security and gentility of
the business, rather than the huge returns on the investments, brought landowning into favor. Columella
praises agriculture as the most desirable calling, better
than military service, commerce, banking, or the law;
but according to him, one could only expect the ordinary
6% on land investments, though at the time he wrote
(some time in the first century[1]) conditions were better
than under Augustus, when Italian land could be counted
on merely for 4%. However, fruit-raising near Rome,
and floriculture also around the city, yielded far greater
profits; and we know that in 227 A.D. a tenant paid
26,000 ses. annual rent for a vegetable garden on the
road toward Ostia.

The government was anxious to do all it could to
promote Italian grain raising, but its zeal was often
more furious than wise. For example, Domitian once,
on the occasion of a good wine and a poor corn harvest,
concluded that it was excessive wine growing which was
ruining grain raising in Italy, and issued an edict forbidding the planting of any new vines in Italy, and
ordering the vines in the provinces to be cut down,
nowhere permitting more than one half to remain. So
drastic a measure as this was sure to be unendurable,
and the edict was very soon revoked. But in its general
policy the imperial government was hardly wiser. If
the landed interests were worth fostering at all, the persons to favor were the struggling class of small free

[1] He seems to have been a contemporary of Seneca.

holders—not the holders of vast estates. But the great imperial domains, whether in Italy, Africa,[1] or anywhere else, were managed in a way to put them on a par with those of the plutocrats. The domain lands were leased out to a few great contractors, who sublet a lesser part of the territory to small tenants, but worked the major part of the lands by slaves. Slaves, to be sure, diminished in numbers[2] and availability as generations went on; but the customs of emperors and great nobles as to leasing their possessions to *conductores* did not abate. Thus the evils of absentee ownership crept in. Tenants took the place of slaves, but these tenants the conductor could grind to the uttermost, while the owner, living in Rome, was only interested in getting as profitable a lease as possible. The tenants presently became in practice, if not yet in legal requirements, bound to their little holdings, unable to throw them up and escape their ever increasing obligations. Thus in 174 A.D., Marcus Aurelius settled many captured Marcomanni both on the imperial estates and on private *latifundia*. These men were essentially serfs; they were called *tributarii,* and are an example of what often happened in modified forms in later periods.

The law came also to the aid of the social proscription that the gentry and nobility should rest the bulk of their fortunes on land. The *plebiscita* of 218 B.C., which prevented senators from engaging in trade, practically compelled every plunderer of a province, and in fact every merchant or banker who hoped to raise the social status of his family, to invest his money in Italian lands; and after the ravages of the Second Punic War Italian lands were held painfully cheap by the impoverished

---

[1] Where the proportion of the land owned personally by the emperor was very great.

[2] For reasons set forth in a later chapter, see page 209.

peasants. But this was only one step in a long series of enactments. A law of Julius Caesar forbade men (except presumably regular bankers) to keep on hand more than 60,000 ses. in specie. Since stocks and bonds or their equivalent, shares in the various tax-farming and trading syndicates, were not so readily purchased as to-day, this was again a compulsion on rich men to invest in lands. A similar law was earnestly pressed by Trajan and Marcus Aurelius. In Trajan's time the earlier laws which required candidates for office to own a certain amount of land in Italy had not been enforced. The vigorous Emperor, however, undertook to prevent candidates (says the younger Pliny) "from regarding Italy not as a mother country but merely as an inn," and declared that all aspirants for office should have one third of their patrimony in land. This being ordered just before an election,[1] every candidate found himself compelled to buy up any real estate on the market, and the price of lands around Rome took a sudden leap upward. In Marcus Aurelius' time practically the same thing happened, but the mere fact that the law had to be reënacted, shows that it had been hard to enforce, and had easily drifted into disuse.

The value of city real estate in the best quarters of Rome compares fairly well with the cost of land in a modern capital. Julius Caesar paid 100,000,000 ses. for the ground of his new Forum. It covered 90,000 square feet, and consequently was worth about $44.45 per square foot, i.e., $4,000,000 in all. But Trajan's Forum—not to name others—was much larger, and the land was surely as valuable as Caesar's. It has been estimated the value of the ground was fully $12,223,000, and the sites of many

[1] By the Senate, of course; the "people" lost their right to elect magistrates in Tiberius' time.

of the great baths and palaces were hardly less expensive in proportion to their area.

Of course these prices were exceptional, and hardly to be put under the head of landed property. It is fairer to look at the prices of fine country villas, of which every magnate possessed as many as possible. Under the later Republic these greatly increased, partly through the general growth in luxury, partly through a well founded belief that Rome was very unhealthy in midsummer. A good villa was a profitable investment. Thus Gaius Marius bought from Cornelia, mother of the Gracchi, a villa at Misenum, for only 300,000 ses.; but Lucullus buying it somewhat later paid a full 10,000,000 ses. for it. We cannot tell, however, how much of this increase was due to new buildings and to other improvements.

But even villa properties were held more for pleasure than for profit. Italian grain raising was a struggling business, except in the North. The real gains came in the one pursuit which prospered in Italy, despite Egyptian and African competition—viz., grazing.

The elder Cato—that personification of the hard-headed money-grasping spirit of old Rome—when asked what was the most profitable use of an estate, replied: "Profitable cattle-raising." "And second best?" "Moderately profitable cattle-raising." "And third best?" "Very unprofitable cattle-raising." "And fourth best?" "To plow the land."

To a certain extent the great Italian landholders of the dying Republic and the early Empire were able to say with the English gentry of the age of the Tudors, "The foot of the sheep will turn the land to gold." The profits from wool were great. The comparison of prices prevailing in Italy and the Orient in the third and the fourth centuries also goes to show that beef and pork were cheaper; consequently, we may assume, more plentiful, while grain was higher—as if there was less of it. All through the imperial period, and in other provinces than Italy therefore, the grazing was gaining upon the agricultural interests. This was possibly to the immediate profit of the landowners, but it was a retrogression in civilization. The first stage in the upward march of man is hunting, the second grazing, the third agriculture; and when wealth means flocks and herds instead of fertile acres, villages are running to waste, a hardy peasantry is being rooted out and driven to the over-crowded cities, and on the fields returning to grass only a few half-wild shepherds are roving. However, the rich owner saw his profit for the time. The cheapest kind of slave labor could be used in managing the flocks, because very little personal attention is really required of a grazier, while a human chattel, a "speaking tool" in the language of the time, could hardly be expected to bestow much care upon the more delicate tasks of agriculture and horticulture. That this cheap labor which replaced the small farmers was of little use for field work, is proven by the fact that we are told the yield from grain in Italy sank during the Roman period from twelvefold to only fourfold—something not to be accounted for by mere climatic changes or the exhaustion of the soil.

By the side of cattle rearing also went the Italian wine culture under the Empire. In fact the wine grower actually played into the graziers' hands, for wine is notoriously exhausting to the soil, and chemical fertilizers and guano were unknown. The depleted land would be allowed to go to grass; or if the wine grower had a large estate most of it would be given up to a great herd in order to supply manure for the vineyard. Even so the grazing gained over this noblest kind of agriculture. In Nero's time it was considered very doubtful whether vineyard property was desirable; meadow land, pasture land, or even forest land were counted better. Columella combatted this view in his book on agriculture, but could not resist the tendency.

Cattle property was of course insecure. The shepherds used were an irresponsible class, if not half bandits. Trajan had to enact a law greatly increasing the penalties for cattle thieving; nevertheless the advantages of the investment continued to present themselves. The other side of the shield, how this supplanting of farming by grazing affected the slave and the peasant, will be presented in a later chapter.

✓

CHAPTER IV

THE EXPENDITURE OF WEALTH

1. *Roman Luxury and Roman Sumptuary Laws.*

THE previous chapters have regarded the men of the Empire as getters; it is now time to examine them as spenders. Roman luxury and prodigality have become so proverbial that the tendency is strong to imagine that frugality and thrift were correspondingly forgotten under the Empire. Divers learned Teutonic antiquarians would have it that the present generation with all its selfish follies are children in the art of enjoyment as beside the ancients; but a closer scanning of the evidence, observes Friedlaender the greatest authority on Roman social history, shows that many investigators have made improper use of isolated facts, and have drawn from them unwarranted conclusions, while the undoubted magnificence of Roman luxury finds some important limitations.

Such a writer as Juvenal, to be sure, would authorize one to draw the blackest of conclusions. "We are now passing through the ninth age of the world," he assures us, "an era far worse than the age of iron, for whose villainy not even Nature herself can find a name, and no metal base enough to call it by." Sensuality, effeminacy, prodigal display of wealth, we are informed, go hand in hand with soulless money-grasping. A gilded vice, he would have it, has stifled morality; money is sought frantically, because it must be spent recklessly to get what the fashionable world called enjoyment. And that there was appalling sensuality, prodigality, wasteful squandering of wealth under the Empire, no sane man can deny. After the feverish rush for wealth, we find coming in the Roman world the feverish rush for excitement, for something new to feed the sated senses; hence the debasing emotions of the arena and the circus; the unspeakable revels of Nero and Elagabalus; the scattering of fortunes on tasteless palaces, race-horses, pretty slaves, elaborate suppers, perfumes and pearls, as well as on many things worse. All this is very true. At the same time in judging the magnitude and wickedness of Roman waste and luxury we must not be led astray by the outcry and prejudices of the censors of the age. Many things once styled effeminate and corrupting are accepted in our day by the most puritanical. The Greeks considered the wearing of hats, save by travelers on long journeys, distinctly womanish; but it does not follow that the hat-wearing nations of to-day are degenerates. So it must be also recalled that the "customs of the fathers," which the Roman moralists ever hold up for admiration, were customs of a barbarous age, which it would have been a grievous thing if later generations had not outgrown. Every century is fond of denouncing the things it considers superfluous. The ancients were a southern people, and able to live in more direct dependence on nature than the more artificial north, which needs many substitutes and helps to make life in its rigorous climate agreeable. Also the typical Roman conservative made it part of his religion to hark back to "the good old days" without regard to the things inevitably altered. Then again, the characters of the chief accusers of Roman luxury are to be noted: Marcus Varro, Seneca, Pliny the Elder, Juvenal, Martial and the like. All except Martial were men of exceedingly simple and strict life, strict probably beyond the average "good men" of their age. Seneca in particular had been a vegetarian in his youth, and despite later relaxations, kept deliberately from such luxuries as oysters and mushrooms. When he died, this prime minister of princely wealth was found to have had a body emaciated for lack of food. Pliny was so conservative as to be of the opinion that the invention of sailing ships was a calamity, as being contrary to the ordinances of nature, and denounced the culture of asparagus as a fearful incentive to gourmandizing. Varro mistrusted the wisdom of the importation of any kind of foreign edibles. Seneca railed against the use of snow for cooling drinks as a most unnatural luxury. As for Juvenal and Martial we can see in the one an upright but embittered moralist; in the other an extremely witty epigramist, fond of puncturing shams; but both more fond of their rhetoric than of exact statement. Their information is true at the bottom, but so distorted and exaggerated that we can use it only with great caution, and must beware of drawing wide conclusions from their unsupported evidence.[1]

We can better appraise the opinions of the critics of luxury, when we note that the elder Pliny's ideal of "the good old times" was a dinner of porridge, a house without plaster, and a single slave to care for a great family. Such "simplicity" was as reasonably demanded in a nation that had conquered all the world, as to try to-day to recall the times when forks were unheard of for dining, and windows were made with shutters in lieu of glass.

[1] It is fair to compare Juvenal and Martial with such satirical periodicals as *Punch* or the New York *Life*. Two thousand years hence a learned critic turning the files of *Life* will learn much that is true of American manners, will see our follies, vices and iniquities revealed cleverly and unsparingly; but if he is a wise critic he will know there is another side to be told—that *Life* shows him the exception and not the rule; that American society is infinitely less artificial and more honest.

Nevertheless when all these abatements from the ancient authors are made, the fact remains that most of their statements about Roman luxury and money wasting are true, and it is only their opinions and the correctness of their epithets that we need to question.

The colossal expenditures of the magnates of the dying Republic, Scaurus, Lucullus, Pompeius, Julius Caesar, not to name others, were made possible by circumstances that did not obtain under the Empire. Men no longer had to throw out vast sums to win popular favor. If they had, the delators would have promptly accused them of lese-majesty. Much public beneficence there was—especially in the provincial towns, as will be shown later; but hardly on the princely scale of the lords of the Senate. Even the emperors could hardly equal the prodigality of Lucullus, whose gardens were the finest in Rome even down into imperial times. Scaurus' outlays on his theater are likened by Plutarch to the lavishness of Caligula and Nero. Under the Empire, however, the *average* of wealth was for a while steadily rising, and with it the easy spending of huge sums on private enjoyments. Men were shut out of politics, and devoted their time to running through the fortunes their fathers had made under the Republic. Luxury, wastefulness and pagan degradation reached its height under Nero. By that time the old republican fortunes had been practically dissipated; wealth had passed to men of plebeian or even servile ancestry, who knew the value of a denarius better. The righteous and economical emperors of the century after Nero discouraged excesses, and set a more moderate pace by their simpler court. The spread of the Stoic philosophy with its approval of abstemious living also had a checking influence. Riches too ceased to be so concentrated in Rome, and while the provincial cities had their spendthrifts and their sybarites, we are justified in believing their life was on the average simpler than in the capital.

That at least one representative Roman gentleman found fashionable society in the eternal city wearying and trivial, is shown by the younger Pliny. He complains bitterly of how excessively bored he is of the vulgar and stupid antics and remarks of the dancers and buffoons commonly brought before the guests at fashionable dinner parties, and clearly hints that he is not alone in his opinion. "When a reader, musician or comic actor enters the dining-room, how many there are who call for their shoes [to go home], or lie back on their couches completely indifferent!" Again he complains of the way in which men of his class must spend their days. "If you take any day singly here in the city, you pass, or seem to pass, your time reasonably enough, when you take stock thereof; but when you put the days together, how dissatisfied you are with yourself! If you say to anybody, 'What have you been doing to-day?' he will rejoin, 'Oh, I have been attending a coming-of-age function'; 'I was at a betrothal or wedding'; 'so-and-so asked me to witness a signing of a will'; 'I have been acting as witness to A, or I have been in consultation with B'." All this, concludes Pliny, is sheer waste of time. "What a number of days I have frittered away with these chilly formalities!"

So much for the opinion of a quiet, kindly man who loved the luxuries of life, but at their true value, and found more comfort in the books of his cupboards than in the plate on his triclinium tables. We know there were many like him. But there were many more who found literature and philosophy a polite nuisance, and considered the chief end in life the spending of large fortunes as rapidly as possible. And why not? There were never more things, strange, wonderful, admirable, to spend money upon, until Columbus unlocked the golden West.   After the Second Punic War the very simple—in some respects almost barbarous—Italian people had poured in upon it all the riches and resources of the known world.   With the riches came a multitude of new wants.   Marble must take the place of travertine for buildings; purple robes from Tyre replaced the homespun woolen togas.   There came tables of Moorish cedar; on these tables were put turbots from Ravenna, oysters from Tarentum, edible snails from Illyria, sea eels from Sicily, roe deer from Ambracia, peacocks from Persia, flamingoes from Egypt, guinea fowls from Numidia. Moralists railed at these imports as soul destroying and making the god of a Roman his belly; yet what would not the elder Pliny and Varro have said of our China tea, Cuban sugar, Brazilian coffee—and these on the humblest table?   The facts were, the Romans were suddenly put to the severest trial a nation can meet, the trial of prosperity.   They endured quite as well as could be expected. The twentieth century opens with America enduring the same ordeal, and it remains to be seen whether we shall bear it better than did Rome.

It is, of course, easy to draw lurid pictures by citing the follies of the worse emperors.   Caligula and Nero, however, simply showed in their expenditures and enjoyments only their general giddiness.   Their aim—if such men can have aims—was to show to every subject the omnipotence of the Caesarian regime—how for them impossibilities did not exist.   Tiberius, Galba, Vespasian and Pertinax were, however, notoriously sparing, and most of the other emperors seldom were lavish save with the army.   It must be granted, nevertheless, that the examples of Caligula and Nero were demoralizing, and set a standard that cast its shadow far and wide. Luxury in Nero's time was by no means confined to

Rome, though here was the seat of the chief abomina-
tions. That emperor banished Suilius, the advocate, to
the Balearic Isles; but there, says Tacitus, he lived "lux-
uriously and voluptuously" even in such a remote region.
The districts around the bay of Naples were also seats
of gilded indolence. Baiae was the Newport of antiquity, and many neighboring towns were barely behind
it in splendor. Pompeii is hardly a type of these pleasure cities; it had too large a permanent artisan population. But probably it was considerably more luxurious
than the districts of northern Italy where life was still
simple if not stern, and where the numerous inscriptions
and records of educational institutions for the young
testify to a sound, unartificial family life. Indeed, to a
dweller of the remote *municipia* of Italy, a visit to Rome
and its sights of depravity came as an unpleasant shock.
Tacitus tells how a deputation to the Senate from the
country towns went home absolutely disgusted at the
dissoluteness they met in the capital. Hither Spain,
Brixia and even rich Patavium were noted for their
austere morality.

The truth seems to be that while the unemployed rich
of the Empire did not possess such great fortunes relatively as their compeers of to-day, they had quite as
much time on their hands and fewer opportunities for
the legitimate spending of their incomes. The actual
necessities of life, rent, wine, bread, etc., were much
cheaper than they are now in the United States. The
southern climate made many of our necessities luxuries.
A man with a moderate income could spend more on
superfluities than at present. When he became really
wealthy, he found it very easy to leap the barrier from
proper luxuries to excesses. The Roman of the Empire
was after all seldom a man of the greatest refinement.
He readily turned his fortune to the most obvious things

—eating, drinking, tawdry display, mere voluptuousness, and moving along the lines of least resistance, no wonder he reached extremes.

The criticism of luxury began almost with the end of the decisive Second Punic War. If repeated and energetic legislation could have made the Romans righteous, they would have been the most Puritanical of nations. The long catalogue of their sumptuary laws is a commentary upon the futility of trying to make men simple and good by statute.

When Cato the Elder was censor in 184 B.C., he undertook to discourage luxury by ordaining that all dresses, carriages, women's ornaments, household furniture, etc., which exceeded 1,500 denarii in value, should be assessed at ten times their worth in order that by the extra taxation such prodigalities should be discouraged. As late as 169 B.C., people would hastily put out their lights when it was reported that Tiberius Sempronius Gracchus the censor was coming down their streets, returning from supper, lest they be suspected of untimely revelry. The task of making Romans abstemious was not left, however, to the efforts of a few officers. The ancient Twelve Tables had a proviso against costly funerals. In 215 B.C., when Hannibal held the Republic by the throat, the *Lex Oppia* was passed, forbidding a woman to wear more than one half ounce of gold, to wear a many colored dress or to ride within the city in a carriage save at religious festivals. This act, however, was a war measure, passed when every scrap of treasure was needed by the state. In 195 B.C., it was repealed. Nevertheless, in 181 B.C. the *Lex Orchia* was enacted which aimed at preventing an excessive number of guests from being invited to banquets. The law was only barely efficient. Ordinances of the Senate on the matter had little effect. Accordingly either in 161 B.C.

or in 159 B.C., the *Lex Fannia* was passed to check the lovers of dainty living. The value and nature of the food permitted at a dinner party was carefully prescribed. The cost of a banquet at the time of the Roman Games, the Plebeian Games and the Saturnalia was not to go over one hundred *asses,* on other festivals thirty, on ordinary days ten.[1] It was forbidden to consume any imported wines, also no more than one fowl could be served and that unfatted.

By 143 B.C. the government found the *Lex Fannia* failing in its purpose, and added the *Lex Didia* to strengthen it. To sharpen the fear of the law, not merely the giver but the guests at illicit feasts, were made liable. The old law had applied only to Rome; the new law was to apply to all the Italians with whom high living presumably was working demoralization.

For more than a generation no further important sumptuary legislation was put on Roman law books, partly because the tendencies of the age made dinners on one unfatted fowl absolutely unendurable, partly because the republican statesmen, in the strife of the Gracchi against the nobles and its long aftermath, had other things to think of. Then the *Lex Licinia* came, enacted in 103 B.C. or 93 B.C.,[2] under the fostering of Publius Licinius Crassus, father of the famous multimillionaire. Again the effort was to check extravagant banquets. On the Calends, Nones and Nundinae,[3] and certain minor festivals, the price of a dinner party was never to exceed thirty *asses,* on greater festivals one hundred, at marriage feasts two hundred. The amount of meat and fish that could be served on ordinary days

---

[1] The value of the *as* in that period was something less than six cents.

[2] There is even a view that it was passed 55 B.C., but this does not seem tenable.

[3] "Ninth-days" i.e., market days.

was strictly limited. A *senatus consultum* enjoined that the law should be instantly put in force, and Lucilius, a contemporaneous poet, saw fit to commemorate its enactment.

Even the *Lex Licinia,* however, could not make the men of the Republic abstemious and unostentatious. Sulla, during his dictatorship, undertook to substitute for it his *Leges Corneliae,* which, besides carefully limiting the amount lawfully to be spent on banquets, laid down restrictions on the cost of funerals, restrictions which the dictator himself set at nought at the obsequies of his wife Metella, after which it is to be feared many a citizen laughed at the law and followed its maker's example. But the legislators were not yet ready to despair. In 78 B.C. a new act, the *Lex Aemilia,* undertook not so much to curtail expenses as to prescribe the varieties and quantities of viands that could be served. A little later a *Lex Antia,* besides returning to the charge respecting expensive banquets, limited the class of persons a magistrate could dine with during his period of office. Then came a lull in the legislation until Julius Caesar—himself a decidedly luxurious liver—undertook during his dictatorship to refurbish the old sumptuary laws and strengthen them. Guards were placed around the markets to seize prohibited meats. "The use of litters for traveling, purple robes and jewels," says Suetonius, "[Caesar] permitted only to persons of a certain age and rank, and on particular days. . . . He some times sent his lictors and soldiers to carry away such edibles as had escaped the notice of the officers [in the markets], even when the dishes were on the table." Augustus followed in his foster father's footsteps. By his ordinances indeed the old limits were somewhat extended—in part possibly because the purchasing power of money had fallen, in part

11

because the Emperor was too clear-headed not to realize extreme laws were unenforceable. On ordinary days, by Augustus' legislation, two hundred sesterces could be paid for a banquet, on festival days three hundred, at marriage feasts one thousand. Tiberius also struggled with the ever recurring problem. He complained in the Senate that the price of Corinthian dishes had become enormous, and that three mullets had sold for 30,000 ses. To put an end to such scandals he proposed that butchers and other food dealers be put under strict supervision by the Senate; that the aediles be authorized to restrain eating houses and taverns so far as not even to permit the sale of pastry. The aediles showed so much zeal in carrying out the Emperor's wishes—issuing edicts as to the price of any single dish, and the number of dishes for each repast—that the Emperor was fain to discourage them lest their regulations prove absolutely unenforceable. In 16 A.D. we find Tiberius also attacking the subject of wastefulness in dress, and having enacted a law forbidding any man to wear silk clothing or golden ornaments anywhere save at religious ceremonies.

The futility of such attempts was not yet clear to the statesmen of the Empire. Claudius, during his censorship, ordered a car plated with silver and of elegant workmanship, which was on sale in the great business street of the *Sigillaria,* to be purchased and broken in pieces before his eyes. Nero—hardly a stern critic of frivolities—also enacted, or allowed to be enacted, laws limiting public suppers to the *sportulae* (i.e., the wicker baskets in which the client's food was carried),[1] and forbidding, says Suetonius, "provision houses from selling any dressed victuals, except pulse and herbs—

---

[1] Perhaps here was an attempt to prevent the rich from political agitation, by means of great feasts to the public.

whereas they had sold all kinds of meat before.''
Hadrian, with his turn for regulating everything, had
ordinances relating to dress, baths, carriages, and
burials. Alexander Severus strove in his day likewise
to check wasteful luxury, and in order to prevent costli-
ness in dress, introduced a regular uniform for all
officials. And once more we find Aurelian attempting
the impossible with more sumptuary ordinances.

It is needless to say all this legislation was ineffectual. No doubt persons were occasionally convicted.
Occasionally a feast or funeral was curtailed, thanks to
the terrors of the statute. But abundant instances can
be found in history of the impracticability of attempting
to change the habits of an age by mere law-making.

2. Debtors and Spendthrifts.

As an almost unavoidable corollary of the huge
Roman fortunes, went the accumulation of huge debts.
Often these debts were, in Republican times, the result
of costly political canvassing, direct bribes to voters,
indirect bribes to them by splendid games in the circus,
public dinners and the like. When a prominent politician of the last days of the Republic carried his indebt-
edness beyond a certain stage, his very liabilities might
redound to his advantage. The influential *argentarii*
and *negotiatores*, who were his creditors, would dread
that if he failed in his program, missed carrying his
law, or getting a wealthy province to govern, he could
never repay them; and therefore worked heart and soul
for his success in the Senate or Comitia. Julius Caesar
was a notable example of a man always in debt, and
always well served by his creditors. The amount of
money spent on a consular canvass was enormous. The
rate of interest on one occasion rose from 4 to 8%
because there were so many candidates for the highest

office. In 62 B.C. Caesar owed 25,000,000 ses.; Marcus Antonius, when only twenty-four years old, owed 6,000,-000 ses.; fourteen years later 40,000,000 ses. Curio did even worse; on one occasion he owed 60,000,000 ses. Milo, Clodius' antagonist and Cicero's champion, capped the climax with 70,000,000 ses. A portion of these vast amounts can be accounted for by mere luxurious and wasteful living, but the bulk had come through political "expenses" and hardly concealed bribes—no pleasant commentary on the condition of the Republic.

But many who were not yet politicians were also greatly in debt. Catiline's gang of young profligates cried for *novae tabulae*—a clean sweep of all obligations heaped up through gambling, wineing, dining and unspeakable vice. Even men of grave and respectable habits caught the mania of their age, that of living beyond their incomes. Cicero was a prominent politician, but he certainly did not scatter his fortune in bribes; still—notwithstanding all the efforts of Atticus, his wise business adviser—he was continually in debt. The orator even jested at it, as a thing to be a trifle proud of, and once wrote to a friend that he was so much in debt he would gladly join in some conspiracy, only since he had punished Catiline, conspirators were not anxious to receive him. His money always flowed off for villas, statues, gardens; though at moments he admits that he has been somewhat extravagant. "Ye immortal gods," cries he, in his paradoxes, "when will men understand what treasures are found in economy!"

Quintus Cicero, his brother, afforded an even more typical case of the easy financial manners of his day. At a time when his creditors almost had him by the throat, he chose the occasion to rebuild his house in Rome, buy one country seat in the suburbs, and another at Arpinum, and greatly enlarge and improve his villa at Arcae.

In the case of Marcus Cicero's son we see what extravagance was taught the heir of a father not notably rich, by observing that young Cicero was given an allowance of 100,000 ses. for annual expenses while he was attending the University at Athens; a sum in actual modern metallic value well up to the highest, though not the maximum allowance, at the largest and most expensive American university, and if translated into the proportionate value, of about $12,000 per year—a generous allowance truly for a youth of unsteady habits!

Certain young men, when they came to their father's fortunes, ran through them with amazing rapidity. Clodius, the son of Asopus the great actor, was an instance. He spent his patrimony as fast as possible, as if possessing it were an intolerable burden. He dissolved in vinegar and so drank a pearl worth $40,000. He bought valuable singing birds and dined on them in lieu of snipe. "All his money flowed into his kitchen." Thus he made away with truly princely riches.

Many a young man, however, was unwilling to await the departure of his parents. The Emperor Claudius, says Tacitus, found the abuse of borrowing money by noble youths on the strength of expected patrimonies was so great that he absolutely forbade money lenders loaning any thing to young men to be repaid upon the deaths of their fathers. Juvenal implies, with his customary exaggeration, but with a dark background of truth, that it was quite customary when a young profligate had almost exhausted all he could borrow, to gather up a small residue and flee to Baiae or Ostia, "quitting the Forum" (i.e., giving one's creditors the slip),[1] an

---

[1] "Quitting the Forum" might sometimes mean going into a more honest bankruptcy; but here there is nothing implied save sheer absconding.

act counted quite as creditable as "removing to the Esquiline from the hot Subura;" while the only inconvenience alleged was that the defaulter must miss for a year the games in the Circus.

Not all noble bankrupts could flee Rome, however. Either their creditors caught them, or they had no residue left. They stayed in the capital and eked out a pitiful existence, literally living on charity. We have another picture of men of good family hovering around the door of some rich freedman to beg their *sportulae*. Juvenal would make us believe that even praetors and tribunes were thus beggars, but such extreme cases were no doubt rare. Caste pride among the senatorial order would have relieved these high born unfortunates, at least enough to keep them from bringing contempt upon their class.

What probably more often happened was that a nobleman pleaded for charity before the very Senate. This befell in Tiberius' reign, when Marcus Hortalus, the grandson of Hortensius the orator, stood up before the Conscript Fathers with his four children, and related how Augustus had given him 1,000,000 ses. to enable him to marry. Now he complained he had run through this fortune by taking a wife and rearing his children; and he implored the Senate and Emperor to have pity on his family. Tiberius rejoined, says Tacitus, that "if all the poor were to come hither and ask for provision for their children, they could never be satisfied, but the treasury would be emptied." However, he said the Senate could vote something for the sons of Hortalus if that body wished. Hortalus was clearly a notorious spendthrift. His money had flowed off anywhere but for the education of his children; but despite the cold reception given him by Tiberius, the whole incident illustrates the latitude Roman "dignity" could allow itself. Can one conceive an English peer making such a plea in the House of Lords?

The typical Roman of birth and fashion may then be imagined as regularly in debt, and frequently on the brink of ruin. Direct political bribery ended at Rome with the Empire, but in the provincial *municipia* vast sums—as we shall see—could be scattered to win popular favor; and even at Rome, aediles, praetors and consuls had to pay dearly in shows for their somewhat tinsel insignia. Houses, slaves, and dinner parties were some of the other things which swept away the relics of the old Republican fortunes. Capital and with it power would then drift to the ex-slaves and provincials whom hard experience had taught the value of money.

3. *Houses and Villas.*

The most obvious way for a rich Roman to spend his money was on city houses and country villas; and in over-ambitious attempts to get and to maintain such properties many a fortune was shipwrecked. Luxury in dwellings began in the last century of the Republic. Sulla (born 138 B.C.) as a young man in decidedly straitened circumstances paid for the rental of a ground floor (the best part of a building) 3,000 ses. per year. A freedman in the story above paid 2,000 ses. Marble was not at that time common in buildings at Rome. Pliny the Elder says that in 92 B.C. no structure in the capital had as yet marble pillars. The usual stone employed was travertine. The Censor Lucius Crassus in that year violently reprimanded his colleague, Cnaeus Domitius Ahenobarbus, for using some columns of Hymettus marble (left over from a theater which he had put up while aedile) in his own house; and Marcus Brutus called Ahenobarbus the "Venus of the Palatine" for this same ostentation.

By Cicero's time dwellings had become far more magnificent. Something has been said of the value of the land Julius Caesar bought for his Forum; we also know something of the value of great city houses at that day. Cicero bought his house on the Palatine from Crassus for 3,500,000 ses. When he returned from banishment, after the house had been destroyed by Clodius, the Senate voted him 2,000,000 ses. indemnity; i.e., the land was worth 1,500,000 ses., 43% of the whole. It has been calculated that real estate averaged to be held four times as valuable in Rome as in the other towns of Italy. The price of the less pretentious houses, of course, varied. Martial says one could buy a house in the capital for 100,000 ses.; but this must have been a very unpretending dwelling indeed. According to Juvenal, a private bath cost 600,000 ses., with a portico attached costing extra, and Fronto—a senator, by no means wealthy—paid 350,000 ses. for a bath. The variegated marbles regularly used to line the walls of the great houses of the Empire surely cost heavily, though we have no precise information. Marcus Scarus built a house on the Palatine which he adorned with the tallest of the marble columns used in his temporary theater. They were of black marble from Melos, a variety introduced by Lucullus. The *eques* Mammura, Caesar's chief engineer in Gaul, had—says Pliny —a house which was a monument to his shameless plunderings in that country. It was provided throughout with marble columns, monoliths of green-veined stone from Carystos in Euboea, or of Carrara marble.

The age of Augustus, when Rome was transformed architecturally, involved a vast improving, not merely of public buildings, but of private palaces. Horace, Tibullus, Propertius give abundant indications of the increasing luxury in private dwellings, as well as of their growth in mere size. The Carrara quarries were now for the first time worked to their fullest extent, and the import trade in foreign building stones was at its height. The poets, as well as Vitruvius the architect, dwell on the kind of a house needful to a man of social pretentions. It must have a high and imposing vestibule, wide atria and peristylia, with parks, covered walks of great circuit, libraries, picture galleries, "basilicas" which aped the magnificence of public buildings. The palace of the friend of Augustus—the *eques* Vedius Pollio—covered "more room than many cities embrace within their walls." In Pompeii we can see the provincial town imitating the metropolis, and in a good many dwellings these features are reproduced, but on such a miniature scale that the area of the houses is not very great.

The mania for bizarre colored marble was very prevalent, and probably increased as taste and good art declined. In the atria of the house of a great man of the Empire would be pilasters of violet-spotted Phrygian marble, while beams wrought of white Hymettan rested on red, yellow or green variegated marble from Numidia, Euboea, and the mountains of Taenarum in Laconia. Amid the precious columns of the courts stood bushes and clumps of trees, plashing fountains, while purple awnings stretched from one line of columns to another, throwing a red shimmer on the pavement or the moss carpet of the floor.

Such a dwelling in the expensive capital demanded a full purse, and the contest between the millionaires in building ever finer palaces continued furiously until the passing of Nero brought back simpler tendencies. Towards the end of Tiberius' reign, Valerius Maximus, perhaps with some exaggeration, says that a palace with its gardens and other dependences, which only covered

four acres of land, was a distinctly cramped dwelling.
The luxury in private baths was possibly greater than
in the halls and the colonnades. Seneca says that he
visited the baths of Scipio the Elder at his villa in
Laternum, and was amazed to find how plain and bare
they were. "Now who would not feel himself a beggar
if the bathing chamber does not sparkle with costly
stones?" Egyptian marble, inlaid with Numidian marble and encircled with mosaics, was coveted for this purpose, also a ceiling paneled with crystal. The water
should flow through silver faucets. There should be
countless statues and pillars. "We have reached,"
concludes the wealthy philosopher, "such a stage of
delicacy that our feet no longer tread on anything but
precious stones!"

Luxury in baths was not confined to Rome. There
were magnificent private baths in Africa, in Britain,
along the Rhine, and, we may presume in every wealthy
community or noble estate in the Empire. Near Cirta in
Numidia there have been discovered ruins of elegant
baths, large and of truly regal magnificence, fit to vie
with any in Rome in almost everything save mere size;
yet these seem intended not for any city, but merely for
the owner of a single great country property. In the
northern provinces also the rigorous climate compelled
the spread of divers luxuries not so common in Rome;
thus in Gaul the use of central furnaces and of glass
windows seems to have been far wider than at the
capital.

A great noble would seldom content himself with one
house, even in Rome itself. Again we may instance
Cicero. Besides his regular dwelling on the Palatine,
and that of his father at Carinae, he had others on the
Argiletum and on the Aventine, whence he drew an
income of 80,000 ses.; so we may presume part at least

of this property was held for profit, not for display.

Life in Rome even for the greatest, however, had the serious drawback of the constant dread of fire. Besides the regular *Cohortes Vigilum,* the public fire department, there seem to have been private watchmen in all the palaces, "a whole regiment of slaves," asserts Juvenal, "on guard with leathern buckets to protect their lord's amber, his beloved statues, his Phrygian marbles, his treasures in ivory and tortoise shell.".

The cost of maintaining his "town house" was thus a sufficient drain on any Roman gentleman; but what he could not conveniently spend in the city, he could readily sink in innumerable villas.

Cicero, we discover, had eight large villas in Italy, not reckoning small houses (*diversoria*) which he, like other Roman notables, owned along the principal roads, as resting spots while he went from one place to another. His Tusculan villa, if no others, was fairly valuable; and when the Senate voted—on his return from exile— 500,000 ses. to repair it, Cicero thought the sum niggardly. The eagerness of the magnates of the Republic and the Empire to multiply country estates is almost incredible. A certain Regulus, whose whole fortune was about 60,000,000 ses., had estates in Umbria, Etruria, Tusculum and in the Campagna on the road to Tibur. Pliny the Younger—of moderate wealth—had landed possessions in Etruria, a large estate at Comum, and several villas near the lake of that name, another estate in the Beneventum district, and another by Laurentum. A man could thus spend all his life in continually traveling up and down Italy, and making sojourns at his own estates.

Horace speaks at length of the great increase of villas and villa property in his time. Soon, he declares, the residences of the rich will leave only a few acres to the plow. Artificial ponds are made bigger than the Lucrine lake. Plane trees are replacing elms. Instead of olive groves are coming shades of myrtle and laurel and the scent of violets. Instead of the greensward, rose-columned halls to give protection against the southern or northern winds.

Statius has much to say of a villa on the bay of Naples, which does not, however, seem to have been pre-eminent in expensive luxury. Its buildings, gardens and parks covered the whole coast for a long stretch. Directly upon the sea arose a warm bath with two domes, a temple to Neptune, and one to Hercules. A pillared portico ran by a winding way to the villa. Its rooms afforded many views of the sea and the islands. Among all the other parts of the building one hall was especially to be noted; it had a view directly across the bay to Naples. It was decorated with colored marbles sought out in Greece, Asia Minor, Numidia and Egypt. Everywhere were costly paintings and sculptures by old masters, and portraits of generals, philosophers and poets. Scanty remains of this villa, its floors of colored marble, its pillars and the like, have been from time to time discovered along the coast; yet it was but one of the many which lined that glorious bay.

Silius Italicus, a consular who died in Trajan's reign, was a man so rich that during a long life he did not succeed in touching bottom with his fortune, despite many extravagancies. "He was such a keen virtuoso," says Pliny the Younger, "that he got the reputation of always itching to buy new things." He owned a number of villas in the same neighborhood, and used to neglect his old ones in his passion for his recent purchases. In each he had any quantity of books, statues and busts, especially of Vergil, for whom he developed a kind of cult, celebrating the poet's birthday more carefully than his own.

The use of costly marbles was hardly less marked in the villas than in the city palaces. In the third century the Gordiani had a villa on the Via Praenestina which contained a square hall upborne by two hundred pillars, fifty each of *Giallo antico,* Cipollino, Pavonazetto and red porphyry. In this villa was likewise a basilica three hundred feet long, baths and everything else on a similar scale. Hadrian's villa was of course the work of an emperor, with its imitations of the architecture of all nations, reminiscences of the owner's journeyings, its "Lyceum," "Academy," "Poecile," "Prytaneum," "Canopus," "Tempe," and even "Hades." But this country palace was hardly more magnificent than the palace also at Tibur of Mamilius Vopiscus, which is described to us as extraordinarily elegant, though Vopiscus himself is practically unknown to history.

As the imperial age waned and art declined, the magnates did not cease building, but they ceased to build in good taste. Bigness took the place of artistic beauty. The emperors of the third century had greater resources than their subjects; but probably they only did on a great scale what many senators did on a smaller. Gordianus the Younger began a portico under the Pincian Hill nine hundred yards in circumference and enclosing a garden of 44,000 square yards. His death stopped the project. Gallienus, who saw more calamities than any emperor of long reign, until Honorius, proposed to build a statue of himself on the Esquiline hill, 219 feet high—twice as high as Trajan's statue— representing him as the sun, holding a rod in his hands. A spiral staircase in the rod was to admit visitors to the very top. This, of course, was not art, but monstrosity.[1] The example of the Caesars was sure to be imitated far and wide. If an *eques* or senator could not erect a colossal statute to himself, he could indulge in even greater absurdities. Galen tells of a rich man who brought to Italy a quantity of water from the Dead Sea to fill up a reservoir.

The rage for villas, and many of them, lasted down to the ruin of the Empire. In the fourth century we find a single senator possessing four villas near to Rome, seven in the rest of Latium, five on the bay of Naples, and it would seem several others about which exact information fails us. Of course some of these properties were larger and more elegant than others, but they appear all to have cost far more than they brought in. They occupied fertile land. They ought to have been producing corn and wine; they stood actually as good as empty. This senator no doubt derived his main income from a host of other farms used strictly for business; but the huge pleasure parks, which formed an appreciable part of Italy, and even of the provinces, economically were hardly more valuable than deserts. They bore nothing but flowers—more flowers than any owner could enjoy. Their purchase and maintenance tied up a very large capital which, if used otherwise, might have averted the long winter which presently froze ancient agriculture, commerce and industry to their undoing.

4. *Gourmandizing, Costly Funerals and other Extravagances.*

The fashionable man of the Empire who did not spend his patrimony on houses or villas usually ridded himself of it by the gratification of his palate. More people

[1] It is worth noting, in speaking of this mania for bigness, that Diocletian's baths at Rome—the largest in area—were also almost the last; but one may ask whether they had the elegance of the earlier *thermae*.

could afford a fine table than could a palace on the Esquiline or country seats in Campania; besides many an individual who did not care for rare statuary and marbles, was quite able to appreciate Ravenna oysters. And finally—as was said earlier—the opportunities for the legitimate expenditure of wealth were less under the Empire than they are to-day, therefore it was easier for men to concentrate their riches and attention upon the mere satisfying of appetite.

These are the main reasons why gastronomy played such an important part in the life of the Empire. As for the early Republic, it seems needless to say that the men who conquered the Samnites, Pyrrhus and Hannibal were extraordinarily temperate both in their eating and their drinking. The Romans hardly realized there was such a thing as the cook's art until 188 B.C., when their army came back from Asia Minor. We know that down to 174 B.C. there were no professional bakers in Rome, and every housewife made her own bread. Down to 100 B.C. imported Greek wine was never passed more than once at the most ostentatious banquet. The Stoic Poseidonius (writing at the beginning of the last century B.C.) commented approvingly on the simplicity of Roman table manners, and on the willingness of Roman boys to eat the simple food their parents set before them and to drink water. But after the period of the Social Wars there came in an era of most elaborate gourmandizing.

Many of the Roman pleasures of the table implied not mere love of good living, but deliberate gluttony. To get a name as a tremendous eater was a very simple way to notoriety, and at no age was notoriety more hankered after than under the Empire. "You are not content, Tucca," says Martial of some fashionable youth, "to be a glutton. You long to be *called* and to appear a glutton." The conditions of Roman society made inevitable that there should be a large class of wealthy or supposedly wealthy idlers. If these idlers were not fond of literary trifling and philosophy, eating and drinking was sure to consume a very large part of their lives. If a would-be gourmand was not wealthy, so much the worse; but he would gorge himself as long as he might. Many men of very modest means, we are informed, seem to have spent their all on their palates. They pawned their last valuables for "a four hundred sesterce fish upon an earthen platter." Their creditors would wait for them in the public food markets where they went to squander their borrowings; while the nearer these gourmands were to ruin, the more daintily they supped, "the most expensive dishes pleasing them best."

The number of rare, not to say absurd, foreign dishes available in Rome was very great; some have been already enumerated. Grouse from Phrygia, cranes from Melos, kids from Ambracia, tunny fish from Chalcedon, sturgeons from Rhodes, acorns from Spain, dates from Egypt, nuts from Thasos—these were a few of the staples. The dinners of the great pontifical colleges were proverbial for serving the best of the products of Roman gastronomy. In 63 B.C. Mucius Lentulus Niger, on entering upon his pontificate, gave a dinner—so Macrobius tells—to his fellow priests, Caesar among them, the Vestal Virgins, and divers others. There was a preliminary meal of eighteen dishes, then a regular dinner of ten heartier dishes; some of the viands sea nettles, roe ribs, boar's ribs, purple shell-fish of two sorts, sow's udder, boar's head, boar's pasties, boiled teals, ducks, hams, hares, and sea hedgehogs. A great feast, but sadly lacking, it would seem, in vegetables, ices and the lighter delicacies; though we hear that starch and "Pontic" pastry were also then served. Presumably a good many state dinners under the Empire could show as long a menu; and of "college" (i.e., priestly) banquets in general, Varro says that their magnificence forced up the price of all delicacies.

The Romans appear to have been more partial to heavy meat courses than were the Athenians, who taunted their Boeotian neighbors as "flesh-eaters;" but down to the end of the Empire, fish was held in extravagant esteem. The most valuable carp and lampreys were kept in fish-ponds, and sometimes became very large. How elaborate the fish tanks of a great nobleman were will be realized when it is stated that the heirs of Lucullus derived 40,000,000 ses. from those which he established; and that Varro tells how one Hirrus made from his 12,000,000 ses. annually, and once gave Caesar six thousand lampreys. Wine cellars, too, could drown or produce great fortunes according as they were used. In the cellars of Hortensius the orator there was a stock of 10,000 jars (33 quarts each) of imported wine; while Italian wine growers generally complained that Greek wines— Sicilian, Lesbian and Chian—often crowded out the Italian wines, even the excellent Falernian.

The efforts of the more famous gourmands, of course, were not merely to gain fame as gluttons, but also as inventors of new dishes and delicacies. Nothing was too bizarre. Many animals never eaten to-day—dormice, peacocks, cranes, flamingoes—graced the silver platters in Roman triclinia. A noble matron once sold five thousand fattened thrushes at twelve sesterces each; and under the first Triumvirate, one Aufidius Lurco made 60,000 ses. per year raising peacocks. Great zeal was shown also in acclimatizing strange and foreign fruits. Lucullus brought the cherry to Italy. In the next century the melon was imported from the Oxus region; while the father of Vitellius—the gourmands' emperor—who was governor of Syria, tried to introduce the fruits of his province at his Italian villa.

Mere desire for the sensations of taste, of course, led to the disgusting use of emetics. *"Vomunt ut edant, edunt ut vomant,"* are the significant words of Seneca. The habit seems to have been passing common. Physicians laid down rules for correct vomiting; and while we have no ample data, it is right to presume that the diseases incident to gluttony were prevalent among the wealthy.

The gourmand's ideal was Marcus Gabius Apicius, whose exploits are now almost proverbial. He lived under Augustus and Tiberius, and made away with a fortune of 100,000,000 ses. in refined gluttony. His case was accounted absolutely marvelous, and quite a cycle of myths grew up about him. Finally, we are told, when he felt he was touching bottom with his fortune, he balanced his books. Only 10,000,000 ses. were left. With such a paltry principal it was impossible to find life worth living. He committed suicide. Apicius' case was regarded even at his own frivolous era with mingled wonderment and horror, as if he were a monstrosity. He was selected by Elagabalus, two hundred years later, as a model for sybaritic living. Yet to-day—if we assume his fortune was worth $12,000,000[1]—a man who squandered a corresponding patrimony would indeed be accounted a wicked prodigal; but his name would hardly pass into a byword, a consideration which should prevent one from thinking that the warnings of Roman waste and luxury have no importance at present save for the antiquarian.

Apicius, while his money lasted, was the first gourmand at Rome, but by no means without rivals. A certain Publius Octavius, a great noble, once paid 5,000 ses.

[1] By assuming that 100,000,000 ses. equaled $4,000,000 cash, and thrice as much in purchasing power.

for a single rare fish weighing five and a half pounds, thereby outbidding Apicius, and even the Emperor Tiberius—a feat that won him much renown, which renown he was probably more anxious to win than he was to taste the delicious finny.

Still the discrimination of Roman epicures was carried to an absurdly fine point. They pretended to be able to tell at the first bite whether the oysters were natives of Circeii, or were Lucrine, or were even from Britain; also at a glance from which coast a sea-urchin had been taken; —nor, when men live merely to eat, is this knowledge entirely incredible. The purchase of costly fish continued even after the fall of Nero. In Domitian's reign it was reported that a spendthrift epicure paid 6,000 ses. for one six-pound mullet[1]—one thousand per pound; and Juvenal, greatly scandalized, cries out that the fisherman possibly could have been bought cheaper than the fish.

As to the cost of the great banquets, it is necessarily hard to strike an average. The Arval Brothers, when they met in one of the famous "Collegiate Dinners," paid four hundred sesterces per plate; but this no doubt included flowers, chaplets and perfumes—a source of great expense. A dinner in Lucullus' celebrated Apollo Hall cost 200,000 ses., and was noted as being an extreme outlay; though a great function of corresponding cost— $24,000—at present would hardly be magnificent enough to pass into history. It is certainly easy to cite more extravagant cases, when we come to emperors; but they were spending the resources of seventy-five millions of people. Thus Lucius Verus gave a feast costing 6,000,-000 ses.; yet even here a large part of the expense appears to have gone off in gifts to the guests—handsome slaves, vessels of costly materials, silver-mounted carriages with yokes of mules and the driver included, and the like.

[1] Very large—according to Horace even one of three pounds was rare.

With such extras it would have been possible to make a dinner party cost almost any sum more.

Considerable sums of money could also be tied up unproductively in silver plate; and considering the fact that the supply which the ancients had of the precious metals was comparatively scanty, this habit rose to a real public evil. Pliny the Elder says that Pompeius Panlliures (the father-in-law of Seneca), while commander of the army of lower Germany (in 58 B.C.), carried about with him 12,000 lbs. of silver. Although no doubt this was exceptional, the Roman officers seem always to have taken large services of plate to their barracks, and even on campaigns; nor could their wealthy relatives at home have been more content simply with earthenware and pewter.[1] Tiberius found it necessary to forbid the use of golden vessels by private persons except in sacrifices and other religious ceremonies, and not till Aurelian's time was their use generally permitted.

Precious stones also admitted very great outlays; though it is hard to judge the values of gems and jewels in antiquity, for we do not know the weights. We hear of Nerva sending Trajan a great diamond as sign of receiving him for successor. We also hear of emeralds of high value. An emerald worth 7,000 ses. was in a ring set on a lady's statue erected (by her son) in southern Spain. The Senator Nonius Struma had an emerald ring worth 2,000,000 ses. for which he was proscribed by Antonius. Pearls from the Indian Ocean and Persian Gulf, and imported via Alexandria, were in extensive demand by the ladies of the Empire for ear pendants. Caesar in 59 B.C. bought a pair for Servilia

[1] In extenuation of the Romans it must be said they do not seem to have possessed our elegant china porcelain table services, despite the beauty of their vases, glassware, etc.

(the mother of Marcus Brutus) that cost 6,000,000 ses.

Perfumes devoured a large share out of many fortunes. No banquet was complete without them. The better varieties were highly expensive. In the loud and flashy society of the capital they were used with very little taste. Pliny the Elder asserts that the approach of a wealthy Roman lady could be told a great way off by the odor streaming from her hair and dress. The use of unguents passed quite early to Rome from Magna Graecia; but the habit does not appear to have penetrated much into the smaller cities. A pound of choice perfume was worth, according to Martial, "ten .gold coins of Domitian;" and certain perfumer's shops in the capital —Cosmus' and Niceros' by name—appear to have been much celebrated. Account, too, has to be taken of the incense and sweet spices used at funerals, which in their turn were sufficiently costly.

Persons, who liked such things, might frequently spend much on troops of pantomimes, kept privately for the amusement of themselves and their guests. In Trajan's time an old lady, Ummida Quadratilla—who died in her eightieth year—kept a band of these freedmen—buffoons, pantomimes and their kind—and showed them all manner of favors up to her end, giving them so much attention that she greatly scandalized her relatives.

A good deal has been said on other pages of the acclimatization of foreign fruits and flowers in Italy. The process was carried on by wealthy people even in the northern provinces. Julian the Apostate tells how around Paris the inhabitants "even rear figs, covering them up in winter with wheaten straw as with a cloth."

The cultivation of flowers was brought to a very high degree under the Empire. Especially the crocus was imported from the East, though Columella considered its cultivation very hard, and sets its raising in Italy on a par with cassia, incense, myrrh, etc. Varro speaks of Italy as "one great orchard," though Greece was at that time very poorly cultivated. The transforming element in Italy seems to have been the slave and freedmen gardeners from Asia—Syrians, Jews, Phoenicians, Cilicians, and others; for horticulture was something in which the Semites had excelled, and they brought their skill with them to the West.

Elaborate houses and villas, of course, demanded equally elaborate furnishings. Nero paid 4,000,000 ses. for some Babylonian embroidered carpets—an extreme price, but showing how high such luxuries could run. In the second century 2,000,000 ses. were paid for a set of the same to cover the couches in a dining-room. "Citruswood" tables (made from the citrus trees of Mt. Atlas) were a terribly expensive fad. Cicero gave 500,000 ses. for one—though he was not a man who threw money away recklessly; and in later times the price went even as high as 1,400,000 ses. Seneca had five hundred citrus tables, though we may guess most of them were not of such extreme values.

Murrha[1] was first introduced into Rome after Pompeius' victory over Mithridates, and at once became a favorite object for expenditure. Small vessels of murrha were sold for as high as 300,000 ses., and Nero bought a drinking cup thereof for 1,000,000 ses., though doubtless he "paid like an emperor." For a ladle of rock crystal, we are told, a lady—not extremely rich—spent 150,000 ses.

Clothes, too, could devour fortunes. In Augustus' time a pound of the best double-dyed purple wool brought over 4,000 ses.; a cheaper grade, "amythestine," or "violet-purple," cost about one third as much. How-

---

[1] Whether this substance was Chinese porcelain, a kind of onyx, or agate, jade or something else has been by no means settled.

ever, Martial makes the price of a mantle of Tyrian
purple of the best color to be only 10,000 ses. So we may
guess that the value of purple had declined in the interval.
The right to wear garments wholly of purple indeed had
been limited since Caesar's time to certain persons and
certain days. Nero actually forbade the sale of Tyrian
and amethystine purple; but this ordinance was relaxed
under Domitian, and probably much earlier, and when
the treasury was in need we see Marcus Aurelius and
Pertinax putting up the imperial wardrobe of purple for
sale.

At great functions the amount of money which the
guests, especially the ladies, could spend on their cos-
tumes would rival almost the extravagant follies of
to-day. The extreme of modesty (in upper society) is
perhaps to be seen in the case of the rhetorician Quintilian's daughter, where the younger Pliny sends her
father 50,000 ses. as part of the expense of her wedding
trousseau; for though Quintilian was wealthy from the
standpoint of the average man of learning, he was in
very modest circumstances for a Senator. On the other
hand, the elder Pliny says that he saw Lollia Paulina,
for a short time the wife of Caligula, and the heiress of
a successfully rapacious proconsul, attend a betrothal
feast wearing on her person the value of 40,000,000 ses.,[1]
nearly all, of course, not in the fabrics, but in the jewelry.

A Roman lady did not have to spend so much as her
American successor on hats, gloves, furs, and hosiery;
furthermore, despite the complaints about money sent
to India to pay for spices and jewels, vast sums from
Rome were not devoured by the modistes of Antioch and

[1] It is very hard to decide whether the jewels worn by the modern
denizen of ''The House of Mirth'' occasionally exceed this figure or not.
It is alleged that sable coats are purchased in America at $40,000 each,
and that the orders at Vienna for the trousseau of an American bride came
to $250,000.

Alexandria, who had no such lucrative market as the "artists" of Paris find in the spendthrift society of New York.

The tendency of the sumptuary laws to restrict costly funerals has already been noted; but in this, as in other particulars, custom and fashion laughed at the statute. The belief of a Roman in the future life was at best a vague one, and he was correspondingly anxious that a memorable funeral and a notable monument should prevent succeeding generations from forgetting him. A man might have been penurious in life, but have no compunctions in saddling his heirs with expensive obsequies. The sums accordingly spent on funerals and tomb-stones were sometimes great.

The city council of Pompeii voted for the funeral of an aedile, excluding the price of the ground for the tomb-stone, 2,000 ses.—and the same sum for a duumvir; so this was probably the average cost of a good funeral in a small city. A veteran of Lambessa, in his testament, devoted 2,000 ses. to his funeral and gravestone. The rich Claudius Isidorus, who left over four thousand slaves and a fortune of 60,000,000 ses., set aside 1,100,000 ses. for his funeral. Vespasian's funeral was reported —possibly not on the best grounds—to have cost 10,000,-000 ses.

But much of the outlay was not through self-glorification, but from a passionate desire to do honor to the beloved dead. Regulus, the notorious advocate and informer of Domitian's and Trajan's time, having lost a son, slaughtered on the pyre the boy's numerous ponies, dogs, nightingales, parrots and blackbirds. He erected a vast number of busts and statues in his son's memory, and kept all the workshops of Rome busy making them in wax, bronze, silver, ivory and marble. He also assembled a large audience, to whom he read a memoir of the boy; had a thousand copies thereof made and sent through Italy and the provinces, requesting the municipal senates to choose one of their number with the best voice to read the memoir to the people—and thanks to Regulus' prestige and wealth, this was actually done.

Tombs and funeral monuments easily represented goodly fortunes. We can gain a rough conception of the cost by the great size of their bases; some were of 225 square feet, and some of 625, 750 and even 910 (in Ostia) are known. And these large ones do not seem to have been uncommon. Petronius' character, Trimalchio, planned himself a tomb with a vineyard and orchard around it, also a porter's lodge; and he set aside 10,000 ses. simply for the land whereon to build it.

Vain glory, and not an honest desire to be remembered, caused many monuments to be erected. A poor messenger of Carthage, who carried official despatches, tells in an inscription how he built himself a tomb, and took great pleasure, while he was crossing the plain, in reading the verses he had caused to be engraved thereon; and these tombs that antedated a funeral must have been fairly common.

The scanty remains of the mausoleums that lined the roads near Rome, and all over Italy, give us an impressive idea of their one-time splendor. A few still survive, as e.g., the tombs of Caecilia Metella and of Plautus on the road to Tibur, and the Pyramid of Cestius. The smaller towns were not very much behind the capital. At Pompeii—for one case—we may observe the ruins of the stately monument of a certain Mamia,—a temple-like building with pilasters on a high sub-structure. At Langres was an elaborate monument to a landowner. Statues of the dead in bronze and Greek marble decorated it, and in an altar of Carrara marble were contained the ashes of the deceased; by the monument was a pond and an orchard with a gardener and three apprentices to keep the charge. All this was provided in the will. At Igel near Trier has been found a monument seventy-three feet high of gray sandstone, and there have been discovered many smaller obelisks of about ten feet in Belgica, Gaul and Roman Germany. In Syria in the region beyond Jordan are numerous Roman monuments, usually with square towers, which have served as dove houses. At Lambessa in Africa, Titus Flavius Maximus, a praefect of the third legion, had an elaborate stone monument about twenty feet high, which preserved his ashes quite safely until 1849.

Of the cost of these monuments we get some information from wills. The cost varied from 200 to 100,000 ses. At Augsburg the gravestone of a decurion seems to have cost 6,000 ses. A great man at Rome would spend far more. Cato of Utica built a monument to his half-brother for 38,000 ses. A praetorian (probably of Septimius Severus' day) had a monument built for him by his brother officers which cost 43,500 ses. When we come to the emperors we of course note the tomb of Hadrian, which was completed by Antonius Pius, that had a substructure which, Procopius declares, was more than one hundred yards to the side, and which can only be compared to such things as the Egyptian pyramids.

Next to the chance of spending money on the tomb, came the cost of the frankincense indispensable at a funeral. Here again the sumptuary laws came in with their prohibitions. For example, at Ostia it was forbidden to use more than twenty pounds of frankincense for the funeral of a young man of the decurion class, or a woman of the local aristocracy. The Elder Pliny says there were three kinds of this incense valued at six, five and three denarii per pound; but one may conjecture that the frankincense which Nero burned at the funeral of Poppaea Sabina (65 A.D.) was even more valuable weight for weight, while the quantity then consumed was declared to be more than all Arabia could produce in a single year. Also when Annia Priscilla, wife of a freedman-secretary of Domitian, died in 95 A.D., all sorts of exaggerated comments were made on the amount of incense wasted.

Unquestionably then, the expenditure on funerals and monuments was decidedly great; yet in justice to the men of the Empire it should be added that they never drifted into absurdities touching the dead, such as marked the Egyptians.

5. *The Delators.*

Many a Roman fortune was ruined, not by costly buildings, peacock suppers, or extravagance in dress, but by the private prosecutor, not to say blackmailer. While the "delators" were hardly cultivated as luxuries by the high-born gentleman of the Empire, there is no more convenient place to consider them than in this chapter, where we are examining the avenues by which the Romans parted with their wealth. Monsieur Boissier, in his valuable book *L'Opposition sous les Césars,* has devoted an entire chapter to the delators, and then by no means exhausts the subject. We, however, have to consider the infamous business from only one point of view— viz., as a means of gain to the accuser, and of financial ruin to the accused.

That the business of these parasites and blackmailers could ever flourish was due to the extreme clumsiness of the machinery which ancient society employed in enforcing its own laws. There were no official prosecutors to take cognizance of crimes, and be responsible for bringing the offender to justice. The task was left to the initiative of private individuals. Practically every citizen of regular standing could bring a criminal action and push it to its issue. The easiest way for an aspiring young politician in republican times to gain fame for himself was to accuse a retiring proconsul of maladministration in his province; and half Rome would listen to the eloquence at the trial. Under the Republic, thus, accusations were usually brought either simply for political ends, or to redress some real injury. The Empire saw fewer set trials for malversation in the provinces, largely because the provinces were better governed; but the motive of financial gain was introduced in a certain important class of cases, which encouraged the delators to come forward.

A "delator" was not always a mere informer—one who gives evidence. He might also be the advocate of the prosecution. He first crept into notice in Augustus' day, when pecuniary rewards were offered to any who secured the conviction of violators of the Emperor's new marriage laws.[1] Then came the *Lex Julia de Majestate*,[2] making disrespect to the Emperor's person, deeds, or authority punishable capitally, while the offender's entire estate was confiscate. A person became liable to the law if he melted down a statue of the Emperor which had been already consecrated, or if he swore an oath by the Genius of the ruler and then violated it. To commit treason, mere intention to commit the offense, not an overt act, was all that was necessary; while Septimius Severus and Caracalla were called upon graciously to issue an edict that it was not lese-majesty if a stone were thrown which accidentally struck an imperial image.

---

[1] Laws quite unpopular, hard to enforce, and hence requiring extraordinary supports to render them effective.

[2] Perhaps enacted in a mild form under Julius Caesar; but it probably took its familiar shape under Augustus.

The worst about this enactment was the means it provided for its enforcement. One fourth of the offender's estate went to the successful prosecutor. In the darker days of Tiberius, Caligula, Nero and Domitian, accusation, even with the flimsiest evidence, was practically the same as conviction. The servile Senate concealed its hatred for the Caesarian regime by its furious zeal to punish all guilty of lese-majesty. A fortunate delator could expect much more than his share of his victim's goods; he was likely to be voted a public benefactor. Thus in Nero's day, to the destroyers of the virtuous Thrasea and Soranus, Eprius and Cossutianus were awarded 500,000 ses. each; and to Ostorius, their companion in infamy, 120,000 ses. and the insignia of the quaestorship.

Fear for one's self, added to cupidity, made delation a terribly popular calling. The extremes were reached as early as Tiberius' reign, when in the case of Sabinus (one of Sejanus' victims) three senators concealed themselves in the cranny between the roof and the ceiling of a confederate's house, while he induced their victim to enter and pour out his grievances against the Emperor and prime minister, seemingly in all confidence and friendship. Or even, in 24 A.D., a son was found accusing a father—Vibius Serenus—of a manifestly absurd plot against Tiberius. These were the times, as Tacitus ominously says, "when the city was in deep alarm, [for] never was there need of greater caution against a man's nearest relatives. Men were afraid to meet, afraid to talk, . . . they even feared things dumb and inanimate, the roofs and the walls."

The plague, of course, abated under good reigns. Caligula pretended at first to discourage the delators. Even Nero reduced their rewards in some cases, however terribly he made use of the miscreants in others. Titus

repressed them severely. Domitian followed his brother's example at first, then allowed the whole breed to
flourish and subserve his tyranny. We are given in
Philostratus' life of Apollonius of Tyana a picture—
possibly fanciful—of the espionage that prevailed under
the gloomy youngest Flavian,—the magistrate of Tarentum languishing in the dungeon for dangerous omissions
from the public prayers, and others suffering with him—
with the stealthy spy gliding into the prison to overhear
their talk. No doubt tyrants like Nero and Domitian
usually allowed prosecutions through fear; but in many
cases the motive of the government, no less than of the
accuser, was simply to get the victim's estate.[1] The
delators' heyday ended when the dagger of Stephanus
slew Domitian, and Trajan ordered their banishment.
But the race could not be rooted out. Comparatively
quiescent under the "good emperors," they sprang to
activity again in the bad times introduced by Commodus.
They flourished under Caracalla, when the bad relations
between that prince and the Senate prepared the way for
many illustrious victims. Under Aurelian the delators
were found to be so active that the Emperor had to pub-
lish a general amnesty in order to close up the many
trials pending for lese-majesty. Constantine issued a
rescript against them; but the repeal of the *majestas*
laws, which alone could draw the teeth of this noxious
tribe, never took place. One may imagine them lingering
on, now repressed, now encouraged by the government,
until the Barbarian darkness.

The same Regulus, who has been mentioned as giving
his son a costly funeral, flourished under Domitian and
Trajan. He was preëminent in his class. Under Domi-

[1] That was so especially under Nero, whose prodigality soon brought him
to such straits that only wholesale confiscations could keep him from
bankruptcy.

tian he seems to have fattened as a mere delator; under Trajan he was shrewd enough to avoid that Emperor's edicts of banishment, and continued to thrive as a more legitimate legal advocate. He was the younger Pliny's *bête noire;* but Pliny hesitated to quarrel with him, despite his wickedness. "Regulus is a difficult bird to net. He is rich; he is a shrewd intriguer; he has no small body of followers, and a still larger circle of those who fear him, and fear is often a more powerful factor than affection." Herennius Senecio, a correspondent of the younger Pliny, had said that "an orator was a bad man who knew nothing of the art of speaking." Pliny was sure all this applied to Regulus. He had weak lungs, a shifting gaze; he stammered, had no imaginative power or memory, no quality at all except a "wild, frantic genius," and yet, thanks to this frenzy of his, he had got people to regard him as a man of vast ability. He is pictured to us as a long-winded speaker, who always induced the judges to allow him as much "water" (i.e., time measured by water clocks) as possible. With all his cunning and unscrupulousness, he had his share of superstitions. He would smear ointment over his left eye before he went into court to argue for the defendant, over his right eye if he was to speak for the plaintiff; and as for his general methods of attack he flatly told Pliny he did not like that urbane gentleman's habit of following up a case point by point. "I lose no time in getting a sight of my opponent's throat, and consider only the easiest way of cutting it."

A man of this type was sure to find abundant means of growing rich in a society so full of scandal, intrigue and dark doings. He was an indefatigable legacy hunter.[1] He would urge physicians to prolong the lives of sick men until they changed their wills in his favor,

[1] For the whole question of legacy hunting, see page 309.

then urge the physicians to give the patient a swift and painless death, since his illness was incurable. From sheer poverty he thus rose by unabashed villainy to riches, and once told Pliny that when consulting the omens as to how soon he could be worth 60,000,000 ses., he found a double set of entrails—clear proof that he was to be worth 120,000,000 instead.

We do not know how much of this fortune was accumulated under Domitian by prosecutions for lese-majesty; it is fair to infer a very large part. "Probably in no other way [than as a delator]," says Professor Dill, "could a man so easily make himself a millionaire."[1] We can speak especially of Regulus because Pliny writes at length of him; but Eprius and Vibius Crispus—other geniuses who combined delation and legitimate advocacy —accumulated far greater fortunes than did he. A little oratorical skill, a stifled conscience, a brazen face, a genius for intrigue and for worming one's self into the confidence of the unwary—these perhaps could breed a tenfold better fortune than a dozen voyages to Ceylon. The successful delator must mark his victims long in advance, allow them to prosper for a while that his own share in the plunder might be larger, and must guard them against the attacks of any fellow accuser. "Don't harm my dead men," said a famous prosecutor under Domitian, meaning that he regarded his victims as his private property.

The volume of the estates divided by the government and the delators of course cannot be computed. It was very large, for only people of wealth were worth destroying.[2] Again, we cannot compute the profit the delators

---

[1] Dill's "Roman Society from Nero to Marcus Aurelius" p. 36.

[2] In this point at least, the Roman lese-majesty prosecutions were more commendable than the *Majestäts beleidigung* cases of modern Germany. The Roman victims were not usually schoolboys, old women and common workmen in their cups.

made by private blackmail levied on persons caught in incautious words or acts, and who purchased immunity by round compositions. Whatever be the similarities between the rich man of Rome and his successor in America, the latter stands in no terror of lese-majesty, and of the centurion come with the order to commit suicide; although, if his life be frivolous, he is possibly open to the blackmailing of scandal-mongering periodicals.

There was another and a pleasanter way in which a Roman gentleman often disbursed a large share of his fortune—on gifts and friendly assistance to compeers.[1] Such gifts might be on quite a large scale. Again, we can cite the invaluable younger Pliny. He writes to a Romanus Firmus that he (Firmus) has already the 100,000 ses. needful to be a decurion of Comum; but Pliny will give him 300,000 more so that he may be a Roman knight. "The length of our friendship is pledge enough that you will not forget this favor." Again, Pliny writes to a young, unmarried lady, Calvina, that he has paid off all her late father's debts, so that she can enter upon his estate unencumbered. He had already given 100,000 ses. towards her dower, and "I authorize you to enter as paid whatever sum was owing from your father [an old friend] to me." Kindly and fairly disinterested acts! Firmus and Calvina would hardly fail at some day to reciprocate; but one thinks none the worse of Pliny. And multitudes of other like deeds must have been done by men who did not record them in letters.

*   *   *   *   *   *   *   *   *

Such in brief space were some of the ways the magnates and favored classes of the Empire gained and disposed of their wealth. We shall now turn to the servants of their prosperity—the slaves, the freedmen, the plebeians.

[1] See Chapter VI.

CHAPTER V

1. *Life of the Lower Classes in Rome.*

THE Roman Empire, like every large society, consisted of a wealthy, a middle and a lower class. Unfortunately the middle elements, the strength of all truly prosperous states, were in a process of elimination all through the imperial period. Rich and poor were being placed in more unmitigated juxtaposition; and he who did not have the good fortune to struggle upward to a place among the favored few was increasingly likely to sink to the unprivileged many. It is the life and economy of these many that now comes under attention. To realize their wants, grievances and condition, it is needful to examine the current life in Rome; for, as repeatedly remarked before, the conditions of the capital were not so unlike most of the provincial cities as to make generalizing therefrom too dangerous.

But this Rome must not be conceived of as the city of marble, of glittering atria and of columned peristylia; of purple-hemmed senators in the golden anterooms of a Caesar; of the extravagant banquets for gourmands; or even of the bankers' offices by the Via Sacra, with the accompanying loaning and keeping of millions and the roar of a world commerce. The vast majority of the free inhabitants of the imperial city dwelt in far less elegant surroundings; their lives formed a dreary routine; they fed themselves by hard labor, eked out by a degrading public charity; their tenements were squalid and unsanitary; their amusements the occasional glimpse of the charioteers and gladiators from the upper benches of the Circus Maximus or the Flavian Amphitheater. A very large part of the population of Rome (about one third, some antiquarians would have it) were slaves, still less favored than the inmates of the hive-like *insulae,* the comfortless apartment houses of the capital.

How large was Rome? Estimates vary even more widely than estimates of the population of the Empire. The conjectures are usually based on certain scattered items of information come to us as to the number of persons receiving free corn-doles in the city at one period or another. But we do not know precisely what proportion of the population received this bounty. Neither do we know the proportion of slaves to free plebeians. These uncertainties give room for divergency in conjecture. Dureau de la Malle will give the Eternal City at its prime only 562,000; Lipsius thinks 8,000,000 not too many; Dyer carefully computes 300,000 public slaves, masons, bakers, etc., 500,000 domestic slaves, and 1,245,-000 free men—2,045,000 in all. Gibbon thinks the total about 1,200,000. Bunsen, Zumpt and Marquardt (the last an excellent authority) put the total around 2,000,000. Beloch—the ultra-conservative investigator of ancient statistics—using almost the same original data as Dyer, reckons the free citizens and resident foreigners at about 570,000, the slaves at 280,000, the garrison at 20,000; in all only 870,000. Edward Meyer, a powerful ally, defends Beloch's opinion; but Seeck, Kornemann and, last but not least, Friedlaender—present day scholars of the first rank—are certain that 2,000,000 is nearer correct. In the absence of any means of arriving at a final decision, the opinion may be advanced that the population of Rome was over 1,000,000 at the time of the fall of the

Republic; that it contiued to increase until the time of
Marcus Aurelius, when it was possibly nearer two than
one million; that then, thanks to the great plague and to
the general calamities of the Empire, there was a marked
decline; perhaps it was not a full million by the time of
Constantine the Great.[1]

Life in the less fashionable quarters of Rome was
painfully congested. There was no "rapid transit,"
and men who had any business in the city must perforce
have lived as close to their place of occupation as possible. It is calculated that twice as many persons lived
—per square foot of soil—in Rome as do to-day in Paris.
The discomforts of the average city dweller were great.
Juvenal is more bitter than he is commonly, when he
arraigns conditions in the Subura, the "East Side" of
the ancient capital. Life on wretched Prochyta (Isle of
Procida) was preferable to existence in that district.
In fact the Subura was worse than any other place, however miserable or lonely. These are all at least free
from the constant dread of fires or of falling houses,
"the thousand dangers of the cruel city and from the
poets spouting in the month of August."

Buildings were very high for an age without ele-
vators. An ordinance of Augustus required that no new
building should rise above seventy feet. Trajan—says
Aurelius Victor—reduced the limit to sixty feet. The
great fire in Nero's time was a blessing in disguise. The
capital had been cursed with a network of incredibly

[1] One consideration that made it difficult to heap up the population
of Rome in a manner approximating that of London or New York, was
the difficulty of feeding great multitudes without rail or direct water
transport. The importance of foreign corn to the capital has been noted.
The supply on hand was always scant, despite great exertions. London,
to be sure, became a huge city before the coming of railways (1,227,000
in 1821), but she had a first-class harbor. Paris on the eve of the
Revolution, had only 600,000 to 900,000 (estimates vary) but everybody
knows the part famines played in the course of the French Revolution.

crooked and narrow alleys. Nero widened and straight-
ened the streets, and ordered the householders to keep on
hand fire-buckets, and to build the lower part of their
buildings of fire-proof materials. The conflagration of
this reign was not however the only like visitation on
Rome. In 111 B.C. a large part of the city was burned
over, and among other things the temple of the Great
Idaean Mother on the Palatine was destroyed. In 3 A.D.
we know this restored temple was burned again. In
83 A.D. the Capitol (just rebuilt), the Pantheon, the Baths
of Agrippa, the Theaters of Balbus and of Pompeius, the
Portico of Octavia, and many other fine public buildings
were ruined. Other cities had their share in these disasters; thus Lyons—in Nero's reign—received 4,000,000
ses. from the imperial treasury to repair the ruin of a
conflagration—a partial recognition perhaps of the liberal
contributions from Lyons at the time of the great fire in
Rome. Buildings were flimsy and combustible; fire
insurance was unknown; the city fire department not
very efficient. Early in the Empire, a certain Rufus
Egnatius, a man of no birth and of very indifferent character, gained the aedileship and praetorship, and even
stood for the consulship, on the strength of popularity
won by sometimes using his slaves to put out fires in the
capital.

Sanitation, too, was wretched in many cities, and
probably in Rome, despite the famous Cloaca Maxima,
and its memories of the bygone centuries. Amastris
in Bithynia was an extremely well built city; but down
its finest and chief street ran a sewer "called a river . . .
dangerous to health because of its shocking smells."
This was presumably an extreme, but not an isolated
case. The water supply in ancient cities would be ample,
but the drainage very bad.

Added to the fear of fire in Rome, was the fear of

falling houses. Inspection of buildings either did not exist or was abominably lax. Many of the apartment houses were put up in the cheapest way possible— "propped up on a slender shore." The steward of the landlord would shelve up the tottering walls, plaster over the gaping cracks, and blandly bid the tenants to sleep secure, "while ruin hung over their heads." Nor— despite the numerous police force organized by Augustus —were the streets any too safe after dark. Besides the mere roisterers who waylaid pedestrians with their coarse horseplay, there were numerous footpads in the capital, and also in the suburbs, especially in the Pontine Marshes and the Gallinarian wood. When the authorities undertook to clean up these localities, the bandits flocked into the city and caused more knifing and purse taking than ever. Their work was greatly lightened by the narrowness of the streets. Martial intimates that from the upper stories of a house one could actually shake hands with neighbors in the dwelling opposite. All this made for squalor and filthiness, as well as for robbery. The lanes of the city were overrunning with a sordid scavenger life, which Martial sums up when he calls a conceited enemy "a buffoon such as wanders around in the quarter beyond Tiber, and barters pale-colored sulphur matches for broken glass; such as one who sells boiled peas and beans to the idle crowd; such as is lord and keeper of snakes [on exhibition], or a common servant of the salt-meat venders, or a hoarse-voiced cook who carries around smoking sausages in steaming shops, or the worst of street poets, or a blackguard slave-dealer from Gades, or a chattering old debauchee."

It is true that, thanks to their genial climate, the Italian masses did not suffer all the miseries of the lowest classes in the North. They enjoyed a wheat diet —something that penetrated northward only slowly.

Wine, oil, and wheat flour were so abundant that Cato could feed them to his slaves. The custom of looking to the rich for gifts rather than for opportunities of work was demoralizingly prevalent. "The mob," says Plutarch, "hates the rich man who will not share his fortune, more than the poor man who steals the public money;" and, as will be shown, the upper classes were not niggards in a certain kind of benevolence. The public and private distributions of food, the slight need for heavy clothing in the mild climate, the generally abstemious habits of the Southern races, made life in the slums of Rome less terrible than in the slums of New York. Yet never was the handicap of poverty more keenly felt than in the Eternal City. When a society begins to rate a man by the answer to the question: "How much has he got?" and to prefer gold to intellect or character, a large portion of its most useful members—men who would willingly be content with small incomes, provided their reward came in other ways—are sure to be thrown into the ranks of the discontented, and are tempted to remove their handicap by any means, even the dishonorable. Juvenal seems to speak out of his own hard experience when he declares that at Rome high birth or ability count for nothing. "Poverty, bitter though it is, has no sharper pain than this—that it makes a man ridiculous." A poor man of good family was mocked by the rich son of an auctioneer.[1] He could not marry to advantage, being unable to match the lady's dowry. The aedile never did him the honor of consulting with him. His name never appears on a will. "All quirites [i.e., citizens of old stock] who are poor ought long ago to have emigrated in a body."

A great many, probably the bulk of the lower classes, did not feel their handicap so keenly. They enjoyed the

[1] As explained above this was an "infamous" calling.

inestimable boon, possessed by Italians and semi-Orientals to-day, of industriously idling away the months, doing just enough to keep breathing. At Thamugade in Numidia a checkerboard has been found, marked on the pavement of the local Forum, where scores of idlers met to gossip and gamble. The sentiment chipped beside it was this:

> *"Venari, lavari,*
> *Ludere, ridere,*
> *(Hoc) Occ est vivare."*

"To hunt, to bathe, to gamble, to laugh, that is living." People who could sum up life's pleasures thus were more contented, but not more commendable, than the class of downtrodden, yet intelligent men, for whom Juvenal is the mouth-piece. The proportion of poor drones or all-but-drones, even in the best days of the Empire, was excessive, and this incubus added sorely to the weight which the honest workers had to carry when the Empire began to decline.

The confusion of races in the Eternal City was almost as general as in Chicago or New York. Probably the proportion of inhabitants who were actually born inside the pomoerium was ever small. "For a long time," says Appian, speaking even of republican days, "the Roman people were only a mixture of all the nations. The freedmen were confounded with the citizens; the slave no longer had anything to distinguish him from his master. In sum, the distribution of corn made at Rome, gathered the beggars, the idle, and the scoundrels from all Italy." Slaves, of course, were foreigners—Gauls, Spaniards, Germans, Britons, Greeks, Egyptians, Syrians—who were sure to bring with them all their native vices, if they often discarded their native virtues. From slavery they usually escaped into the ranks of the freedmen, but

the manumission before the praetor would not make
them more chaste or honest. The Roman "mob" is to
be imagined like unto our "foreign masses," whatever
the shortcomings of the latter. Besides the vagabond
strangers and starving artisans—the ordinary malcontent elements—there were the crowds of freedmen,
demoralized by servitude, and given by liberty simply
more chances for evil doing; the gladiators training to
fight the beasts or each other and making nothing of
bloodshed; and lowest of all the fugitive slaves, who after
robbing and murdering on the country roads of Italy
would drift to Rome to hide themselves in its sinks and
slums. From these creatures Clodius and his ilk enlisted
their gangs of professional rioters, and these constituted
the dangerous "mob" down to the fall of the Empire.

In the fourth century A.D., the Roman proletariat had
not improved in quality. Ammianus Marcellinus pours
out his wrath against them. They "spent the whole night
in the wine shops. Some lay concealed in the shady
arcades of the theaters or else quarreled incessantly over
dice or [favorite pursuits of all] from sunrise to evening they stood gaping through sunshine or rain, examining most carefully the good and bad points of the
charioteers and horses." The passion for the circus
races was intense, and there seems to be nothing at the
present day—even in communities most given to "sport"
—like unto it.

As has been earlier remarked, the export trade of
Rome was trifling, the import trade tremendous. The
manufactures carried on in the city were few—mainly
glass and paper, and, perhaps more important, the making of the armor, weapons, etc., needed by the army.
There was, we know, a special guild for the manufacture
of catapults and other casting machines. But the great

population of the city gave rise to a vast retail trade, and this in its lower branches was mainly in the hands of the ubiquitous foreigners. Greeks and worse than Greeks, in the opinion of good Romans, had taken possession of Rome. *"Syrian Orontes has long since poured into the Tiber,"* cried the satirist in lines to-day threadbare, "and brought with it its language, morals, and the crooked harps of the flute-players, the eastern tambourines and the girls made to stand on hire at the circus." The Greeks were bad enough and numerous enough. Intruders from Sicyon, Samos, Andros, Tralles and Ephesus abounded. They were ready to hire themselves for any service—that of grammarian, rhetorican, mathematician, athletic trainer, painter, soothsayer, rope-dancer, physician, wizard—all in one. "Bid the hungry Greekling to go to heaven—behold! he will go!" And these coarse, thrusting, clever creatures pushed themselves in ahead of others for all the privileges and honors due to the native born Roman.

With less bitterness Martial in one of his epigrams to Domitian tells how in Rome great multitudes meet to watch the gorgeous spectacles. There was no race, he says, too distant to send its representatives, Thracians, Sarmatians, Egyptians, Arabians, Sabaeans, Ethiopians, Germans. They spoke many languages, but all blended in one common shout of praise to Caesar.

Martial is under no illusions, however, as to the discomforts of a poor man in Rome. Like every capital city, life in it was excessively expensive. In his old age, says the epigramist, he would like to retire to the country, and leave those banks of the Tiber, "where even hunger is expensive, where you may wear out four togas in a summer, while in the country one lasts four seasons." The life of the poor plebeian in the great tenement houses of the capital is represented as such that it was no merit to despise life in the Stoic fashion. The poor man's room would be "up two hundred steps," with a ceiling so low that one could scarce stand upright. The sole furnishings would be a hearth often cold, "a jug with a broken handle," a sleeping mat overrun with vermin, and some straw. A single toga must cover the poor creature both by day and by night. His food was wine, sour as vinegar, and black bread, eked out with a few cheap vegetables. On a few festivals there might be a sheep's head with leeks or a smoked pig's head as an extraordinary luxury.

Leases for these miserable tenements expired commonly on the first of July. Many poor families were then flung into the street by the pitiless house agents after they had pawned all their household stuff of any value. Martial again draws a brutally humorous picture of a man and three women wandering through the alleys tugging a bedstead with three legs, a table with two, a lamp, a horn lantern, a few broken plates, with divers like articles, having been driven from their quarters, and now wandering about in search of a new tenement.

The number of professional beggars was excessive, even for southern countries. They haunted cellars, bridges, doorways, and resorted to all the tricks and mutilations of modern Neapolitans to catch the coppers of the gullible. In winter they were almost shelterless, save for archways. Dogs were their companions; rough bran-bread their regular diet; their only property a staff, a blanket and a knapsack. These men were of course at the bottom of the proletariat. The government stood in awe of them, for they were creatures with absolutely nothing but life to lose, and that life worth to them very little. Nero—the emperor who poured out the blood of his imperial kinsfolk and of the great senatorial houses like water—trembled when these men began to mutter that he had started the great fire in Rome; therefore he made the Christians his scapegoats.

The picture must not be made too dark. The public corn-doles and the *sportulae* of the great patrons had their advantages. Rome did not have the "wage-slavery" which modern socialists denounce. She had her slums, but hardly her sweat-shops. Most of life was passed in the open air under the blue Italian sky. The Forum, the elegant porticoes of the Campus Martius were always open to the public, as were many fine gardens. As for the baths—great general club houses—they were open to every one who could find a trifling fee.[1] A man who slept in absolute squalor could spend his day in a huge building decorated with all the heavy magnificence of the imperial art. It was no slight thing to have free access to the marble halls of the Baths of Caracalla. At the end of the third century A.D., there were in Rome eleven large public *thermae,* and 926 smaller privately conducted *thermae.* Caracalla's baths could accommodate 1,600 bathers at once, Diocletian's 3,600. Lanciani has calculated that if each public bath could hold 1,500 and each private 50,[2] 62,800 people could bathe in Rome at once.

And again, if the sanitation of ancient cities was bad, the water supply was bountiful, probably better than in most European cities to-day. In Pompeii all houses not of the smallest kind had water in superabundance. In the house of the Vetii were sixteen streams. A great number of inscriptions from many points in the Empire testify to the water supply, and to the great care bestowed upon it. Libanius boasts of the excellent water

[1] Agrippa bequeathed his *thermae* to the people to be open gratis; and probably other public baths nominally charged no admission. But a *quadrans* (a very small coin) seems to have been a usual fee to defray the cost of oil and attendance.

[2] It must be said that these averages seem too high.

of Antioch—how every one had it in his house and how clear and sweet it was. Smyrna made equal boasts. In Alexandria at Caesar's time the Nile water was very bad; but later, care was taken to supply the whole population with duly purified water. Thysdrus, Verecundia and other African cities had noble aqueducts. At Segovia in Spain the water came fresh and clear from a Roman aqueduct eighteen hundred years after it was built. The northern cities were even better supplied by the Alpine or mountain streams. Trier and others were thus fortunate. Cologne received excellent blue-green water through a subterranean channel said to have been nearly forty-five miles long.

The water supply is one of the things for which we can draw data from the provinces, so there is less need to dwell on Rome. Yet the capital was probably even better supplied than any of her rivals; from the Aqua Appia of 312 B.C. to the Aqua Alexandrina built by Alexander Severus, the government was always improving the water system, and to-day the lofty gray arches of the aqueducts are an inseparable part of the Latin campagna.

2. *The Slaves.*

A traveler in Australia reports a native as remarking grandiloquently, "white fellows work, not black fellow; black fellow gentleman." It is sentiments like these, uttered or more commonly lived out by almost all uncivilized peoples which constituted the justification—so far as there could be justification—for slavery. The ancient German spent half of his life lolling on his bearskin, putting his vast physical powers to very trifling account. The Latin words for work and for vexation have the same root. To the Greek of the Odyssey, the ideal life was that of the Phaeacians—an existence of unbroken feasting, dancing, merry-making. It takes a high grade of civilization to justify the proverb: "Labor sweetens life." To the average barbarian labor implied only shame and compulsion. And compulsion was surely necessary if any work was to be gotten out of most of the semi-civilized races subjected by Rome.

Ancient economy was founded largely on slave labor. The earlier philosophers justified it. We never hear of any ex-slave, upon rising to the riches of the proverbial freedman, trying to mitigate the general lot of his former comrades. On the contrary the wealthy freedmen were probably the most harsh and brutal of masters. Only as the Empire advanced, first the Stoic doctrines, then finally the Christian came to attack the venerable institution; and more decisive still—the decline in the supply of slaves forced a shifting of the basis of Roman society.

'The Romans drew their slave labor from ever widening circles. The most obvious source of supply was from the captives in war. Where the legions went, thither went the dealers, ready to crowd around the quaestor's auction stand after a raid or battle, bid for the captured wretches, then ship their shackled purchases off to the markets of Italy, whence they were soon transferred to the houses or farms. In some of the wars of the Republic, slaves were thus sold in the conqueror's camp for mere trifles. "Cheap as a Sardinian," was a proverb for the age following the conquest of Sardinia by the elder Gracchus in 181 B.C., when he took prisoner or slew 80,000 on that not very populous island. In Lucullus' camp in Asia, on one occasion prisoners sold for only sixteen sesterces each.[1] Every successful war would mean a supply of a new kind of slaves. Thus at first the Romans made slaves of their captives in South Italy, then of those in Sicily, Greece, Greek Asia, Provincial Africa.

[1] Of course the purchaser had to stand the expense and risk of getting these captives to a distant retail market where they could be sold at profit.

Aemilius Paulus sold 150,000 Epirotes at one time. Then as the lines of conquest were spread wider, and the civilized nations were subdued, the Romans had to conquer and draw their slaves from the semi-civilized—from Gaul, Spain, Thrace, Numidia, and presently Germany and Britain were laid under contribution. The rude, raw creatures from these regions were naturally less amenable and less skilful than, say, the Greeks and Asiatics. They could only be used for the roughest kind of work and be controlled by sheer force. This fact did not make slavery any the milder.

At times the supply of slaves would be so great as to glut the labor market and make the "speaking tools" the very cheapest kind of machinery. Plutarch asserts that in Gaul Caesar in ten years took by storm eight hundred towns, subdued three hundred cantons; and of the 3,000,-000 men who opposed him, he killed a million and took captive a second million. Whole tribes would be rooted out, as in 25 B.C. when the Alpine tribe of the Salassi, 36,000 in all, were sold into slavery, man, woman and child, by Augustus, the purchasers being bound not to grant to any their freedom within twenty years. In certain unsettled provinces the local propraetors deliberately would pick quarrels with ill-subdued tribes in order to grow rich by kidnapping expeditions into the interior.

The supply of slave labor at the time of the Gracchi seemed inexhaustible. Many provinces then had hardly been tapped, and the human commodities did not have to be taken too far to market. The Alpine regions north of Italy were still full of wild races that were counted excellent plunder. The elder Cato never paid at retail for a slave more than 6,000 ses. The consequence of this abundant supply was that it was cheapest for the owner to push his slaves to their uttermost working capacity, to let them die, then to buy new ones; rather than resort to tender treatment and the breeding by natural methods of a new stock at his homestead.

By the beginning of the Empire, however, it was plain the supply was beginning to drop below the demand. The *Pax Romana* protected the conquered provincials against violations of liberty. The last civil wars also had interrupted the flow of slaves from the frontiers. Augustus had to break up with a strong arm the practice by landowners (probably in the more lawless parts of southern Italy) of seizing isolated travelers and imprisoning them in their *ergastula* (slave-prisons), then putting these luckless freemen to work precisely like the meanest slaves.[1]

Of course there were plenty of slaves who were not victims of the conquests. The abominable practice of abandoning unwelcome children was generally prevalent; slave-dealers would be on the lookout regularly for foundlings, then would bring up these children as slaves and sell them where lay the best profit. In this way some of the best patrician blood of the Empire can be conceived as suffering ignominy and chains. Sometimes, of course, the free parentage of these foundlings would be discovered long after their exposure. Were they still slaves? A case arose during the governorship of the younger Pliny in Bithynia. He referred the matter to Trajan, who replied—with the humanity that characterized the "good" emperors—that these persons were free, and that their fosterers could not even demand pay for bringing them up. But in how few cases could this free origin be proven! And too frequently children were deliberately sold by their needy parents as slaves. The practice was fairly common in Italy, and even at the most

---

[1] Persons fearing to be impressed for the army had sometimes taken temporary refuge in these prisons, and had afterwards been forcibly detained by the unscrupulous keepers.

enlightened period of the Empire a father was allowed this direful resort in cases of great necessity. Many children thus sold by their parents became freedmen of great prominence, and possibly had a little better social standing than had the bulk of ex-slaves.

But despite these adventitious aids, the slave supply would dwindle. Every conquered province meant a new "man-crop," but after the thorough first reaping by the legions, there was hardly a second harvest in that quarter. Settled, obedient communities could not be raided wantonly. On the fringe of the Empire there was for long much kidnapping. The buyer at the city market would seldom press the vendor for the precise origin of his wares. Still pirates and law-breakers were steadily cleared away. The Roman law threw its aegis ever more plainly over the subject peoples. In Cato the Elder's writings the price of labor seems to play no part at all; with Varro and Columella it is a very serious item. Occasional campaigns, as that of Drusus' in Germany and of Trajan in Dacia, gave temporary relief by bringing in a horde of stout captives. But generally speaking the stock of able-bodied slaves for field labor ran down rapidly. It was easier to get house slaves from the nearer Orient, because in that region the struggle for bread was so hard that men were often willing to sell their children, or even themselves, simply to get a master to feed them. But the sly, soft-footed Syrians were not suited to rough farm work. The landowners were forced to look elsewhere.

One outcome of slavery must not be overlooked—the way in which the institution aided the commingling of races. The remote villages in every province, no doubt, kept their peasant stock pure—Kelts, Iberians, Illyrians, Phrygians, etc.—for here the imported slaves would be few; but in all the larger towns—and not Rome merely—

14

no matter where, thanks to the coming of foreign slaves, strange races were commingled; blonde, bronzed and black were settled, then propagated in regions very far from their native habitats. The process might not have been bad for society, had these foreigners been good representatives of their own peoples; but, as might be imagined, the slaves usually came from their lowest classes, which were naturally most exposed and helpless before conquest or kidnapping.

Their morals were not bettered by the life they often had to lead in their new homes. Fortunate was the prisoner who became the house slave of a magnate; his more common lot would be that of a farmslave in the *ergastulum,* on one of the great man's innumerable farms. This slave prison itself was under ground, and, Columella says, was properly lighted by narrow windows too high to be reached by the hand. The biped cattle confined there worked in the daytime among the fields in chain gangs under the whip. House slaves who displeased their masters might suddenly be taken out of the light duties and relative luxuries of the city mansions, to be plunged into these living hells. According to Apuleius, fifteen slaves was the minimum number that could be profitably kept in an *ergastulum.* To the average wretch in these filthy, sweaty kennels, death must have been usually a release. Such creatures could be made to work by nothing save blows. It was the *ergastula* that made possible the oft-repeated proverb "so many slaves, so many enemies." The slave in the chain gang would seldom become a freedman. He was lucky if he died by mild disease, and if the owner or farm steward did not some day in anger nail him upon a cross. Hadrian reformed the *ergastulum* system; he placed the prisons under the strict supervision of the police, to check the grossest abuses. He even contemplated abolishing the *ergastula* altogether, but his death prevented the completion of that humane project. Antoninus Pius carried his reforms a little further. It was not, however, the legislation of the emperors, but the final decline in the supply of slaves which ended the cruelties of the system at the last. The brutality of the Roman worldly wisdom, as well as its real·ignorance of economic laws, is shown by the counsel of Varro, that hired free labor should be used on farms in unhealthy localities, so that the master need not lose by the dying off of his human live stock.

Again the Roman owners might allow their servants such license that they even became a menace to the public peace. In the second century B.C. the censors on one occasion sold the right to gather pitch in the Bruttian forest to a syndicate that proceeded to fill the region with bands of slaves who were allowed to rove like bandits; numbers of desperate freemen joined them. The district became unsafe. The Senate had to order the consuls to investigate and restore order. Almost the same thing seems to have happened with the slaves used by the contractors for the mines in Macedonia in 167 B.C. From this permitted license to the open slave wars of Sicily and finally to the direful servile revolt of Spartacus (73 B.C.) in Campania, it was only a step. The Romans were right—if they were to perpetuate their society—in regarding a slave revolt as the first of calamities. Every man's servants might turn against him. Every man might expect to be murdered in his bed, and to have his wife and daughter given over to unspeakable outrage. It was the most damning count in Cicero's indictment of Catiline that he was trying to enkindle the slaves. Slave property was very precarious during the disturbances of the civil wars. Augustus carefully vindicated the rights of owners to their human property. In his memorial at Ancyra he boasts that besides clearing the sea of pirates, he restored 30,000 slaves to their masters. The slaves he captured, who were not reclaimed, he ruthlessly crucified. The danger of a slave revolt did not pass during the early Empire. In 24 A.D., a servile war nearly broke out in southern Italy. An ex-praetorian, Titus Curtisius began to conspire with slaves around Brundusium, then by public proclamations called the rural slaves, employed in the forests in those parts, to strike for liberty. A great explosion was imminent, when by good luck three government galleys entered the port, and the local quaestor, drawing marines from their crews, broke up the rebels before they were fairly in arms. Tiberius hurried a large force southward, but it was not needed—while, till the alarm passed, panic reigned in Rome, everybody expecting the worst. Again even as late as 265 A.D. when the feeble reign of Gallienus seemed to be allowing Roman society to dissolve, a regular slave-rising harassed Sicily, the hotbed of such outbreaks.

The separation of farm and city slaves was sharp. A farm slave with hard hands and weather-beaten face was unendurable about the city palace; though a young child of marked beauty, born on the farm, might be sent to the city, to be trained for the master's domestic service. In the palace itself, so long as the great man was not irritated, there was little work and much idleness. Excessive subdivisions of domestic labor prevailed; duties were so slight that their discharge took a mere fraction of the day, e.g., the slave employed to caponize poultry could dispose of his duty in ten minutes. The upper slaves had underslaves to do the disagreeable necessities. Six girls would be needed for the toilet of the mistress. If a man of middle station was served by only three slaves at dinner, he was counted remarkably simple in his tastes. Servants were used for every possible purpose, to reduce the care and efforts of their owners to a minimum. "Let slaves serve you like the members of your body, each for this or for another end," Demosthenes had said centuries before the Empire. In Augustus' day the singer Tigellinus, who had once had two hundred slaves, fell into extreme poverty—he showed his poverty by only keeping twenty servants. Pedanius Secundus, the city praefect of Rome, who was murdered in 61 A.D., had four hundred in his palace. All this meant more than silly luxury; it meant the multiplication of useless hands and their deduction from the economic energy of the Empire—a deliberate handicap upon the industrious who directly or indirectly had to feed them.

The price of slaves, of course, varied with the age, health, education and handsomeness of the commodity. A good ordinary male slave in Horace's time brought about 2,000 ses.;[1] but girls, unless somewhat beautiful, were cheaper. Martial thinks 600 ses. enough for a girl of indifferent character. Handsome girls were sometimes bought for no worthy purposes—in this case the price would be higher. Also slaves who were trained as secretaries or librarians or physicians would bring a good price. It was a profitable speculation to train slaves to be actors, for these sold readily. A *morio,* a professional fool or jester—especially if he was quaintly deformed—might fetch a round 20,000 ses. And as for beautiful boy eunuchs, if the rich purchaser of such luxuries took the whim, he might pay as much as 100,000 or even 200,000 ses.—but this was entirely exceptional. The price of slaves seems to have risen under the later Empire, showing that the supply was not keeping pace

[1] It is difficult to say how these prices compare with the cost of negroes in the South before the Civil War; $1,000 then seems to have been a usual price for a "prime hand." Probably ancient slaves were both actually and relatively much cheaper.

with the demand, although, owing to the inferior quality of the servants offered, it ought to have declined.

Handsome slaves were naturally in great demand about the palaces. They would be marshaled in groups by race, age and color; boys of extraordinary beauty, "the bloom of Asia," would serve as cup-bearers at banquets. The masters liked to wipe their hands upon their hair. Boys of Alexandria were in demand— they were reputed to be very quick-witted, and apt at merry repartee. Mere human monstrosities were often required for purposes of vulgar amusement, just as later at medieval courts. At Rome there was a "Market of Natural Wonders" where one could buy legless, armless and three-eyed men, and the like; while, according to the evidence of statuettes, the art of mutilation seems to have been brought to a hideous perfection. Despite the prohibitions of imperial laws, the making of eunuchs was on the increase. Their numbers grew in all the palaces. Septimius Severus' Praetorian Praefect—Plautianus— had one hundred boys reduced to this condition, and gave them to his daughter at her wedding.

No house slave was secure against a brutal or irritable master. If he did not order him off to the farm-prison, he could have him whipped even to death, or crucified. Vedius Pollio in Augustus' time—the son of a freedman—was notably cruel to his slaves. He kept in tanks huge eels, trained to eat men, and fed them with slaves that displeased him. He was, however, regarded even in his own day, as an exceptionally cruel master. In the main, the lot of a house slave with a temperate master was not at all miserable. He was the member of a little kingdom, subject to a despot, but often a very benevolent despot. Pliny the Younger writes a friend that he is quite troubled because some of his slaves have died. "I am aware that some people call such misfor-

tunes a mere loss of money, and plume themselves as
great men and wise; whether they are great and wise I
do not know, but certainly they are not men.'' Pliny
allowed his slaves to make wills, so long as they left
their property to their fellow slaves in his *familia*. Of
course the fear always hung over such servants of being
sold away to a brutal master; but one gathers the
impression that such danger was not so great as with
the favored house slaves in our southern states before
the Civil War.

Cicero was also very fond of his slaves. At the end
they would have defended him against his pursuers, but
he would not suffer it. When one of his ''readers'' died,
he wrote to Atticus: ''I am more grieved than perhaps I
ought to be over a slave.'' Tiro, his confidant, almost
his companion rather than his servant, was for many
years Cicero's slave before being manumitted.

But the friendly relations were likely to die out when
the palaces swarmed with hundreds of menials. It was
remarked of Galba, by Suetonius, that he ''kept up an
ancient, but obsolete custom—and now nowhere observed
except in his own family—which was to have all his
freedmen and slaves appear in a body, twice a day before
him, morning and evening, and offer him their salu-
tations.''

Some of the uses a rich parvenu might make of his
slaves were indeed extraordinary. Seneca tells of a
Calvisius Sabinus, wealthy but uneducated, who came to
pass for a highly cultured man, though actually somewhat boorish. He had taken three bright slaves, had
one of them learn all of Homer, one Hesiod, a third the
chief Lyric Poets. When he dined, the trio waited on
him, and whispered to him quotations proper to inter-
lard the conversation with his guests.

Diligence and faithfulness have been in a servant's

favor ever since Joseph was sold into Egypt; but under the Empire it is to be feared the most honest and potentially deserving slaves did not always prosper. The Germans and other northern barbarians were too rude and slovenly to be admitted to the house *familia*, with its excellent chances of freedom. They would be banished to the chains of the *ergastulum,* while Orientals more corrupt but effeminate, supple and handsome, would get into the house and win the owner's good graces. Exceptions there might be if the German had a sightly head of fine blonde hair, but the chances were against him.

Those in the upper strata of slaves might rise to really important positions about their master; just as Tiro did before manumission. To be a favored slave in the imperial household meant to have more influence than not a few senators. We hear of a trusted slave of an emperor going on a journey with a lordly retinue at his service—a body physician, three secretaries, an agent, a treasurer, a body servant, two cooks, two money-changers and two lackeys. A slave at the court could easily enrich himself if he served close to the emperor and used his wits. One of Galba's slaves gave Otho (during Galba's brief reign) a bribe of 1,000,000 ses. for securing an imperial stewardship. A slavery where the bondsman could afford to give more than the equivalent of $120,000 as a bribe could scarcely have been harsh!

A house slave could reasonably anticipate becoming a freedman. The Romans indeed felt the latter class was growing too numerous. A *Lex Aelia Sentia* limited the rights of enfranchisement; a master could only emancipate a certain number by will, and a tax of 5% was laid on every slave manumitted—the master had both to lose the slave and pay the tax. Augustus—says Dio—in his last testament advised his successors "not to liberate many slaves, and thus avoid filling the city with a rabble." But as will speedily be made plain, these restrictions were not very effective. The house slave continued to get his liberty on somewhat easy terms. The farm slave continued to be whipped and worked to death in the *ergastulum,* until the whole institution of slavery ceased to be the basis of society.

Not the least baneful effect of the supply of cheap slaves during the later Republic and early Empire was its discouragement of mechanical progress. Why invent elaborate machinery when so much physical labor was to be had for a trifle? During the whole period of the Empire we find no improvement in technique, nor in processes of manufacture, and only a very few inventions. The water-mill had been known to Mithridates the Great; but four hundred years later men still ground with the hand-mill, or millstones turned by cattle. The products of the Empire at length showed a distinct retrogression rather than improvement. The supply of cheap labor had dwindled; but in the interval the spirit of invention had died.

3. *The Freedmen.*

The legal position of an emancipated slave in Rome was in many ways not bad. He was put practically on an equality with the run of plebeians, and the formal limitations of his legal status fell away with his children and grandchildren. The chances of a house slave becoming free were excellent. Cicero speaks of it as exceptional if an industrious, well-behaved servant had to wait more than six years for manumission after entering the *familia.*[1] The average man was anxious to have a host of clients follow him to the funeral pyre, and so to

[1] Of course these six years would not include childhood, or the time when a speculator was training the young slave for some accomplishment, etc.; but simply the time after he fairly went into the service of his master.

proclaim his importance; and the easiest way to get these clients was to be liberal in manumitting slaves.

Freedom also was not always given out of pure benevolence. A slave cost his master for support; but not so a freedman. A nobleman manumitting a tutor, doctor or barber, could stipulate that his children should be taught, or he himself be physicked or shaved free of expense. All sorts of service were compacted for with a freedman, as a condition for his release. Sometimes the burden was unreasonable. As early as 105 B.C. the praetor Rutilius had to carry through a law limiting the demands of a patron upon an ex-slave. But the relation of patron and freedman was often near and dear, especially when the patron himself was not a noble, but a shop-keeper or small manufacturer. Many gravestones were erected by faithful freedmen to their patrons, and a patron thus by inscription commemorates a freedman who was a goldsmith: "He never wronged anyone, nor did anything against the will of his patron. A great quantity of gold and silver was always by him, but he never let himself hanker for it." A rich man again felt bound to keep his ex-slaves from poverty. Damasius, a consular of Trajan's time, left an estate of 6,000,000 ses. His will gave a list of slaves to be manumitted, and each was to be paid 4,000 ses., so that none might come to want. The estate was also to pay the 5% manumission tax on them, and to form a fund to supply the freedmen with clothes so long as they should live. This obligation to maintain a horde of sometimes very idle dependents was often a drain on a modest estate. The younger Pliny left a legacy of 1,866,666 ses., the annual interest of which at 6% was 111,999 ses., or 1,119 ses. per year for each of his hundred freedmen—that they might never come to want after him. The same kind-hearted gentleman gave a piece of land, worth 100,000 ses., to an old family nurse, and when its value deteriorated, took pains it should again be put in good order. He even begged the Roman citizenship from Trajan for one Harpocras, a freedman physician of Alexandria, who had done him great service; and in behalf of another freedman, who seems to have been his body surgeon, and who was a citizen already, he begged the franchise for his numerous relatives.

The great disability of freedmen was their exclusion from the Senate. Nero would not even enroll sons of a freedman on the Roman album. But in the municipia they seem occasionally to have gotten into the local curia, despite prohibitions; e.g., an inscription boasts how a freedman rose "from the lowest order to the very highest." The upper classes felt the danger of contamination. In 24 A.D. the *Lex Visellia* ordered the criminal prosecution of freedmen who usurped the rights of free-born, or even thrust themselves into the decurionate.[1] To keep the freeborn sheep socially separate from the manumitted goats, Augustus is said to have introduced a system of naming which marked the freedmen from the free, and so prevented false pedigrees and other impostures. Claudius pretended to check the freedmen, —he confiscated the estates of all of them who posed as *equites;* he returned to slavery such as were ungrateful to their patrons, and he announced openly that in suits between patron and freedmen he would favor the former; but despite these brave efforts, it was notorious that the freedmen of his following ruled him as a band of menials ruled few other emperors. The reign of Claudius, as all know, was practically the joint rule of Pallas and Narcissus.

The freedmen were detested by the freeborn. They were vulgar, ostentatious with their wealth, unscrupu-

[1] The decurions were the senators of the provincial towns.

lous in their business methods, not handicapped by modesty—in short they were not gentlemen; but practically the whole economic development of the Empire rested on them and their children. They had not been taught to despise trade and manual industry. The highborn must mend his fortune only by inheritance, a lucky marriage, an indirect speculation in a syndicate, perhaps by the pickings of a rich province. The freedman had every avenue of gain open to him. He had probably won his freedom by faithful, industrious service. He kept his hard-working habits, and grew rich. Probably he would remain humble to his patron; but his children would spend his money freely and hold their heads high. His grandchildren would reach out towards consulships, and deny with wrath that an ancestor of theirs was ever auctioned off in the slave market.

Even under the early Empire the first generation of ex-slaves could climb to the front, when they showed supreme ability. The nobility of the Empire was not yet a closed body like the old noblesse of France. "He is a son of his deeds," said Tiberius, justifying himself in exalting a parvenu. In Pliny's time Largius, the son of a freedman, was praetor. Finally Pertinax, of like parentage, became emperor. Under Caracalla a slave was suddenly exalted to the Roman Senate.

Since in the highest circles childlessness was painfully prevalent, the favorite freedmen of a great man, his indispensable confidant as it often happened, would be willed the fortune of one of the proudest houses of the aristocracy. The riches of some freedmen were proverbial: "*Libertinae Opes*" was the byword. The higher one went at the capital, the more important one found the ex-slaves. Pliny the Younger, in his Panegyric on Trajan, speaks thus of their influence at the imperial palace. "The majority of our emperors, those masters of the citizens, were the slaves of their freed-men. They understood only by means of them; they spoke by them; and by them were awarded the praetor-ships, the priesthoods, the consulships." Nevertheless Pliny thinks great praise should be given to Trajan's freedmen.[1] They formed a permanent body beyond doubt of valuable men, and were passed on from Caesar to Caesar as so much family property. Claudius Etruscus, who died in Domitian's time, eighty years old, had served ten emperors and had held secretaryships of great responsibility.

That the freedmen should have great power in the imperial palace was inevitable unless the rulers were willing to effect a decided change in the form of govern-ment. According to strict theory the emperor was no more than the chief of divers magistrates. He had no standing corps of regular ministers to execute his policy, and administer the Empire. Yet he had a vast deal to do; he was the responsible head of what was in fact a vast monarchy. He could find plenty of high nobles to command his legions, and hold court in his provinces; but Claudii and Cornelii scorned to sit day after day in offices at Rome auditing vouchers, conducting routine correspondence, and arranging the thousand petty details which taken together make a successful administration. The emperor was therefore obliged to do as did the other magistrates, who employed slaves, freedmen and ple-beians for their routine clerical work. Only to be secre-tary to a Caesar was different from being secretary to a quaestor in a petty province. The business was vast; many of the details highly important. Be an emperor never so conscientious, a great deal must be left to his assistants. And these assistants were commonly freed-

[1] Was this not prudent flattery, from a man who expected many favors from the influential members of the government?

men. If the Caesar was a weak, easy-going man, he would be at his servants' mercy—as was Claudius. To hold one of the four great secretaryships of the palace was to be one of the four first ministers of the state. The secretary *a rationibus* attended to the details of trade, public works, finance, and the imperial household. The secretary *a libellis et cognitionibus* sifted petitions and complaints, and decided what things needed the personal attention of the emperor. The two secretaries *ab epistolis* divided the provinces between them, one taking the Greek, one the Latin-speaking half; they attended to the details of wars, the interior department and foreign affairs. Even if these men were strictly supervised to prevent their abusing their office, their power as permanent ministers, cognizant of all the machinery of their bureaus, was vast.[1] Hadrian showed his wisdom by introducing *equites* as secretaries—for by his time the upper classes were forgetting partly their contempt for clerical work; and his successors followed up his reforms, which involved a decline in the power of the "Caesarians,"—as the imperial slaves and freedmen were called—but it was a reform too long postponed.

Augustus revealed his usual sagacity when he ordered the legs of one of his secretaries, Thallus, to be broken, because the fellow had taken 2,000 ses. as a bribe for disclosing the contents of one of the Emperor's letters. Only the sternest measures could keep the "Caesarians" in any kind of check. The same *princeps* also tried to stand upon his dignity by never admitting any freedman to his table; a fact which Valerius Messala, and from

[1] It ought to be said that this use of freedmen did not always extend to the administration away from Rome. Of about eighty financial procurators traceable through inscriptions, only eight appear to have been freedmen.

him Suetonius, notes in such a way as to indicate that
this was exceptional, and later emperors had no such
prohibition. In the very next reign one of the greatest
offices in the gift of the Empire was bestowed on an
ex-slave, when a Spanish freedmen was made praefect
of Egypt by Tiberius; and consequently a man who had
once no doubt stood with chalked feet in the slave market
was clothed with vice-regal powers, as the deputy of the
Caesar and the successor to the authority of the deified
Pharaohs.

As repeatedly intimated, freedmen ruled the world in
the reign of Claudius. When that Emperor was com-
plaining of his scanty exchequer, it was remarked
pointedly that "the treasury would be full enough if
those two freedmen of his would only take him into
partnership." The adulation which the Senate offered
Pallas was almost equal to that offered the *eques*
Sejanus in Tiberius' day. "The eulogies of Marius,
Sulla, and Pompeius," said a man of the next generation, "rolled into one would fall short of those showered
on Pallas. The Senate voted him 'the most worthy and
scrupulous guardian of the imperial finances that an emperor ever had;' decreed him 5,000,000 ses., and when he
declined them, 'implored the Father of the State (Claudius) to compel Pallas to acceed to the Senate's wishes.' "
Pallas, however, haughtily refused; a greater affront to
the Senate—it was said—than if he had accepted; but
the decree of the Senate in his honor was engraved on a
bronze tablet and set up beside the statue of Julius
Caesar.

During Vitellius' brief reign, Asiaticus, a freedman,
ran the Empire for his patron. He had been a runaway
slave, a vendor of cheap wine, and had been sold to a
master of itinerant gladiators, but afterwards he became
Vitellius' factotum, and was actually enrolled by him

among the *equites,* to the scandal of all the emperor's supporters.

More than a hundred years later the Empire had another freedman ruler. Cleander, the all powerful minister for several years of Commodus' weak reign, was a Phrygian slave and porter who rose to be praetorian praefect. He was frightfully venal—selling all the great offices many times over, so that in 189 A.D. there were twenty-five consuls, whereof Septimius Severus was one. He finally perished in a popular outbreak when the mob charged him with causing a scarcity of corn, and Commodus sacrificed him to save himself.

The number of freedmen who at one time or another rose to public prominence was great. Some were able men who deserved their good fortune. Some were like Felix,[1] governor of Judea, who kept St. Paul in prison hoping "that money should have been given him by Paul, that he might loose him."[2] The vast majority of the ex-slaves assuredly rose to no such heights. They were the handicrafts men, the shopkeepers, the small merchants, even the small farmers. Some slowly worked upwards; the bulk would intermarry with the mass of the plebeians, and in a few generations lose the taint of slavery, even if they never won the narrow purple stripe of the *eques,* or the broad stripe of the senator.

4. *The Condition and Rise of the Lower Classes.*

It is a trite proverb that one man's loss is another's gain; like all proverbs it is only partially true. It is undoubtedly true, however, that the follies and easy spending of the Roman rich did a great deal to fill the pockets and better the condition of the trading classes. At the darkest period of the Empire there was a solid,

[1] The brother of Pallas.

[2] Acts 24:26.

substantial class, content with a worldly sufficiency—
even with a small sufficiency. One of Juvenal's characters says that 20,000 ses. is enough yearly income, provided he had a few silver vases, and a pair of stout
slaves to care for him in his old age. We have the
record of how a certain slave physician rose to modest
honorable wealth. He was a Publius Decimus Eros
Merula of Assisi, a specialist in surgery and eye diseases.
His gravestone tells the way he spent his money. First
his master let him accumulate a *"peculium"*[1] of 4,000
ses., with which he bought his freedom. To get into the
local board of *seviri*[2] he paid 2,000 ses., to set up a statue
of Hercules 30,000 ses., to the paving of the streets of
the town 37,000 ses. When he died he left 520,000 ses.;
no bad fortune for a self-made professional man in a
small Italian city.

There were many like him. An inscription from
Mactaris (Tunis) Africa tells a similar story. The man
who erected it this time was free born, but his father left
him penniless. He tells how he was a field reaper for
twelve years, then by his diligence became head reaper,
and served eleven years. Finally he became owner of a
house and farm "which lacked nothing." He became a
decurion and the highest magistrate in his provincial
city. He was not ashamed of his small beginnings, and
concluded by commanding; "learn, mortal, by my example to live a life above reproach, and like me to merit by
an honest life a gentle death."

The emperor Vespasian was again an instance of
how high a man of very modest origin could rise. He
was neither highly born nor very rich. When he

---

[1] The personal property and earnings of a slave, which he had a moral
though not a legal right to keep for himself.

[2] A board of six priests named annually by the city senates. They
were commonly freedmen, who were thus given public honors, though
barred from political office.

returned from the government of the province of Africa, he came home none the wealthier, though governing very well. He was then so much in debt that he had to mortgage his whole property to his brother, and was reduced to dealing (no doubt through an agent) in mules; hence the nickname fastened on him of "the muleteer." Yet this man rose to the chiefest commands under Nero—despite his crime of snoring at one of the Emperor's musicales—and ultimately wore the purple right worthily.[1]

Non-Latins very rapidly won their way to prominent places in the imperial government. The first transition was when Rome took her statesmen, not from the capital, but from the towns of Italy. This occurred under the Republic. "How many of us [senators]" says Cicero, "are not sprung from the Italian municipia!" Under the Empire the rulers came from a far wider circuit. Trajan gave the consular toga to Lucius Quietus, a Mauretanian; Hadrian was descended from a Galatian tetrarch; Marcus Aurelius, from several Africans. Two Numidians—Fronto and Proculus—obtained the proconsulship of Asia—the most honorable of the provincial governorships. In 146 A.D. the proconsulship of Africa —the second post for such honors—fell to a Paphlagonian. Arrian Herodes Atticus, and several others of Greek birth, received the consulship. Dio Cassius' father was a Bithynian, but he came to govern Cilicia and Dalmatia. Marcus Aurelius married his daughter to an *eques* of Antioch. If provincials could thus prosper within the exclusive goverment circles, how much lesser prejudice must have prevailed against them in the less conservative world of commerce!

Balbus is an early example of how a mere provincial

---

[1] Vespasian's grandfather had begun as a subaltern officer at Reate, a Sabine town, yet rose to the rule of a proconsular province.

could rise. He was Julius Caesar's invaluable business man and wire puller. He was born in Spain, yet he mounted, says Paterculus, "to a triumph, a pontificate, and from a private station to a consulate; [though he was] not a mere 'sojourner,'[1] but a native Spaniard."

Likewise, as the Empire advanced, even the custom of requiring a man to be a senator before he could be capable of high public honors waned also. A notable instance of this was seen in Hadrian's act when he gave Quintus Marcius Turbo a great command in Pannonia and Dacia, though Turbo seems to have been a mere *eques*. Finally Macrinus, the usurper after Caracalla, who had risen from the rank and file of the army, put on the purple, had himself adopted into the families of the Severi and the Antonini, and lost his crown and life at last, not because he was low born, but only because he was incompetent.

In the brisk public life of the smaller cities, people of very unaristocratic occupations could make their influence count politically. Witness the wall inscription at Pompeii. One Primus, a fuller there, took great interest in the local elections, and in front of his fullery were several notices; e.g., "Vesonius Primus requests the election of Gnaeus Helvius as aedile, a man right worthy of a public post." "Vesonius Primus requests you to choose Gaius Gavius duumvir; (he will be) a valuable public servant. Do, I pray you, elect him!" "Primus and his friends are doing their best to make Gnaeus Helvius Sabinus aedile," etc.

Life, nevertheless, for the lower classes was rude, harsh, uncouth, even when the large criminal classes, heretofore mentioned, did not intrude themselves. In Rome the city rabbles were liable to strange outbreaks

[1] A Roman who had colonized in Spain.

that had nothing to do with the government. The elder Pliny—who seems to be copying from the daily gazette—tells a tale that illustrates the passions and prejudices of the plebeians. On March 28th, 35 A.D., a shoemaker killed a raven which had soiled a pair of new shoes. The bird had possessed a remarkable gift of speech, and was loved and even revered by the whole quarter. The district rose in a storm against the slayer. He was driven from the quarter. Later he was murdered. The bird was pompously buried, borne on a bier by two Moors, and accompanied by flute players. It was given a funeral pyre specially erected on the Appian Way, which was surrounded by a great multitude offering garlands.

Such incidents show the excitability as well as the superstition even of the more comfortably settled portion of the masses. But dense ignorance, in the medieval sense, was not one of their worst handicaps. Elementary education seems to have been reasonably extended in ancient times. In a wretched mining colony of Lusitania we find a school. Primary schools would rarely be wanting even in the smaller towns. The larger towns had always their schools of higher instruction, especially in rhetoric. The teachers were poorly enough paid, as has been made plain; no doubt the instruction was very faulty; still the youth of the Empire were commonly not illiterate. The elder Statius conducted a school in Naples, whither came boys from Lucania and Apulia. The father of Horace, though a freedman and of quite limited means, sent his son even to Rome from Venusia to get an education as good as a senator's boy. The great lack of the Roman school was the entire lack of industrial training, at least in the higher sense. The social stigma attached to manual labor accounted in large part for that. We have agricultural treatises preserved; but next to no books on any industry or process of manufacture.   Yet the Empire would have prospered longer if her inhabitants had written more works on the arts and crafts, and fewer on Epicurean philosophy.

The education of the lower classes was no doubt distinctly crude.   The poor spelling and grammar of the guild inscriptions testifies to that.   Gellius speaks of a strange word as "plebeian," and belonging to the speech of the artisan classes.   But verses of Vergil were in everybody's mouth.   A sign of a game dealer bore an extract from the Aeneid; and attempts, not always bad, at verse making, hexameters and the like, are to be read on very humble tombstones; while in Pompeii, among the numerous wall scribblings, besides extracts from Vergil are bits of Ovid, Propertius, Tibullus and Lucretius. We there can still read, *"Arma virumque cano,"* scratched, it would seem, by some schoolboy.

5.   *The Roman Guilds.*

The institution of slavery prevented the labor problem from presenting features in the Roman Empire similar to those of our modern society.   In the place of the strike one finds commonly the slave revolt; in the place of sweat-shops the *ergastulum*.   The labor problem, however, is perennial.   At no period of ancient history was the free industrial class entirely extinct.   A record is said to have been found of a strike of workingmen in Egypt in the days of a Pharaoh, of hoary antiquity even for Caesar and Cicero.   Especially as the slave supply dwindled, the plebeian classes won back, albeit painfully, their rightful place in the industries and agriculture.   Circumstances never permitted the artisans to become powerful through their organizations, after the manner of the medieval trade guilds or the modern labor unions.   They nevertheless rose to a life active enough to call for more than passing comment.

The most venerable of the guilds of Rome traced their antiquity back to Numa. Goldsmiths, coppersmiths, builders, dyers, leather workers, tanners, and potters thus perpetuated a long corporate life; but they seem to have existed more as mere religious organizations—for the worship of a common guardian god—than for any of the belligerent purposes of present day labor societies. In fact the ancient guilds, even at their highest development, remained relatively weak. They were societies of men of like profession, but they enjoyed no monopolies like the old French guilds; they controlled no apprentices, did not direct the processes of manufacture, and do not seem to have been very hard to enter. Still, mere numbers are strength. They were able here and there to win a certain power, thanks to common action; for example, the fullers of Rome were given the use of a piece of public land by Augustus without the need of paying rent. But in the main the government looked askance at the "collegia" of the lower classes. This was not through fear they might use concerted pressure for too high wages, or make other unreasonable commercial demands on their betters; but because the Roman government dreaded by instinct every kind of an organization or even of a gathering, as a possible center for secret political intrigue or for open riot. An inscription at a market place in Africa gives notice that here twice a month the people of the region and also strangers might meet,—"but only for the purpose of buying and selling"—all associations and formal gatherings being evidently prohibited.

Trajan, the most enlightened of princes, frowned on the "collegia." He wrote to Pliny that since Amisus in Bithynia was a "free city"[1] with special laws, a collection might be taken up *for the poor,* "since that does

---

[1] The Roman government had granted it internal autonomy.

not bring people together, and form illicit societies.   But in other free states beneath our jurisdiction collections of this kind are not to be permitted.''   If Trajan could thus distrust mere charitable collections, it is no wonder he and other emperors disliked the semi-secret organization, the meetings and rites of the Christians.   Trajan carried his dislike so far that when Pliny suggested forming a guild of firemen one hundred and fifty strong at Nicomedia, pledging himself to see that only *bona fide* members joined, and urging that the city had just suffered for need of a fire department, the Emperor would not listen, because ''Bithynia, and especially city states like Nicomedia, are the prey of factions,'' and the most that can be allowed is to provide the householders with fire-buckets, and arrange for some slight neighborhood coöperation.

Trajan's prejudices were not entirely idle.   At times the guilds could become the touch-word for serious civic explosions.   The best known case of a riot started by artisans is that which involved St. Paul at Ephesus.   It began by Demetrius calling the ''workingmen of his occupation''[1]—i.e., the silversmiths' guild—together, and harranguing them on how Paul's doctrines were ruining their trade.   A riot that shook the city followed.   The ''town clerk,''[2] who finally dissolved the tumult in the theater, stated the peril of the whole community in his last sentence: ''For we are in danger to be called in question for this day's uproar, there being no cause whereby we can give an account of this concourse;'' in other words the Roman government might investigate, conclude that the Ephesian senate and guilds stimulated rioting, and cancel the city's liberties.

More than two hundred years later in Aurelian's day

[1] Acts 19:24.

[2] The recorder for the local senate; a man of importance.

the numerous artisans of the mint at Rome joined in a semi-political riot in which thousands of soldiers and citizens perished.

Nevertheless, the collegiate principle gradually won its way in the Empire. Despite frownings from above, the bare right to found fraternities and associations was, according to the jurist Gaius, recognized in the ancient Twelve Tables, and in the Later Empire the tendency to form collegia was very great; so great that such a firm ruler as Septimius Severus tried in vain to prevent their formation even in the army. In the main the most the law could do was to prevent collegia from being organized for any but public interests—not as mere associations of pleasure. Their numbers were kept as small as possible. Unauthorized ones could be broken up by the police. The number of organizations we find traces of in Gaul, is far from representing the whole commercial and industrial life of that great region. In Narbonne and other southern localities guilds seem to have been lacking. They were numerous in Lyons, but passing farther north they again appear somewhat rarer.[1]

By 150 A.D. the only guilds with a firmly recognized legal existence were those of the farmers of taxes, workers of gold, silver and salt mines, the old guilds at Rome previously named, and a few others, as e.g., of the bakers, and the Tiber boatmen.

Marcus Aurelius was the first emperor to favor the guilds. He gave them and the numerous funeral societies[2] the right to receive legacies, making them "civil persons" able to possess property, capital and slaves.

[1] They may simply seem to have been rare, because our inscriptional evidence from North Gaul is generally scanty.

[2] Coöperative societies which existed to supply the members with decent burials, and to keep alive their memories by occasional feasts, etc.

He however enacted that no one should belong to more than one college at once—thus checking the chance of the guilds to serve political ends. Finally the Syrian emperors, strangers to the conservative Roman traditions, gave the collegia a vastly enlarged scope. Alexander Severus deliberately formed all the trades into guilds; and during the later Empire the guild system proved a convenient organ for the imperial government. It could use the guild officers to aid it in collecting taxes in money, kind or labor from the members; and the result was that under the declining Empire the collegia sank more and more under the state control, and finally became regular engines for fiscal oppression.* No person following a given trade such as coining, the making of arms or of various precious fabrics, mining, etc. could escape enrollment. He was held close to his guild, and to the officers set over it by the government. ˙Certain trades were less regulated than others, but a man had still to be enrolled for taxation purposes, nor could he quit his guild, lest the government should lose his tax; until at last a fugitive from a guild could be reclaimed by force, as a fugitive from a kind of ˎ servitude.

Of course there were compensations—divers exemptions from military service, municipal service, local taxes and the like. The collegia too were recognized as honorable public bodies, and had a large part in civic fêtes and ceremonies. In 311 when Constantine the Great made his entrance into Autun in Gaul the guilds made a noble procession for him in the streets with their banners.

The number of collegia presently became great, all justifying themselves to the law by their public utility. Trades were much subdivided. There were several kinds of carpenters, ship-builders, lumbermen and watermen along the Rhone, Saone, and Seine in Gaul. "The most Splendid Order of the Watermen of the Rhone and Saone" had its seat in Lyons. At Arles besides the watermen however there was one of regular sea mariners. There were other guilds of watermen on the Rhine, Neckar, Moselle, and Aar and we know that as early as 43 B.C. the pall-bearers of Rome belonged to a kind of organization, and bitterly resented it, if any "non-union" outsider ventured to put his shoulder to a bier.

The desire for a decent burial and for being kept in remembrance was extremely great under the Empire. This led to associations, where under pretext of honoring the dead many good meals were eaten, and much good fellowship enjoyed. At Lanuvium an inscription tells us of such a "Funeral Collegium." To join it one must pay 100 ses. and an amphora of good wine (about six gallons); the monthly dues were six *asses*. In return every member was entitled to a funeral worth 250 ses., besides 50 ses. to be distributed as reward money among the members who attended the last rite.[1] Suicides were not entitled to a society funeral, but provision was made for paying for the undertaker in case a member died at a distance from Lanuvium.

The funeral societies would meet for common banquets. The fare was plain, as was natural where the members were common plebeians, freedmen or even slaves. In one case the staple menu was four sardines, a bottle of wine, and a loaf for each guest. There would be stringent fines to punish disturbances at the meetings. The society was commonly under the protection of a patron god or gods. Thus the Lanuvium collegium was called "The Worshippers of Diana and Antinous." Sometimes the rules and regulations would be extremely

[1] The distribution was evidently made to ensure as full attendance as possible.

complex. "You who for the first time enter the collegium," commands the Lanuvium inscription, "read first of all the statutes, and so behave that you will not be complained of and leave to your heirs a law-suit."

Much genuine fraternity might prevail in the collegia, whether they be for trade or only for funeral purposes. Women could belong. Members were known as "brothers" and "sisters." "He was devoted to his family and his collegium," is said on not a few tombstones. The collegia, too, gratified the hankering of very humble persons for high-sounding titles and tinsel insignia. The guilds would be organized as petty republics, with a "*populus*," a hierarchy of magistrates, and at the head usually two *duumvirs,* elected for one or five years,[1] also curators to attend to the financial arrangements and under them quaestors. Under the later Empire, when the guilds became units for taxation, they would have a praefect, named by the state, set over them,[2] but commonly the government did not meddle. Every five years the "album" of members would be carefully compiled. The collegium would usually be managed by the free votes of all within it; but its officers received the customary honors of a double portion of food at the banquets. Often, too,—by vote of the city decurions—the guild members would be given seats of honor in the local theater. The political influence of the collegia in the city elections could easily account for this. The "labor vote" was not to be despised. "The fishermen nominate Popidius Rufus as aedile," reads a Pompeian inscription.

From Oxyrhynchos, in Egypt, comes some curious information as to the guilds in that little community.

[1] In this latter case called *quinquennales.*

[2] As with e.g., the Rhone watermen.

Coppersmiths, bakers, beer-sellers, oil-sellers and bee-keepers all had their organizations. Each elected a president who held office only one month; each month also they were obliged to report to the authorities, prob-ably for assessment purposes, the value of the goods they had on hand—and one finds the coppersmiths reporting that they had six pounds of malleable bronze, worth 4,000 ses., and four pounds of cast bronze.

The collegium would have its *schola,* a house situated preferably in the center of the trade district where the members lived; the building might be elegantly furnished with elaborate banqueting halls, and a statue of the patron god.[1] This would especially be the case if the guild was favored not merely with a divine patron, but also with a powerful and wealthy human one. The patronship of a guild was a highly honorable thing to get. Usually the patrons were great merchants, or mem-bers of the *augustales,*—rich freedmen; but regular city magistrates would not despise the honorary presi-dencies. At Arles the sailors' collegium once had as *eques,* the procurator of the public corn supply in Nar-bonnensis and Liguria for its protector. Such honors were expensive. The patron and the actual working officer, like the ordinary city magistrate, paid his *sum-mum honorium* on assuming office. At Narbo one Fadius Musa, patron of the builders, gave 16,000 ses. as a fund for an annual dinner in his honor; yet as often perhaps a gift would take the form of enlarging the club house.

The Roman guilds then were social fraternities rather than economic units. They did much to break down the distinctions between bond and free, and gratified the social ambitions of the lowly. They existed down to

---

[1] The great banquet of the year would be in honor of the patron god; thus in Rome on March 19th, the weavers held high festival to Minerva; on June 19th the millers and bakers to Vesta.

the end of antiquity. It is even claimed that they perpetuated themselves and survived in medieval Paris, and were in vigorous life in the reign of St. Louis.[1]

6. *The Small Farmers and Coloni.*

In a former chapter the landed interests of the Roman world have been considered from the standpoint of the magnate owner. It is now right to examine the lot of the small freeholder, of the tenant, and of the class presently known as the *coloni.*

The Italian small farmers never recovered from the devastations and demoralization incident to the Second Punic War; but although this and similar calamities pressed them sore, and drove them in shoals to the metropolis, the emigration of peasants to Rome did not at first make them forget their origin, amid the greater allurements and greater discomforts of the capital. Tiberius Gracchus found 77,000 poor citizens who gladly went off to hard field labor on the new country estates his laws were assigning. Caesar, in distributing the Campanian lands, limited the grants to the fathers of three children, so great evidently was the demand for snug farms. But in time the Roman masses forgot their peasant ancestry, if indeed the infiltration of outlandish elements left them much of the old Italian stock at all. They were loath to quit the games of the circus, the roaring amphitheater, the free corn-doles, even if they must sleep in the hideous *insulae.* After some generations it became almost impossible again to make peasants of them simply by offering a few stony acres upon the hills. The agricultural life of Italy was largely doomed, and farming became more and more a thing for the provinces.

No doubt without a protective tariff against foreign

[1] No one pretends this survival is clearly proven. St. Louis (Louis IX) died 1270 A.D.

grain—something that the pressing need of cheap corn
in Rome rendered impossible—Italy could hardly have
competed with African and Egyptian grain growing, no
matter what the system of agriculture. The younger
Pliny speaks of the meadows and fields near his Tuscan
estate, "which only the most powerful oxen and the
stoutest plows can turn. The soil is so tough and
composed of such thick clods that when it is broken up
it has to be harrowed nine times." The Tuscan farm
was not exceptional. Much of Italy was thus. No wonder the owners of many *latifundia* preferred to give up
their grain crops, and turn their stony fields to pasturage.

The small farmers, without the capitalistic support
of the great owners, then seemed waging a losing battle
during the later Republic and early Empire; but not all
of them became half-fed idlers in Rome. The provinces
opened wide to them. There was as constant a stream
of sturdy peasants from Italy to almost every subject
region in the north and west, as there has been from
impoverished Ireland to the United States. These peasants did not all remain peasants. They became traders,
petty officials, soldiers; but their strength was lost forever to Italy. The provinces were open to their exploita-
tion. The wars of conquest had devastated many fields,
left many farms tenantless. Probably one of the reasons
why the Romans were able to assimilate their subjects
so rapidly was because the ablest part—physically and
intellectually—of the conquered peoples had perished in
the wars of conquest or subsequent revolts. When Pompeius broke up the Cilician pirates who had burned four
hundred towns and launched thirteen hundred ships, he
destroyed almost the last refuge of the bold spirits who
would not bend the knee to Rome.[1] So the conquest of

---

[1] The refuge away from the Roman power in Augustus' day, was
Parthia, a very dubious sanctuary. For a civilized man to have fled to
the barbarian north was unthinkable; he would have preferred suicide.

the provinces worked to facilitate the emptying of Italy. The old Italian stock scattered itself over the world, became diluted and lost. It did its work, but after a little we cannot trace its current in history.

The troubles of the Italian peasantry had probably begun before the dread coming of Hannibal; and these troubles repeated themselves with the free peasantry of the provinces at a later stage of Roman history. The typical small farmer of ancient times—whether he lived in Asia Minor, Etruria or Gaul—fed himself from his own land. The clothes he wore were spun from his own sheep. He needed to buy very little. He was almost independent economically. But when war or anything else disturbed him, he would be suddenly forced into debt for the most trivial wants. He usually had kept no ready money from one end of the year to the other. Then he would fall into the clutches of the money-lender. It was no longer enough to raise corn to feed himself and his family; he must raise more corn, sell it, pay the debt. Seldom—with price of grain falling—could he do this. The little estate would be swallowed up.

As early as 180 B.C. there began to be gaps among the free farmers of Italy. In that year 40,000 Ligurians of the Apnanian people were dragged from their homes with their wives and children and settled in Samnium. This was done nominally because they made trouble in their old habitat; but it would have been impossible, had there not been much vacant, arable land in Samnium. Under the Empire various bold attempts were made to drive the Roman proletariat back to the soil. The number of recipients of the corn-doles would be cut down; laws would require a certain percentage of the farm laborers on *latifundia* to be hired freemen, not slaves; but the Roman populace had been weaned of its love of the soil, and could not be forced back to it.

Trajan became alarmed at the decline of the population of Italy. He took measures to promote marriage, arranged for the support of the aged and of orphans; he admitted five thousand children to the Roman corn-doles (a form of orphan relief); his great public buildings at the capital gave employment to the worthy poor desiring work; but above all he tried to promote the farming interests by a great extention of roads—thus he built a highway through the noxious Pomptinian marshes, and his Via Trajana from Beneventum to Brindisi. Unfortunately the best of Roman roads were poor substitutes for water transport. It surely cost far less to bring a load of grain from Alexandria to Ostia, than to haul a similar amount by wagon from Lucania. This added to the handicap given by the greater fertility of the African provinces. By Trajan's time South Italy was dying by inches. Tarentum, Capua, Nuceria and the other once famous towns, were only being kept from complete decline by artificial additions to the population; while the open country—in Greek days one of the most highly cultivated spots on the earth—was becoming a desert.

The ousting of the struggling small farmers by the *latifundia* owners went on almost as long as there were any small farmers left. As late as Juvenal's time we have a hint of the unscrupulous greed of the magnates. If the owner of a coveted little farm would not sell at the offered price, the poor Naboth might wake some morning to find a herd of cows in his cornfield, and his entire crop mowed clean.

Certain forms of agriculture always yielded some peasants a modest profit, especially market gardening near the city. Varro speaks of this as bringing very fair returns. Fruits and flowers could be sold in the markets of the capital "for gold;" and he tells how two old soldiers with only a half an acre of land made 10,000 ses. per year by bee culture. Columella thinks a small vineyard properly managed ought to yield 18%; to start one there was needed 32,800 ses., which could buy seven acres of wine land, and pay the interest for two years on the capital while the land would not bear crops. In Upper Italy (as remarked before), in Gaul and Spain, and generally in the East, slave labor did not get the upper hand of free labor so completely as in Central and South Italy; and even in Central Italy the hard peasant stock, tenacious as the soil it plowed, would here and there make a long, almost successful stand against the *latifundia*. At Caere, Martial says the richest farmer had only nine acres, yet the inhabitants managed to make a living. At a community near Beneventum we find about fifty farmers. Two of these were wealthy men, rated at 451,000 and 501,000 ses. each, nine possessed 100,000 to 400,000 ses. each; the rest were much poorer.

The decline of the slave supply forced a modification of the *latifundia* system. Columella advises employing free tenants if possible. The younger Pliny used to hire out his land; and the use of free tenants in fact can be traced back to Sulla's time. The revolt of Spartacus, when myriads of slaves used on the Italian estates were lost to their owners, accelerated the transition. The influx of captives from Caesar's Gallic conquests halted the process for a few decades; but by Nero's reign the letting of parcels of land to tenants was fairly common, though agricultural writers sometimes complained it put property in the hands of men who had no standing interest in it, but ran through it as fast as possible for the greatest immediate profit, and ruined the vineyards, buildings, etc.

It was seldom that a son would be a tenant, it is said, in his father's place. That was a rare piece of good

16

fortune for the landlord, and as a rule the tenant farmer was always on the move from estate to estate; so the country laborers as a class were very unreliable, and many an owner or farm bailiff must have sighed for a gang of stout "speaking tools" who could be worked in chains all day, and locked in the *ergastulum* at night.

Notwithstanding these drawbacks, small tenant farmers, often paying a quota of the produce instead of a fixed rent, were becoming in some parts of Italy the usual way of working property during the first century A.D. An experienced man like Columella might be able to go without their help and get a good profit out of the land; but most landlords, it would seem, could not afford to keep a large gang of slaves—always growing more difficult and expensive to replace—and were glad to get a moderate return from rents.

The average wages of the common laboring class in Roman days are not easy to ascertain. In Jesus' parable of the workmen in the vineyard, they are paid one and all a "penny," i.e., a denarius (4 sesterces) per day; and that appears to have been a good and sufficient wage. In Egypt wages seem to have risen somewhat—at least nominally—under the Empire. In 78 A.D. laborers at Heliopolis, Egypt, obtained three to five obols per day; but about 150 A.D., in the Fayum, the average pay was eight obols.[1] In 215 A.D. the bricklayers at Arsinoë obtained two and a half drachmae per day. In 255 A.D. wages at Memphis varied from six to nine drachmae. We have no similar data for other provinces, but it is safe to conclude this seeming increase in wages was only nominal. The third century A.D. was a time of greatly depreciated coinage; the day laborer was lucky if his pay rose as the value of the money fell.

---

[1] Six obols made a drachma, or denarius; therefore an obol was about two-thirds of a sesterce.

As to the proportion of crop or the rent, a landlord could exact from a farm tenant, we have again information from Egypt; but it is unsafe to generalize much from conditions in that province as to those in all the Empire. In Egypt, leases of farms fell into two distinct classes; but both systems were in use side by side in different farms. On some farms the tenants paid a fixed number of *artabai* or corn per *aroura* of land; on others they paid a stipulated proportion of the whole produce, however great or small it might be. The best terms we hear of a tenant making were, that he should have to pay one half his gross crop to the landlord; he might have to pay as much as four fifths, in which case his lot would have been hardly enviable. Sometimes a special contract would be made, by which he would pay, say three fourths of the ordinary produce and five sixths of the hay. In other provinces, however, there is some reason for feeling that the landlords were not for a while able to drive such hard terms.

Gradually a yet newer system supplanted the roving tenantry, which the landlords of the early Empire complained of. "The most prosperous domain," says Columella, "is that which is tilled by laborers who were born on it." The *latifundia* owners began to regret the dwindling of the free peasantry. Efforts were made to induce the laborers to stay on the farms. Southern Italy had been finally ruined, and the same conditions which had destroyed its prosperity were threatening to encroach on northern Italy, Spain, Gaul, Africa; the very lands which had profited temporarily by the decline of the peninsula. A new attitude was taken towards free laborers. They were to be preserved at all hazards and kept out of the cities. Inscriptions tell how some of these toilers remained on the same land twenty, thirty or even fifty years. As is usually the case when the great try to control the lower classes, a mixture of bribery and compulsion would be used to accomplish such ends. The farm laborer would be often an ex-slave; he would be given a little hut of his own, encouraged—as slaves in the palmy *ergastulum* days were not—to marry, and rear many children. He would be protected in the use of his house and small farm plot so long as he did his duty by the owner; on the other hand, it was made increasingly difficult for him to leave the estate. He could not sell his house and lot of ground. Probably neighboring landlords would hesitate to employ a deserter from a nearby property. Living on the farm, paying and taking pay mostly in kind, the tenant had very little ready money to start life anew with, if he wandered away. In time he or his children would become almost bound to the soil, though there was not yet a single law legalizing serfdom.

The state, however, discouraged frequent removals. A tenant with a fixed farm could be easily found for his poll tax, for the obligatory labor he owed as part of his taxes, for his military service. A wanderer was likely to escape his public duties. The government therefore favored the landlord as against the tenant.

And in time the attitude of the law formally changed. The first signs thereof appear with the settling of bands of Germans by Marcus Aurelius on the frontiers, who were given lands in return for which they were bound to pay certain taxes, and more especially to give military service. Obviously if they could migrate at pleasure, this military service would become worthless. Therefore they were bound to stay where they were; and their lands, and also their duty to stay on them and defend the Empire, were inherited by their children. These military settlements on the frontiers grew greater in the third century. Sarmatii were thus planted in North

Italy, showing how the movement was no longer confined to the boundary lands. Even around Ravenna were some barbarians again planted by Marcus Aurelius, seemingly under like conditions. But in the Empire at large, without direct intervention of the government, the masses of small farmers—tenants and petty freeholders —were being forced into permanent subordination to the great. The privileges of the senatorial order had something to do with this. A Roman senator, and many more of his near kin,[1] could be tried on criminal charges only by the emperor himself or the praetorian praefect. They were thus assured a great immunity in their encroachments on weaker landowners or tenants. The petty farmers could only defend themselves at law by seeking some other great man as a helper. They "recommended" themselves to him; became his clients, almost bondsmen; while he became their patron and defender at the tribunals. The emperors launched edicts against this demoralizing practice, and set up *defensores*—legal officials—to vindicate the rights of the lowly against the strong, but to no purpose. The tendency of the times, the confusion into which the Empire presently fell, aided the process of "recommendation," and to complete its handiwork came the *"praecarium."*

A small landholder—and small landholders still hung on a long while in the provinces, if not in South Italy— would fall into some kind of difficulty. Bad crops or even a raid of barbarians might ruin his little capital. He would therefore transfer his estate to a creditor who would, however, supply new capital, and give him the right to use the farm and buy it back if he could pay the loan with interest. If the small farmer did not repay—

---

[1] As well as many who had only the qualifications and rating to be a senator without belonging to the regular body.

and how seldom he could!—he became a sort of tenant
to the creditor, and so continued, and his children after
him. If the creditor was a great territorial lord—as
was commonly the case—the petty agriculturist who
"recommended" himself to him, and entered into this
tenant-like condition called "the *praecarium*," would be
better off in times of trouble than if he were independent.
His patron would keep him going over the times of
drought; if the barbarians raided again, this *"colonus"*
could find a certain refuge in his lord's fortified manor
house. But he was not likely ever to disengage himself
from his subject condition. As the state pressed the
master ever harder for taxes, he in turn must press his
coloni harder for their rents. The *colonus* furthermore
was liable to the poll tax, the military tax, the dues for
the transport of his produce to market—something light
at first, but later very heavy. The government policy
of settling barbarians in the Empire—in return for rents
and corvèes—a policy in which Claudius II, Aurelian,
and Probus especially imitated Marcus Aurelius—tended
to harden the sanction to the extension of the power of
the landed nobility. In theory a *colonus* remained in an
endurable legal position. His marriages were valid;
sometimes he could heap up quite a property. But
usually he was a poor man. If he ran away from his
land he could be recovered, in the later Empire, like a
runaway slave. When the recruiting officer came to levy
his contingent on the estate, the proprietor could indicate
which *coloni* he preferred to get rid of, and the malcontent tenant would be sent off "to bend the back under the
centurion's vine rod."[1] Worst of all, however, was the
colonus' real inability to get a fair hearing in the courts.
The local governor was morally certain to favor the

---

[1] The cat-o'-nine-tails of the Roman army.

egregius or the *clarissimus*,[2] his master, as against his *colonus*. On the great estates of Gaul, Spain or Africa, even the governor's courts in the provincial cities would be far away. The lord of the *latifundia,* or his bailiff, did what was right in his own eyes, just as the feudal barons, their successors, were to do in the centuries to follow.

When the *coloni* were fortunate enough to hold their tenant lands on one of the numerous estates of the Empire, their condition was probably somewhat better. Few Caesars favored deliberate oppression, and they usually would redress grievances, if fairly brought to their attention. In Africa we find a "*saltus*," a great landed estate of the crown, leased out to *conductores*. In Commodus' day the *coloni* on it complained that these were oppressing them. Hadrian earlier had ordered that the *conductores* could exact two days of field labor, two of weeding, two of harvesting, but by the connivance of the emperor's procurator the *conductores* were exacting more, and even punishing the authors of a petition to Rome. However, a second petition was sent the emperor, obtained his consideration, and he ordered that the rights of the *coloni* should be strictly respected.

The lower classes were not always, however, so passive under oppression. In Gaul, late in the third century A.D., the *Bagaudes* were like the Jacquerie of later France—genuine peasant risings which it needed regular campaigns by Maximianus to crush in 286 A.D. As early as Septimius Severus' reign there had been much brigandage around Lyons, possibly of a similar nature; and in the fifth century, when the Empire was breaking up, rebel peasant bands appear in Gaul and Spain, even thrusting on a usurper to the throne, and adding their outrages to the horrors of the times.

[2] The titles of an *eques* and of a senator respectively under the Empire.

CHAPTER VI

1. *The Ancient Idea of Beneficence.*

THOUGH the Roman Age was no age of charity, it was certainly an age of remarkable—nay, lavish—munificence within certain lines and for certain objects. Men beggared themselves in making gifts to their fellow men. To understand the spirit which underlay this generosity, to assess it as an economic factor at its true value, it is not, however, enough to enumerate typical instances of large or small benefactions; it is necessary also to understand the ancients' idea of generosity.

The definition of generosity by Aristotle is a comparatively noble one. Generosity, he asserts, is to be measured, not by the amount of the gift, but by the spirit of the giver. It is most seemly to hasten to aid a needy friend without awaiting his solicitation; but the motive for giving still remains far behind the Christian ideal of giving from pure benevolence and love. One must give, says the Stagirite, "because it is beautiful to give," i.e., in order to adorn the giver with virtue. "Of everything praiseworthy, the generous man takes as his share the best;" in other words, he is generous for his own sake; not for the sufferer's, but to keep himself from being reproached with avarice.

Aristotle lived in a country and at an age when benevolence to the class that needed real benevolence was hardly a national virtue. There was a certain amount of poor relief in Athens, however; possibly because, with the democratic government, the voice and vote of the humble were worth reckoning with in the ecclesia. Cripples, infirm folk, and the blind, who had less than three *minae*[1] of property, were awarded two obols per day allowance, by vote on each separate case of the Attic Assembly, after due investigations by the Council. Orphans of certain warriors were cared for by the state, and orphans in general were not liable to the property tax. But these forms of poor relief do not seem to have been extended much outside of Athens. Isocrates makes it a peculiar boast for Athens that in her—unlike other Greek cities—there was never the shameful sight of a citizen begging for bread from strangers.

There was less real benevolence in Rome than in Greece. The Italian nation that made Cato the Elder its ideal, and nodded assent to his advice to cast away old slaves worn out by labor, was not likely to waste time or money on unfortunates who could neither be dangerous as foes, nor repay with interest any material kindnesses. "Compassion," says Boeckh, "was no Hellenic virtue;" and Ulhorn rightly adds that it was no Roman virtue either. "Canst thou by any means," says Quintilian, "condescend so far that the poor shall not appear loathsome to thee?" And Plautus has a more savage wisdom still: "He does the beggar no service who gives him meat and drink; for what he gives is lost, and the life of the poor is but a prolonged misery."

Seneca, with his sometimes honest searchings for high virtue, came nearest of the pagans to the Christian concept; but he seems to hint that only the man likely to be grateful should usually come in for generosity. "I would choose out," says Nero's prime minister, "a blameless simple man, and one who would be grateful

[1] About $54.00.

and mindful of benefit.'' Still he is not without a deeper, nobler note: ''Kindness persisted in subdues at last even the wicked;'' and again, ''It is not the sign of a noble spirit to give and to lose, but it is the sign of a noble spirit to lose and still to give;'' and to crown all, ''If you ask what I receive in return for my benefactions, I reply 'a good conscience'.''

However, charity and mere liberality were by no means identical. A man of the Empire would be frequently liberal to his equals, his fellow citizens, his guild members, his municipality—persons or institutions to whom he was grateful, or from whom he might hope for something good in return. Of all persons in his day Augustus stood least in need of benevolence; but when his house on the Palatine was burned, his veteran soldiers, the judges of the tribes, and even the Roman populace contributed individually to the rebuilding, each according to ability. But the Emperor graciously refused to accept the subscription, and consented to take no more than four sesterces per person. Where again it was the community and not the individual that was to be relieved, a rich Roman would open his money-bags eagerly. The praise of one beggar was nothing, but the cheers of a closely packed forum, when some public benefaction was announced, was incense to the demigods of plutocracy. Money was freely given to supply free distributions of corn, to rebuild cities ruined by fire or earthquake. A large mass of starving beggars becomes a menace to order and property rights. It was worldly wisdom as well as kindliness that prompted Trajan when he urged the cities to husband their money, and spend it on poor relief. The government recognized that the rich should bear the bulk of the taxes—at least during the better days of the Empire; e.g., the 5% inheritance tax did not apply to property worth less than 100,000 ses. And once or twice we meet with sentiments worthy to be uttered by Christians. The lovable Pliny the Younger uttered one when he said, "It is a duty to seek out those who are in want, to bring them aid, to support, and make them in a manner one's own family." And on a certain tomb is another: "There is in life only one beautiful thing, and that is beneficence."

But despite scattering hints like these of the dawn of a new concept of the duty of "him that hath," the motive for liberality long remained mainly, if not solely, the praise of men.[1] There is a vast difference between the Christian *caritas,* which sought to make the world permanently better, and the pagan *liberalitas.* Gifts were placed not where they were needed, but where they would gain the most of passing applause. The beggar is almost always more grateful for an alms in money than for an opportunity to do honest work. Those men, too, would obtain gifts who were able to give something in exchange. A citizen received a corn-dole from a magnate; he did not need it, but he could help elect the magnate to a city office. A non-citizen might be starving; he had no vote; he got no corn. Or if the non-citizen was admitted to the distribution, to the banquet, to the free bath, it was simply to earn the giver paeans for extraordinary liberality. Those who could help the giver most—the guild president, the city magistrate— were sure of a double or triple portion in any distribution.

The occasions when the favored classes could expect the bounties of the rich were truly many. If a magnate celebrated a birthday, caused his son to assume the manly toga, gave his daughter in marriage, entered a

[1] Pindar in his odes seems to intimate that noble actions were not worth doing unless the world could praise them; a sentiment almost as truly Roman as it was Greek.

city office, did a score of other things, he would probably
have to dispense some lavish charity. Public opinion
would turn against him if he failed. Frequently he
must repair or even erect some public building. At the
dedication he must feast the local senate, and often the
greater part of the citizens, hundreds and thousands of
persons, either inviting them to an actual dinner or com-
muting it by a gift of money. Or he might be expected
to supply games and gladiator fights. The demand that
a rich man do his duty by the public which protected him
in his riches was louder than at present in the United
States; and again there seems to have been a certain
willingness to condone the methods of getting the wealth
provided a part of that wealth was spent on the community. Unfortunately the citzens of the provincial
towns seldom clamored for hospitals, college endowments and public libraries. In one of Petronius' scenes
we find the inhabitants of a town on the bay of Naples
declaring that they expected from a local notable a three
days' gladiator fight, costing 400,000 ses.—something he
could well afford, being worth a round 300,000,000 ses.
And what things the average city folk really lusted after
will presently be made plain.

One other point in ancient generosity is striking.
The lower middle classes seldom took part in it. We
hear of public subscriptions to pay for a funeral or to
erect a statue to some famous man, but little evidence
comes of the community devoting itself *en masse* to the
relief of the poor and needy. What public praise comes
to *one* of five hundred subscribers on a long list of modest
sums? The Christian Lactantius rightly said that the
pagan philosophy, as truly as the pagan religion, did
nothing to promote charity. "Of such things your philosophy teaches nothing." In fine, the admonition of
Jesus "to give and ask not again," was based on a keen

knowledge of a major failing of the age—a failing of Jew, Greek, Roman—to be generous to foolish lavishness where reward was in view, whether from a friend or the community; and to shut up one's purse from the truly needy.

2. *The Benefactions of the Rich.*

Within these limits the rich men of the Empire were undoubtedly remarkably generous. There was never a time perhaps when the duty of spending wealth for the benefit of the community was more clearly realized than between 31 B.C. and 180 A.D.—the "good years" of the Roman imperial system. The emperors by example and admonition spurred on rich men to lavish their money on the public. Nerva, in a set speech, urged the wealthy to show munificence, and not to deceive the cities as if these were legacy hunters. Trajan ordained that every promise made to a city, e.g., of erecting a new public building, should be binding on the promisor and on his heirs. Augustus' buildings in Rome were considerable, but it was not by his unaided effort that the capital became changed in his day from a city of brick to one of marble. Under his prompting Statilius Taurus built the first permanent stone amphitheater in Rome; Balbus built a stone theater, and in connection with it a curved portico; Lucius Philippus built the Temple of Hercules Musarum and surrounded it with a portico; Lucius Cornificius built a Temple of Diana, Asinius Pollio an *Atrium Libertatis;* Munatius Plaucus a Temple of Saturn. Agrippa, Augustus' prime minister, especially was a princely builder. In Tiberius' reign Lepidus, the head of the great Aemilian family, rebuilt and beautified the old Basilica of Paulus, asking special leave to do this at his own expense, as being a peculiar monument of his family; "for even *at that time,*" says Tacitus, "it was usual for private men to be magnificent in public works"—a plain indication that the age of Trajan was one of remarkable generosity.

Great public calamities were naturally occasions when the rich could show their liberality. In Nero's reign a huge amphitheater at Fidenae fell, burying beneath its ruins 50,000 persons. The wealthy Romans at once despatched physicians,[1] with all kinds of medical supplies, and received the wounded in their houses; also after the eruption of Vesuvius in 79 A.D., when Pompeii was overwhelmed, the refugees met with very generous help and kindness.

The lord of a great country estate was under moral obligation to deal bountifully with his tenants and the rustics of the lands around. Perhaps, however, it is unfair to cite the younger Pliny as being of only typical generosity. With pardonable vanity he tells how on one of his estates was an old temple of Ceres, much frequented by the country folk. He rebuilt it handsomely with four columns, a marble pavement, and a portico to shelter the worshippers in storm or heat. This, he says, will show "his generosity and also his piety." Pliny was not at all a "pious" man in the strict sense; in fact he was decidedly unreligious, though not a scoffer, and his "piety" probably consisted more in discharging his duty to men than to gods. More notable was his gift of 1,600,000 ses. to his native town of Comum; and when a friend died leaving a bequest—technically invalid—of 400,000 ses. also to Comum, Pliny, though heir to one third, resigned his share and urged the other heirs to waive their claims also.

Another letter of Pliny's tells in a most interesting way about a friend who was planning a public endowment for a feast in his own memory. He asks Pliny how

[1] Very likely their house slaves.

he shall arrange it. The genial consular writes back telling him not to give the money in a lump sum to the community; it will be squandered; nor in land, for "it will be neglected as all public owned lands are." His own gift of 500,000 ses. to Comum to endow schools has been arranged most satisfactorily; first, he transferred some land to the state agent; second, he received it back as a tenant, paying 30,000 ses. per year for it. Since the land was worth more than 500,000 ses., it will be good, thinks Pliny, always to have a tenant to keep it in proper order.

Memorial feasts were decidedly favorite things to endow. A community was likely to cherish the name of the man or woman who provided them every year with a good dinner; and if the belief among pagans in the immortality of the soul was dim, the desire not to be forgotten by the living was great correspondingly. A certain Salvia Marcellina bequeathed to the "College of Aesculapius and Hygeia" 50,000 ses. wherewith to perpetuate the memory of her husband, an "overseer of the imperial tablets." In this instance a *sportula* was to be distributed twice per year; the higher officers of the college were to get 24 ses. each and eight jars of wine; the lower 16 ses. and six jars; the common members eight ses. and three jars. Besides this each and all received three loaves of bread. This was not charity. It was giving "to him who hath." The most necessitous got least! The idea was solely to secure the maximum of honor to the memory of the donor and her husband.

But not all endowments were thus selfish. Among the noblest were the foundations for the upbringing of children. Trajan and other emperors did something in this direction, but private benevolence accomplished a great deal also. We hear of one such foundation at Beleja in Upper Italy. It had a capital of 1,044,000 ses., standing at 5% interest. This income provided for 281 children—245 legitimate boys, 34 legitimate girls; and one of each illegitimate. The boys were given an allowance of sixteen ses. per month, the girls twelve ses. The subsidy continued for the boys till they were eighteen, for the girls till fourteen. In Cirta Sicca (Africa) we meet the rare case of a similar institute maintained by general contributions, providing for the education of three hundred boys and two hundred girls. The girls were allowed 96 ses. per year, the boys 120 ses., and, an exception in ancient society, the children of non-citizens might enjoy the benefits as well as children of full burgesses. In Spain we find Fabia, a benevolent lady, making a somewhat similar foundation. She left 50,000 ses. at interest. Twice a year, on her husband's birthday and her own, there was to be a distribution out of the income to certain boys and girls. The boys were to get 30 ses. each, the girls 40 ses., but if the income sank the girls' share was to be reduced. The large share for the girls shows that this gift was really made out of pure benevolence, and not out of "good citizenship"—to provide a race of recruits for the army.

More often, however, the gifts to the community would take the form of a public building. An endowment can be scattered by incompetent trustees; a dinner is soon consumed; but a suitable public building—barring fire or earthquake—needs only a moderate amount of care to keep its giver in long remembrance. Gifts of this kind could be cited *ad infinitum*. Ummidia Quadratilla built at Canusium an amphitheater and a temple; Secundus at Bordeaux an aqueduct costing 2,000,000 ses. One Perigrinus, mentioned in Lucian, gave thirty talents —his whole fortune—to his native city. Crinas of Massilia spent 10,000,000 ses. on its walls. A certain Hiero, a native of Laodicea, gave two thousand talents to that city. Finally one may name the princely Herodes Atticus, the tutor of Marcus Aurelius. His family boasted noble origin from Aegina, and regal wealth. He spent his money on the Italian cities, on Corinth, Thessaly, Euboea, Boeotia, Elis and Athens. He built an aqueduct at Canusium, a theater at Corinth, at Delphi a race course, and dreamed of completing Nero's canal across the Corinthian Isthmus. At Athens, the city of his love, he restored the ancient shrines and stadium; in memory of his wife he built the roofed theater by the Acropolis that still bears his name; by his will he gave every Athenian citizen the gift of a *mina*.[1] Considering the relative wealth of the imperial and the modern age, it is not likely that his giving has been surpassed by the most lavish of American millionaires.

Avarice then was not one of the vices of the imperial age. The humble were taught to look to the bounty of the rich; to expect to receive much for nothing; to prefer a life of idle indigence, relieved by decidedly indiscriminate alms giving, to a career of honest toil. The beggar who whines his *carità* at the cathedral door in Italy to-day is the heir in spirit, if not by blood, of the proletariat of the Empire who ate the doles of the great man. It is as dangerous to give too much as too little— a truth that the world slowly comes to understand; but the bountiful magnates of the early Empire thought not of this. Presently the magnates ceased to be able to be bountiful. The poor had forgotten the joys of honest work. It took all the miseries of the Dark Ages to learn them over again.

The age of the early Caesars was, as has been made evident, an age of active, prosperous civic life. Communities had money; they spent it freely. Pliny tells Trajan of the great building activities of Prusa, Nico-

[1] About 400 ses.

17

media, Nicaea, Claudiopolis and Sinope during the two brief years he governed Bithynia. This money hardly came from heavy local taxes. It was contributed more or less freely by the rich citizens, especially under the terms by which they were elected to the local magistracies.

A citizen of a municipal town was a *municeps*—one who shares the public duties. He could not renounce his origin, or escape doing his full share in the community. "What is a city if not an association founded on justice?" demands Ulpianus. The community was looked on as a parent; we meet the terms "son of the Senate," "of the city," "of the people." The relation was one of the same filial loyalty to the town that the alumnus of an American college has to his *alma mater*. The old magistracies still lingered on in the communities despite the tendency of the imperial system to reduce all institutions to a level uniformity. In Hadrian's time there were still praetors in Etruria, and dictators in the towns of Latium, as well as duumvirs.

It is a frequent complaint that present day American conditions make it hard for a poor and honest man to win high political office. A branch of our national legislature has been rightly or wrongly nicknamed "the millionaires' club." Whatever be the truth of this caviling to-day, it is perfectly certain that wealth was usually a prerequisite for the holding of municipal office under the early Empire. The requirement was made in entire frankness, and no one imagined there was anything discreditable about it. To enter one of the municipal senates, the *Splendidissimus Ordo*—filled up every five years by the appointment of the two *quinquennales*[1]—a certain property qualification was necessary. At Comum we know it was 100,000 ses.; but the rating

[1] Practically the same as the old censors in republican Rome.

varied according to the importance of the town. At Rome to be a member of *the* Senate, par excellence, a man, besides his other qualifications, had to own property worth 1,000,000 ses.,—a "millionaires' club" in very truth—though a sesterce was far from being a dollar. On the other hand, salaries for local senators and magistrates did not exist. The imperial governors and procurators were well paid—to take away pretexts for extorting from the provincials. A governor would be openly spoken of as a "one hundred thousand sesterce officer," or a "two hundred thousand," according to the greatness of his rank; but the municipal official served for the honor, not for the reward. Nay, more, men were willing to pay into the public chest 4,000 or even 8,000 ses. for seats in the local curiae; or—as once at Tarsus— 2,000 ses. for the right merely to vote in the local assemblies.

After election the unpaid municipal magistrate found his expenses beginning. He had to pay into the town treasury a fixed honorarium. If he would do the thing handsomely, the required sum would be doubled. Dio Chrysostom reminded his fellow townsmen how his grandfather, his father and himself all compromised their fortunes in such ways. A lady of Calarna in Numidia paid as much as 400,000 ses. for a theater in return for a "life priestess-ship." The average price for an office lasting one year in a small city was, of course, far lower. In Pompeii the fee was 10,000 ses. for being duumvir. In larger towns the dignities came higher, running up to as much as 55,000 ses. From Africa come not a few data as to these expensive pleasures of municipal office. In one African town in Elagabalus' time a certain man found that it cost him 82,000 ses. to be a flamen; 20,000 went as a required gift to the decurions, 30,000 for a statue to adorn the city,

the rest for public games and a general distribution of
money. Not all this, of course, was required by the
letter of the law, but it gave an impression of noble
generosity. At another rather small African city a candidate gave double the required honorarium (1,600 ses.)
—i.e., 3,200 ses.—which money was used to repair a
temple. It was insufficient, and his granddaughter gave
an extra contribution to complete it. . This man also paid
for his brother to enter the curia. All in all his venture
into politics in a very small community cost 12,000 ses.
At Rome the matter of fixed honoraria was worse than
elsewhere, although not all the magistracies were liable
to it. Even in republican times the curule aedileship
had been ruinous to many through the obligation to give
elaborate games. Even scions of the imperial family
had to pay heavy contributions when they entered upon
some of their honors. During Caligula's reign, Claudius
—hardly yet recognized as his successor—was taxed
8,000,000 ses. on entering a priestly office, and the future
emperor was so reduced that to clear off his bond to the
treasury, he had to have all his estates set on sale by
order of the praefect.

It was inevitable that with the city voters expecting
such payments and gratuities from magistrates, they
would elect men from whom much could be hoped. The
laws strove to regulate candidating in colonies and
municipia as best they might. There were regulations,
e.g., forbidding under forfeit of 5,000 ses., the giving of
any public festivities by a candidate for one year before
the election, or even the inviting to his house more than
nine persons at once—and then such an invitation must
be given only on the evening before. After entering on
an office the new magistrate had to give heavy bonds for
its faithful performance. He was responsible for the
leases of public property; for public buildings, built

under him, for a period of fifteen years; and for all public funds under his care. He was liable for prosecution
as to his accounts for twenty years after quitting office,
even if those accounts had been audited. His colleagues,
his father, his direct supporters in the election,[1] were all
liable along with his bondsmen. If he made any profit
out of his office he confronted a ruinous fine; and a
hardly less severe mulct if he broke one of the municipal
statutes.

And yet so great was the personal vanity of the
imperial age; so eagerly did men crave the purple hem,
the curule chair, the lictors, the first seats in the theater,
the tinsel and the petty remnants of actual power, that
so long as the municipia were wealthy there seem to have
been no lack of office seekers. Canvasses were brisk.
Fortunes were poured out freely on these unconcealed
bribes to the public. When the office was more or less
formal, as for instance, a priesthood, a rich man might
buy such a magistracy in more than one town. We thus
find one individual *flamen perpetuus* simultaneously in
Thamugade and Lambaesis in Numidia. The provincial
towns indeed were not content with the payments made
by the local property owners, but under the guise of
electing wealthy outsiders, preferably genuine Roman
nobles, Scipios, Marcelli, etc., "patrons" (a very honorable distinction if the town was important) they levied a
double tribute. In return for the statue in the forum
and the honorifics, the noble patron would feel in duty
bound to repay with feasts, public buildings, and down-
right distributions of money to the community that
elected him. In the capital were frequently men of
family who had ruined themselves discharging their obligations as patrons, and by a turn of fate the client

[1] Such an inclusion in our American laws against malversation in office,
might produce startling changes in our "practical politics!"

cities had to advance money to help the patron's heirs.

When a man was continuously posing before his fellow citizens, holding an office or feeling out for one, he could readily run through a goodly property, even if his single payments were not very great. We have such an instance with a citizen of Philadelphia in Lydia. At one time or another he gave in all 2,440,000 ses. for the purchase of public grain; 40,000 ses. for building a roof to the theater, 28,000 ses. to the seven collegia in the city, for each to erect a statue; a total of 2,504,000 ses.

When we come to such princely personages as Agrippa, we pass obviously out of the range of mere municipal life, yet it is worth noting what he did in 33 A.D. when he acted as aedile at Rome, at a time when it was of the greatest moment to win public good-will for himself and for Octavius his master. Besides executing many public works, repairing buildings, sewers, aqueducts, etc. his games lasted fifty-five days without interruption; he opened one hundred and seventy baths for the public enjoyment, and distributed an unlimited allowance of oil and salt; also for the whole year supplied the population with the services of barbers free. Agrippa's own fortune was heavily drained by this, though no doubt Octavian contributed *sub-rosa,* to eke out his friend's resources. A few years later they were amply reimbursed out of the treasures of Cleopatra, but Agrippa's munificence must long have remained the ideal of city plebeians, who dreamed more of *donativa* than of opportunities for honest work.

Besides these payments, legally or only morally obligatory upon office holders, the cities of the Empire had a considerable income from simple legacies. When Pliny was in Bithynia, a Julius Largus of Pontus, "whose face I have never seen, and whose name I never heard," left the governor himself 50,000 ses. to pay

for the trouble of dividing the rest of the estate between
the cities of Heraclea and Tios. Pliny was left to judge
whether it was better to erect some buildings with the
money and to dedicate them to the Emperor, or to
institute an athletic festival to be held every five years
and be called "the Trajan games." The cautious
governor referred the decision to the Emperor. We do
not know whether Trajan decided in favor of the buildings or the festivals, but the suggestion of these contests
leads naturally to a consideration of that subject
through which more private money was poured out
on the community than through any other single way—
the games, especially the contests of gladiators.

3. *Private and Semi-private Exhibitions of Games.*

There is a famous passage in Juvenal which will bear
repeating. "The sovereign [Roman] people that once
gave away military commands, consulships, legions,
everything, now . . . . limits its longings to two things—
bread and the games of the circus." An example of
degeneracy no doubt, but also an example of what may
come to a people that looks to the governors and the
wealthy for what they may give it, rather than seeks
what it may get for itself. The corn-doles of Rome and
the provincial cities, as well as the contests in the circus
and arena, were in large share provided by the government and constituted a heavy drain on the public purse;
but the wealthy more privately supplied a very large
proportion. This was peculiarly true of the gladiatorial
contests. There was no swifter, easier, and—proportionately speaking—cheaper method for securing popularity, than by providing a suitable butchery. So great
was the desire for this kind of festival that when Marcus
Aurelius desired to punish Antioch for taking sides
with the rebel Avidius Cassius, he could think of nothing

better than to prohibit any more arena combats and like exhibitions in the guilty city.

Of course horse-races, and other similar contests often took the place of contests of men and beasts; but the gladiatorial combats remained the special favorites. The cost for the public games was at first defrayed from the public treasury; but about the time of the First Punic War the expenses began to fall on the private purses of the presiding magistrates, especially on the aediles. On rare occasions, the Roman public indeed bestirred itself to take this burden from an exceptionally deserving official. This took place in 186 B.C. in the case of the games given by Scipio Asiaticus; and again a certain Oppius, who saved his father under circumstances involving great filial piety in the proscription of 43 B.C., was elected aedile by the admiring people, and the participants in the aedile's games gave their services for nothing, while each spectator threw money into the orchestra for the magistrate. This example of the Roman plebs *giving* something to a poor and worthy man, is however almost unique.

The scale of lavish display in public spectacles was set under the Republic. When Marcus Scaurus was aedile in 58 B.C.[1] his games were the finest ever seen in Rome. He erected a temporary theater able to hold 80,000 people. Three hundred and sixty columns decorated it. The lowest story was of white marble, the middle of glass, the highest of gilded wood. Between the pillars were three thousand statues, besides paintings and other ornaments. One hundred and fifty panthers were shown, five crocodiles, and for the first time in Rome a hippopotamus. It is needless to say these games exhausted Scaurus' entire ill-gotten fortune,

[1] He had been Pompeius' quaestor in Syria, and had used his opportunities for profit.

and drove him into difficulties with the money-lenders.

The consuls were expected under the Empire to give public games, and to pay for the same themselves; but when a poor but worthy favorite of the emperor was advanced to the consul dignity, the government would help him out with the expense, although it expected ordinary aspirants to defray the cost privately. Here is what Valerian ordered his treasurers to allow Aurelian for the games he was required to give as consul in 257 A.D: "Three hundred pieces of gold, three thousand of silver, ten silken tunics, fifty of Egyptian linen, four Cyprus table cloths, ten African carpets, ten Moorish coverlets, one hundred swine, one hundred sheep, and the food and serving of a public feast for the *equites* and senators;" also for the sacrifice, "two large animals and two small ones." The gladiators, the jockeys, the race horses, and the wild animals to be slain in the arena, Aurelian must evidently find himself.

Naturally there was a vast difference between the games given in Rome by a consul, praetor or aedile and those given in a country municipium hardly above the grade of a hamlet.

In 51 A.D. the "Roman Games," which lasted sixteen days, cost 760,000 ses., and the "Apollinarian Games" lasting eight days cost 380,000 ses. The state probably paid part of this; but a praetor was responsible, e.g., for the "Megalesian Games" to the extent of 100,000 ses. and much more, if he wished to make a really respectable display. On the other hand an inscription at Pisaurum makes it probable that a simple gladiatorial fight (in which perhaps no one was actually killed) could be had for 150 or 180 ses.

Gladiators sometimes were extremely cheap, especially after a successful war. Says a panegyric of Constantine the Great: "The perfidy of the Bructeri [a Germanic tribe] does not allow them to be used as soldiers, their savage nature prevents them from being sold as slaves; by exposing them to the beasts you have made these enemies of the Empire serve for the pleasures of the people. This was your grandest triumph.'' Constantine's games naturally were under government fostering; but it may be safely surmised, if he did not require all the luckless Bructeri for his amphitheater at Treves, that they were sold on easy terms to amuse the populace elsewhere; and so with other conquerors.

The demand that magistrates should give and pay for periodic gladiator fights spread far and wide over the Roman world. Gaul, Spain, North Africa, shared the mania; the lands impregnated with Hellenic humanism a little less. If possible some innovation was needed to make the combats remarkable—e.g., a fight with silver weapons. In Gaul and Africa the contests were especially in favor because in those provinces it was easy to get wild beasts for the killing. Only in Greece the old athletic contests in a measure held their own.

But many a gladiator died in combats entirely apart from any regular city games. A wealthy funeral was incomplete without their presence. The populace would demand the contests as a right. In Tiberius' reign Pollentia was the scene of riot. The people refused to allow the corpse of a high rank centurion to be taken from their forum till they had wrung from his heirs money for a public show of gladiators. Tiberius sent two cohorts to the city, arrested many disturbers, and imprisoned the culpable local magistrates for life; but the affair showed the popular temper.

It is easy to multiply instances of gladiators officiating at funerals. A duumvir of the Latin town of Sinuessa, at the death of his father, gave a combat admitting all the villagers from far around. One Maximus, in Trajan's reign, lost his wife. He asked the people of Verona, her native city, how he should honor her. They demanded a gladiator fight. The fight was given, and a friend wrote to condole with him over the fact that the panthers ordered had not arrived in time.

Again, fights might be given on no particular occasion, but it would seem, simply to court applause and popularity. An inscription at Minturnae tells of a man who gave a four days' fight. Twenty-two gladiators joined; half were killed; "besides," runs the inscription, "he gave a hunt of ten terrible bears; noble fellow citizens, you will remember this [service]!"

The glory of presiding over games given by one's self was very great. Men ruined themselves, seeking the seven days' popularity. In Tiberius' time the Senate passed a *consultum*, forbidding anybody with less than 400,000 ses., i.e., a fairly ample fortune, to give public games; but the rule seems to have been a dead letter. Martial ridicules even a shoemaker and a fuller who undertook to give gladiator combats.

Another way in which combats were provided was by will. The testator would wish to leave a good impression on his fellow citizens, and would provide in his will that some of his slaves should fight in the arena. This was a cheap if brutal way of meeting the cost. The slaves thus doomed would commonly be the least desirable. The testator was through with their services; their value was slight to the heirs. Marcus Aurelius, however, forbade honoring such infamous provisos, and broke up the practice.

The best gladiators, of course, were not worthless slaves. Their services came high. The givers of games in provincial towns had to import "guest artists" from a distance. We hear of a gladiator coming to Pannonian Sirmium after he had won laurels at Thessa-

Ionica and Rome—and presumably he charged the master of the games a round fee.

The slaughters of the arena continued—as all know —down to the reign of Honorius. It was a rare year when a plebeian of the Empire went without several free chances for his favorite excitement; yet despite the great numbers of private and government-given contests, there seems to have been a profit in arranging gladiator fights as purely commercial ventures "for the gate." To this end, one Atilius, a freedman, erected his insecure amphitheater at Fidenae, whither in 27 A.D. great crowds came out from Rome to perish when the fragile staging collapsed. Tacitus declares that Atilius' motive was not "exuberant wealth, nor desire to win local popularity, but mere sordid love of gain." Despite occasional speculations of this kind, however, the gladiatorial combats must have ruined twenty of their promoters where they enriched one.

4. *The Sportula. Receipt of Donatives by the Rich.*

There was in the Roman world very little of that pride which makes the poor of the present day willing to steal, but to remain "above begging." Laziness and mendicancy were not merely widespread, but honorable. It is improper to minimize the great number of honest toilers, farmers, artisans, shopkeepers, merchants in imperial times, without which indeed it would have been impossible for the drones to live. But the proportion of drones to workers was exceedingly great—greater possibly than in any large society which the world has ever since known. In the capital and the great cities the system of clientship wrought directly for idleness. All men of public pretensions had to appear in the forum, at the courts, and almost everywhere with a numerous following. One's greatness in fact could be judged by the number of retainers trudging behind the litter. If a man had abundant wealth, such a cortège was easily supplied. In return for dancing attendance on him, he was willing to make a distribution every morning of money or food to a horde of shabby gentlemen, or bustling freedmen. The usual money fee was twenty-five ses. per morning, or 2,280 ses. per year—no small item in the revenue of a man of a genteel past but an uncertain future. It might be eked out by occasional gifts, an old toga possibly, or an invitation at rare intervals to a vacant seat at dinner. Martial, the poet, who was an obsequious client, received once the gift of a little field from a patron, though he complained it was too small for any real use. The system worked upward even to the palace. The Caesar had his clients—"his friends" —who ate at his table, received his gifts, and traveled with him. So great was the number of these imperial clients that they would be graded according to intimacy and rank, into friends of the first, second and third degree.[1] In the houses of rich senators, or still richer freedmen, little courts would be held on somewhat the same model, though of course far smaller.

Juvenal draws one of his most striking pictures when he portrays the clients at Rome bustling in the morning for their sportula. They have risen at gray dawn or earlier, hurried from their unsanitary tenements, and now press around the doors of the great man. A steward surveys them carefully to see that no spurious "friend" has come to claim a share. Then the dole, food or money is dispensed from the threshold. Praetors and tribunes, the poet declares,—probably generalizing from a few extreme cases—are there; but a freedman born by the Euphrates, with pierced ears, who came to the city

---

[1] Something after the manner of the members of the first, second, and third *lever*, etc., at Versailles under the old Bourbon monarchy.

with chalked feet as a slave, is preferred even before the magistrates, and is given first access, when the doors fly open, to the presence of the patron.

Besides the money or food distribution, the client always lived in the hope that faithful marching behind his patron in the forum, and equally faithful clapping in the basilica when his patron argued a case, would lead to an invitation to dinner. At length the invitation would come; but the client must be prepared to put his pride in his pocket. He could expect only the lowest seat in the triclinium, miserable wine and viands, while his master and the honored guests partook of dainties. Behind him—for the patron had no illusions as to his client's character—stood a special slave, not to serve him, but to watch that he did not, with his finger-nails, pick out the gems set in the golden cup grudgingly allowed him. In return for this early rising, this cring-ing servility, this receipt of alms, this insulting hospi-tality, what was the client's reward? The right to keep his hands from toil!

But it was not merely the broken gentlemen, and the clutching freedmen who gladly took something for nothing. The habit of receiving gifts—not as personal tokens, but as mere bestowals of charity—penetrated even to the rich. The evil grew worse as the Empire grew older. The willingness to receive "tips" is an insidious evil working upward from the bottom of society. At the present day it manifests itself in America in the "honest graft" which makes public and corporation officials willing to receive presents where law and unwarped conscience forbid such receiving. In Rome this willingness of people who ought to have been above such pickings was entirely unconcealed; nor was there the slightest feeling that a "tip" should at least be in return for service. The millionaire on the Caelian

was as willing as the beggar from Janiculum to stretch
forth the itching palm. Ammianus Marcellinus sums up
conditions among the rich and noble at Rome in the
fourth century, a generation before the advent of Alaric.
After speaking of the effeminacy and absolute indolence
of the upper classes, he thus concludes: "but some
[noble] persons, if they are invited to a wedding, be
they ever so weak, yet when the gold is offered [as fees
to the guests] in the hollow palm . . . away they will
go briskly as far as Spoletum [a good seventy miles]."
Obviously the good historian is here using a little rhetoric; but it is easy to marshal facts. In the first century
Piso, a rich senator, was accustomed every year to raise
a certain number of his poor friends to the rank of *eques*
—a gift requiring sometimes as much as 400,000 ses.[1]
A generous act, no doubt; but what of the self respect of
the men who were thus favored? One of the letters of
the younger Pliny gives a more striking instance than
this. "It is the custom for those who assume the manly
toga [in Bithynia], or who marry, or enter upon office,
or dedicate any public work, to invite all the [local]
Senate, and even a considerable number of plebeians,
and to present each person with four or eight sesterces."
Gifts of sixteen or thirty-two cents—or considering
values of money, fifty cents and a dollar! And the city
fathers, the men of high property rating, the wealthiest
citizens in the town, stretching forth for these trifles
eagerly! But the substantial facts are beyond all dispute. Even this is not the most extreme case. Every
Roman senator was by statutory requirement a millionaire; yet Suetonius tells us that in the reign of Domitian
a rich man, one Ruscus Caepio, left a proviso in his will
that his heirs distribute a regular gratuity annually

[1] That was the required equestrian property rating. Of course, most
of these people would have owned something themselves.

among the body, this one-time "Assembly of Kings."
The Emperor balked at this and canceled the will.
Unless the senators were of better stuff than their age,
such an act added nothing to Domitian's popularity.
Yet another time, while at the theater, he took pains that
the senators should get their share of the lottery tickets
for which the vulgar crowd were scrambling.

The evil was as rampant in the provinces as in the
capital. In the declining cities of old Hellas it aided to
impoverish the numerous givers, and did the recipients
no good. "To the increased aversion for labor,"
remarks Mommsen, "and to the decay in the means of
good families, this noxious practice contributed its full
share." It contributed also to the vain glory and
quest of empty civic distinctions which was the bane of
municipal life under the Empire—for what is to be
thought of a city where in return for a money distribution among the decurions and leading plebeians, the community votes the donor a "public benefactor," and
allows him to erect a statue of himself in the forum,
paying for the statue himself?

As at almost all such times, in every money distribution those who needed the gifts least received the most,
because—it is obvious—they were the people to vote
offices, honors, and memorials to the donor. Thus an
inscription at Lyons shows how at one distribution the
decurions obtained sixty ses., while members of the
equestrian rank had only fifty-two. At Gabii, in 163 A.D.,
a silk merchant wished to glorify the memory of his
daughter. He erected a temple containing a bronze
statue of the dead woman as Venus, with bronze doors
and other elaborate decorations. This, however, was
not enough. The inevitable distribution of money followed. To the townspeople of the highest rank was
given twenty sesterces each, to the second rank eight, to

all other local citizens four. Yet even this did not suffice. The father paid into the treasury of Gabii 100,000 ses. to be put at interest, the income to pay for an annual feast in honor of the dead woman's memory, in which feast only the two highest classes of townsmen could participate. An honest effort to honor a dear child's memory? No doubt. But what shall be the commentary on the system of munificence where the rich were filled with good things and the poor were sent empty away?

5. *The Presents on the Saturnalia.*

The Saturnalia, the Roman festival falling toward the end of December, corresponded with much similarity to the modern Christmas season. The courts were closed. No public business could be transacted. Schools were dismissed. Even the sentences of criminals were suspended. As on certain American holidays, extraordinary liberties were allowed the servants. There are accounts that the slaves of a household were allowed to wear their master's dresses, and were waited upon by their owners at a banquet. This statement is to be taken with large grains of salt. It is enough if we believe the license was very complete, and that Roman masters and mistresses waited on *themselves,* as do the householders of other great societies on divers national holidays. The riot and jollity in the servants' hall of a Roman palace or villa was apt then to be excessive; so that Pliny the Younger had a special sitting room built at his Laurentine villa—"where I find it delightful," says he, "to sit during the Saturnalia, when all the rest of the house rings with the merry riot."

All this, however, is by way of preface to some comments on the exchange of presents among friends at the Saturnalia; a custom that presents amusing parallels to what happens at twentieth century Christmastides.

The presents that might be exchanged were of all kinds and values, though naturally certain gifts predominated. Wax tapers were a familiar gift, for reasons not wholly obvious. Little terra-cotta figures or figures of dough baked hard—possibly symbols of an old, nigh forgotten human sacrifice to Saturn—passed from hand to hand; but a great many presents were simply objects of ordinary use or value, just as our Christmas gifts are not confined to holly wreaths and sugar cakes.[1] Silver vessels seem to have been a fairly common gift. Martial complained in one of his epigrams of the way a friend was treating him on the Saturnalia. Ten years before he had given the poet a silver dish, weighing four pounds; on the fifth year a little bowl of two thirds of a pound; in the sixth, another of barely one half pound; in the ninth a little spoon "no heavier than a needle;" in the last year, nothing. "Therefore," says the poet, "return to your four pounds." Game, cakes, linen, clothing, books, all sorts of trifles and valuables would be given.

The emperor both received and gave presents. The festival given by Domitian on the Saturnalia is called by Statius "a day of happiness, a night of intoxication." The Caesar did not indeed provide a gigantic Christmas tree for the Roman people, but the top of the amphitheater (presumably the Flavian) poured down on them fruit of all kinds, nuts, figs, cakes and cheeses. The whole was followed by a great banquet to all the citizens, to which they sat down as guests of the Emperor. But the latter usually had his share of the good things also.

[1] Gifts were also given on New Year's day, and the kind of presents differed in some degree from those on the Saturnalia, but I have not thought it necessary to distinguish minutely what special presents were appropriate for each occasion. The spirit and general tendency were identical.

The crazy Caligula made proclamation that he would receive on New Year's day (the other great occasion for the bestowal of gifts) such presents as people might bring him; and accordingly the purple-clad imperator actually stood in his own vestibule to clutch the gifts which persons of all ranks threw before him by handfuls and lapfuls. His predecessor, Tiberius, was more munificent. He was accustomed to return Saturnalia and New Year's gifts fourfold, but since it annoyed him to have late comers bringing trifles to the palace all through the month of January—in the hope of getting the profitable counter-gift—he returned none that had been brought after New Year's day. Hadrian also, though no spendthrift, took advantage of the Saturnalia to send his friends all kinds of impromptu presents, as well as to return bountifully all presents made to him.

The Romans had their habit of making birthday presents too. Martial, who evidently kept a careful account of favors received and bestowed, says that he failed to send a certain Sextus a present on his birthday, and that Sextus has retaliated by not inviting him to a dinner party. The emperor's birthday was, as may be imagined, celebrated all over the Empire; and he was supposed to receive presents more or less valuable. But perhaps the most costly gifts were bestowed neither on the Saturnalia, nor on birthdays, but at banquets,—by the host—whatever the reason for the feast. It was almost an insult to allow a guest to depart empty-handed. He must at least be allowed to take with him his napkin. Commonly, however, the host was expected to do far more than this. At a small dinner party of select friends much more valuable presents could be looked for than a mere distribution of a few wretched coins, as at the "public dinners" given a municipality by some magnate. The gifts might be distributed by lot, so as to add to the merriment of the dinner, and there were other variations possible. Lucian suggests that when presents are given, a note should always accompany, telling of the contents lest the receiver be robbed by his slaves, who might rifle the package after they had carried it to his home, before he could open it. The value of such presents was only limited by the donor's wealth and generosity—a candelabrum, a statuette of Corinthian bronze, clothes, furniture, books, domestic animals, slaves. Caligula once gave a favorite charioteer 2,000,000 ses. at the end of a mad banquet; but this was imperial frenzy.

Through all this giving sound comically familiar notes—"I give to him because he gave to me;" "I give to him that he may give to me." Such sentiments are still uttered, or at least thought, fifteen hundred years after the passing of the Saturnalia.

6. *Certain "Modern" Phases.*

There are certain other phases in the life of the Roman world that show a strangely "modern" aspect. Roman society was in many respects brutal and crude; its polish was often a thin veneer for effeminate sensuality or sheer barbarism; it worshipped money and outward rank as have few other civilizations; yet we find in it—even at the age when it seemed most sordid and repellant—a consciousness that lucre could never quite replace intellect,—that it was well to *seem* cultured, even if one were not.

The most ready means at the present day for distributing mere information, which a great many people take for education, is beyond doubt the newspaper. Printing presses did not exist under the Empire. Yet the citizens of the capitals, and possibly of some of the other large cities, found a very feeble substitute for modern journalism.

First of all there was maintained at the Temple of Saturn at Rome a regular record, the *Libri Actorum* —alleged to have been commenced by King Servius Tullius—of all births in the city, marriages, divorces, deaths, and divers other details that might naturally go into a public register. Probably anybody could consult this who wished to, but far more important was the publication known as the *Acta Diurna,* which was a daily gazette published by the Roman government during the later Republic and under the Empire. Various clerks and subordinate officers of the magistrates drew it up. It was posted presumably in the form of placards in some public place, where anybody who listed could read and make copy; and in Cicero's time a good many scribes called *operarii* made a fair business by copying the gazette, or making extracts from it for the use of wealthy Romans, especially for such as were away from the city and wished to keep in touch with the Forum gossip. After the gazette had been up a certain time, it would be withdrawn and deposited for reference in the record office, or in the great public libraries.

It is very unfortunate that we have no really authentic fragments of the *Acta Diurna,* though we possess a parody upon it in Petronius' *Trimalchio;* and by means of this and other hints we can guess at its contents. First of all the births and deaths in the city were recorded; a statement of the receipts by the treasury from the provinces; and—very important for the hungry capital—information as to the supply of grain. Besides these things note would be made of the edicts of magistrates, the wills of prominent men, reports of trials, acquittals and condemnations; also a list of new magistrates after elections. If the Senate had passed any important decrees, especially any in honor of the emperor, they would be given. The court news—the doings of the imperial family—would be chronicled as faithfully as by the semi-official press of Berlin. What might be termed sensational news would be added—prodigies and miracles—the birth of a two-headed pig at Praeneste, the fall of a meteor at Tusculum, conflagrations, important funerals, great sacrifices, erection of new buildings; and—raciest of all—reports of love adventures in the upper crust of society, with the names of the parties boldly given. There were even personal items, communicated to the official editor, by way of advertisement, though we dare not say that such mention was ever paid for.

The means of publishing the *Acta* obviously prevented any literary style. The statements were bare, unadorned; the lively southern imaginations of the readers would supply the rest. One can picture the bustle in the Forum after the new tablets were posted; the eager gesticulations, the craning necks, the scores of busy scribes, the brisk messenger of the grain merchant running away to inform his master that the Alexandrian corn fleet was delayed, and that his stock in hand had doubled value.

Of course it would be wrong to exaggerate the scope and importance of the *Acta*. We cannot tell how much they were imitated in the provincial cities. The usual means of spreading public information remained the chatter of the market places until the eighteenth century or later. The Athenians, with their fondness "for hearing or telling some new thing," had many rivals, if few peers. In the provinces, however, if there were few or no dailies, there was a large educated upper class, eager to read "the latest books," and to keep in touch with literary celebrities. Tacitus one time was sitting with a strange gentleman at some games in Rome, and after some general conversation, the man said: "Are you from

Italy or the Provinces?'' ''You know me quite well,'' said the historian, ''from the books of mine you have read.'' ''Ah!'' said the stranger, ''then you are either Tacitus or Pliny''—a remark which would have been impossible save in a society where at least a surface of culture was very general.

The government naturally encouraged schools in the provinces, as diffusers of the Latin language, hence of Roman civilization. Agricola, in Britain, set up Latin schools for the children of the conquered native chiefs, and his biographer boasts that they soon became ''enamored of rhetoric.'' Many cities, especially in the east, would rise to dispute Rome's claim to intellectual supremacy. Besides Athens and Alexandria, other university towns still kept their fame. Apollonia, Rhodes, Tarsus, Ephesus, Antioch, Tyre and Sidon were all centers of a would-be ''cultured'' society. Apart from the cities even, ''book learning'' had penetrated into the rural estates. Pliny the Younger tells of ''mere country squires, [in Italy] who were men of deep erudition;'' and mentions a certain *eques,* Terentius Junior, who had buried himself on a farm, yet was a master of the most polished Greek and Latin. Pliny the Younger himself added to his large fund of good works by founding a public library at Comum—an act he wisely considered more advantageous than the endowment of gladiator shows.

Unfortunately a society whose foundation is wealth, not genuine refinement, is likely to be more anxious to appear bookish, than to be literary. Everybody—from the decrepit consular of a long line of ancestors to the newly rich freedman with no ancestors at all—felt it good form to dabble in literature—preferably in poetry. The amount of bad verse composed under the Empire was fearful and wonderful, and only matched by the patience with which every friend harkened to the reading of every other friend's efforts—at set "audiences"—knowing that repayment would come when the loudly applauded reader would have to listen in turn to him. The want of taste, the absolute lack of proper standards of criticism allowed to prevail at these public readings account in part for the long night that came over ancient letters, following upon the death of Suetonius.

The manufacture of epics obviously was not sufficient employment for men of real talent and ambition. Politics had been reduced to palace intrigue; but an orator could still distinguish himself by arguing in the courts. Here again money showed its baneful influence. A young advocate to succeed must be sure of sufficient applause to impress the praetor or justices. If he had wealth, his agent would fill the basilica with a claque of worthless loiterers, whose applause from the center seats —at the proper points in the oration—would be deafening, and to whom at the end the agents would hand out their money fees as openly as they would doles of food to clients. The trade was profitable; for sometimes as much as twelve ses. per head was paid to the applauders, who—the lovers of genuine oratory complained—never listened to the harangue, but stupidily waited for the signal of their leader. The oration ended, these parasites hastened to another court house, to repeat the operation and pocket a second fee.

If a man of pretensions did not write poetry, or argue in the courts, he was fairly sure at least to indulge in writing memoirs. Here indeed history would be glad if some of the numerous autobiographies could have been preserved. How interesting would be the "commentaries" of Trajan; the memoirs of Agrippina, mother of Nero; the life history of Septimius Severus, that hardheaded African *eques* who founded a dynasty. There is little to condemn in such a pastime; but that Severus and Trajan—busy fighters that they were—found leisure to meddle with it, shows how wide-spread was the literary habit.

At the other end of the social scale, but also calling themselves devotees of letters, were the poor wandering students whose escapades remind us of the itinerent scholars of Luther's day in Germany. The class was very numerous, very profligate; and often enough used the name of student only as a pretext for leading a vagrant life. As late as Valentinian I it was necessary to issue an edict against these youths at Rome, that if they went too much to the theater, and indulged in night revels—in a word, if they did not conduct themselves as "the dignity of a liberal education demanded"—they were to be put on ship and sent home.[1] But the genuine desire for knowledge was often great. The sacrifices of Horace's father to obtain for him an education has been mentioned, and such acts were not unusual. A tombstone at Calama, Africa, presents a father lamenting the death of two boys to whom he had given an education: "but now after so much expense he could not enjoy either of them."

The demand for the latest books in the provinces was constant. Horace in one of his "Epistles" tells how when the first rage for a book was over in Rome, the extra copies would be shipped off to Ilerda in Spain, or Utica, where they would be readily disposed of. During the next century as the provinces became more Romanized, the demand probably became greater still, and Gaul particularly must have furnished an excellent book market.

The ancient world did not even escape certain features

[1] Usually that "home" would be Africa, which seems to have sent an unusual number of students to Italy.

that are accounted exclusively modern. There was a "spelling reform" under Claudius. The pedantic Emperor undertook to introduce three new letters into the alphabet for the purpose of making spelling more scientific, but as might have been imagined, this "improvement," though used in some inscriptions, in his reign, did not survive its author.

The early imperial age was also the period of the development of a freedom among women, that was hardly again equaled until the nineteenth century. Women were a power at the imperial court almost as great as at the French court of the later Louis. They mingled in local elections—witness their appeals to voters in the Pompeian wall inscription. They dipped into philosophy and literature. Juvenal shudders at their learning. They even indulged in "physical culture" exercises; to Juvenal's infinite horror they verily put on light armor and studied fencing with trainers, and learned to swing dumb-bells, to work up a healthy glow at the baths. But it is not necessary to follow the worthy satirist in all his invectives, or to ask why he placed the sin of fencing (for women) only a little above the sin of adultery.

A culture that is really a pseudo-culture is certain sooner or later to run to seed. By the fourth century A.D. all the sap in the ancient learning had dried up. It was no longer genteel even to *seem* learned. In 400 A.D. Synesius, attending the lectures on philosophy at Athens, says that the lecturers despaired of getting audiences by ordinary means, and by the mere excellence of their discourses; and so distributed to faithful attendants jars of the famous Hymettus honey. With conditions come to this, it is indeed a pity that Arcadius did not close the philosophy schools, instead of leaving it for Justinian to do more than a century after him.

7. *"Back to the Country."*

The age of Rome was the age of large cities. We have considered their probable population in an earlier chapter; also how the capital and its mighty rivals were huge magnets drawing to themselves native and alien, patrician and slave. We rightly think of the typical man of the Empire as a "city man" who breathes the air of a forum, whose sandals are worn amid the innumerable dark alleys of an ancient metropolis. If he was not a dweller in the great Rome, he was very possibly a dweller in one of the numerous lesser Romes. The provincial cities—especially where there was no time-honored local tradition to maintain—imitated the capital in their manner of temples, arenas, baths, theaters and curiae. Even the names of the streets were copied. Antioch in Pisidia had a "Velabrum," Lyons a "Vatican," Toulouse and Cirta a "Capitol." The imitation was probably as slavish as the imitation of Berlin by Stettin, of Paris by modern Amiens. And yet with all this city life,—warp and woof, it would seem, of the society of the age—the idea that man made the city, but God the country; that brick walls, narrow streets, darkness, noise, dust and filth were not an ideal environment, was almost as strong among certain classes of the ancients as it is in America in the twentieth century. To settle whether the idyls of Theocritus, Bion and Moschus represent more than literary byplays,—whether they indicate that Hellenistic society was beginning to weary of the crowded glitter of Alexandria, Antioch, and Syracuse—would take this discussion too far afield. Under the Empire we find the Latin idyls of decidedly poorer poetic quality than their Greek prototypes; but the cry "back to the country!" begins to find a louder utterance. The gentility and desirability of farming for Romans has been sufficiently set forth, and this partiality died hard, if it ever died at all. Under the later Republic, when to wield political power one must be within easy walk of the Forum, it is no wonder the great as well as the lowly crowded the capital. Under the Empire political power belonged to the Caesar and his freedmen. Then it was that men of quiet taste and true refinement as well as men of slender purses, began to find life in the great city irksome with no corresponding political advantages; and a movement the other way really started.

First of all, life in the smaller towns was far cheaper than in the Italian Babylon. "At Sora, Fabrateria and Frusino"[1] says Juvenal, "you can purchase a pretty house merely for the year's rent of a cellar in Rome." The "pretty house" was likely to be a very simple one. Pompeii shows us what the dwellings in a provincial city were like. Not more than three or four in that town belonged to really rich men; most were extremely small and modest. But they were not tenements buried under piles of rickety upper stories; the gates and the green fields were near at hand. Compared to the dark, foul *insulae* of Rome they were Elysium. However, Juvenal would probably have said he wished to live near, not *in* even the smaller cities. The tart censor of wicked luxuries becomes enthusiastic while drawing his picture of rustic delights. "There [by these towns] you will have your own little garden—you will have a well so shallow that you need no rope or bucket, whence you can easily draw the water for your sprouting plants. Live then [in such a place], enamoured of the pitchfork, and the dresser of your trim garden, from which you can provide the feast to a hundred [vegetarian] Pythagoreans. For is it not something to be able in any spot, in any retreat what-

[1] Towns in the Volscian country of South Latium.

soever, to make one's self lord of just a single lizard?''

But there is more than the economy of money to be gained from rural life. Here, we are told, one can dine off coarse earthenware plates and not lose social caste, nor have to put on the cumbersome ''dress suit''—the toga—save to go to a burial; here the old style theater still stands, here the good old-fashioned dramas are acted, and the unsophisticated children bawl at the grinning masks of the actors; and here a white tunic is a good enough festival dress even for a magistrate. Here too a friend can come and sup. He will not want a tedious city banquet, but a little juicy kid, asparagus which the farm steward's wife has just picked upon the hillside, some big eggs ''still warm in the twisted hay,'' grapes from one's own vines, and pears and apples ''smelling very fresh.'' The servants will be without the fine flourishes of city carvers and cup bearers; they will understand only Latin, not Greek; the wine they will serve must come from the hills close by; and among the guests there will be no talking about investments and the rates of interest in the Forum.

Thus Juvenal; and if we think he is overstating after his wont; that he is giving his own views, not those of many others around him, listen again to the typical ''good gentleman,'' Pliny the Younger. He writes to Caninius Rufus, a native of his own town: ''How is Comum looking, your darling spot and mine? And that charming villa of yours—what of it, and its porticoes where it is always spring, its sturdy clumps of plane trees, its fresh crystal canal, and the lake below that gives such a lovely view? How is the exercise ground, so soft yet firm to the foot? What of the large dining halls, and the little rooms, and the retiring rooms for night and day? . . . Lucky man that you are if you can spend your leisure there!''

Pliny was unable to spend as much time as he liked in Comum. He had presumably a handsome palace at Rome; but he often preferred playing the "suburbanite" and going each day into the city for business. His Laurentine villa was seventeen miles from Rome; near enough, he says, "so that after getting through all your work, and without any loss or curtailment of your working hours, you can go out and stay there."[1] . . . "You will [there] see abundant flocks of sheep and many herds of cattle and horses."[2]

Or again, take the Spaniard Martial who found the roar of the capital so fascinating, yet in the end so dreary. He contrasts the miserable life under the "cold marble porticoes" of the city with the joys of rural life, where one can be "rich with the spoils of grove and field; unfold before his fire the well filled hunting nets; lift the leaping fish from the quivering line; and draw forth the yellow honey from the red cask, while a plump housekeeper loads his table, and his own eggs are cooking over the fire which has cost not a farthing. My wish [concludes Martial] is that the man who loves not me, may not love this—let him drag out life and grow pale with the woes of the city!"

About fifty years later Lucian draws somewhat similar contrasts between the simple life of the small Greek cities and the "burdensome banquets and still more burdensome brothels" of Rome. "How could you," asks one Greek in Rome of a fellow Hellene, "leave the light of the sun, Hellas, and its happiness and its freedom for the sake of this crowd?"

Last of all we may quote not a poet, nor a refined

[1] A testimony to the speed and convenience of "suburban transit" at least for the very rich.

[2] An incidental witness to how the grazing interests had menaced farming even in the outskirts of Rome.

letter-writer, but a knotty, iron-handed centurion, a favorite of Trajan, and commander of the praetorium under Hadrian. He deliberately retired from his high office and spent his last seven years in the good green country. On his tombstone he caused to be engraved: "Here lies Similis who existed seventy-six years, and who lived seven."

The Roman world was pompous, gorgeous, supremely artificial. It was a sign that all was not bad in it when men turned away their faces from the scramble for place and pelf in the metropolis, and remembered that besides the arch-deity Plutus, there was still the hoary Ceres.

CHAPTER VII

MARRIAGE, DIVORCE AND CHILDLESSNESS

1. *Money and Motives in Marriage.*

THE old question whether the ancients knew of lawful "love" in the modern sense of the term, is hardly one to be threshed out in a book having to do primarily with the Roman money power, however much some of these pages seem to have wandered from purely financial problems. It is sufficient here to note that under the Empire, as under the Republic, and in the Greek period, the ancients married while yet the women were exceedingly young. And early marriages are manifestly likely to hurt the romantic tendency, or rather to cause it to flow in very undesirable directions—such as the adoration of married women. In ancient times a marriage for love was usually with a widow or a divorced woman.[1] The possibility of a purely sentimental attachment for a wife, who was perhaps only ten years old when affianced, was not very great. The result was that nearly all the plentiful erotic poetry we find is addressed to married women.[2] Seneca therefore advises the wise man to "love his wife with the head, not with the heart, [for] . . . nothing is more hateful than to love one's wife as one loves one's mistress." That Seneca could

---

[1] Not always—witness in Athens—the love-match of Elpinice, daughter of Miltiades with Callias the Rich.

[2] Just as was the case with most of the medieval troubadours' lays.

might then rule her husband with a rod of iron. Her husband was her guardian, but not a scrap of her property could he alienate or contract away without her consent. He became the slave of his wife's fortune. "I have sold my authority for the dowry that I've accepted," whimpers one of Plautus' comedy characters. And Cicero more seriously in a set oration asserts: "Our ancient laws intended to put the woman under the guardian; but the *jurisconsulti*[1] have put the guardian under the authority of the woman."

As for the dowry in general, it was as indispensable in marriages of good society as a *dot* is to-day in France. The contract between the parties stated how much and what nature it was, when to be paid, etc. With a girl of the highest class, e.g., a wealthy senator's daughter, the bridegroom might look for even 1,000,000 ses. Such at least was the sum Messalina, the wife of Claudius, brought Silius, in that infamous mock marriage which ruined both bride and bridegroom; an occasion when there seems to have been every effort to conform to all the usages of polite society.

2.   *Divorce, and the Causes Thereof.*

If such authors as Gellius, Valerius, Maximus and Dionysius of Halicarnassus are to be believed, divorces in early Rome were extremely rare; in fact all but unknown. When in 233 B.C. Spurius Carvilius Ruga put away his wife merely because of barrenness, his act was disapproved by public sentiment. But a hundred years later his act would have been nothing exceptional. A hundred later still, he would have been a somewhat

---

[1] Whose decisions developed this application of the Roman Law. The object of the dowry was of course to protect the wife against being wantonly divorced. If she were sent away by her husband, he must restore her the dowry.

unusual man if he had not thought himself entirely justified in divorcing his spouse on such grounds, even if he had been wedded or divorced twice or thrice already.

The weakening of the religious rites which were wont to solemnize an old Roman marriage, no doubt had something to do with this deplorable change; but with the religious and legal side of divorce we have little to do. That the marriage tie had become frightfully lax by the time the Republic fell, is one of the best known facts of Roman history.

No doubt it was usually the husband who took the initiative in dissolving an ungrateful compact. Often enough he must have been wanton and guilty. But the blame was not always on his shoulders. Mention has already been made of the tyranny of rich widows. Such a spouse was frequently able to drive her partner close to distraction. "Wives with dowries are the executioners of their husbands," affirms Plautus. The man could indeed divorce her, but how—unless she were clearly at fault—could he repay the heavy dowry she had brought to his house? Haughty, imperious, she ruled everything; she drove about boldly in her chariot; she filled the house with tradespeople and creditors. Often she had a manager, a handsome young fellow, who meddled with everything, who gave orders to the husband, and who very likely was his mistress' lover. "She bought her husband for a million sesterces—that is the price at which he calls her chaste," says Juvenal with more than his wonted cynicism. A rich wife could write a love letter in her husband's presence, and flirt brazenly. "A rich wife with a covetous husband has all a widow's privileges." There is ample evidence to show that the satirist was right. A lady of this type often affected literature. At table "she praises Vergil, excuses the suicide of Dido;" confutes grammarians and rhetoricians, and "no one in the company can put in a word, not even another woman." She could give her husband lectures on oratory, and correct his slips of grammar. Again, [many women] "sit and see Alcestis on the stage, enduring death for the sake of her husband —though, were a like exchange granted to them, they would willingly sacrifice a husband to purchase a lap-dog's life."

So long as the fair ones who so conducted themselves were wealthy in their own right, they might enjoy themselves in some safety. When the money they wasted was their husbands', they trod on slippery ground. The ladies of the Empire did not win a name for French frugality. We hear of men misers; almost never of women misers. It was charged that the typical society woman would pawn the family plate to ride in a sedan chair to the games, not to speak of rewarding a paramour. Even if she was poor, she would be a spendthrift. Men with all their faults, we are told, can dread the future. Women take the last coin and squander it, "as though money, with a kind of vegetable power, would bloom afresh from the empty chest." And that money matters and extravagance were probably at the bottom of a great many divorces does not require elaborate proof.

In Tiberius' reign the whole question of feminine conduct was solemnly debated in the imperial Senate. It began by Caecina Severus proposing to the Conscript Fathers the forbidding of magistrates going out to a province to be accompanied by their wives. He said he himself had lived with his wife forty years, and by her had six children; but that he had always confined her to Italy. Women, he asserted, were naturally prone to fatigue, and if they had the least chance were cruel, ambitious and greedy of authority. They became cen-

ters of profligate intrigue in the governors' courts in the
provinces, where there were "two courts of justice, but
the orders of the ladies were more peremptory and
capricious. The old laws against women had been discarded, and now they ruled everything—their families,
the courts, and even the armies."

Valerius Messalinus, the son of a noted orator, arose
to answer for the majority of the Senate against the
proposal of Caecina. He aserted that it was just as well
the ancient laws had been softened. Magistrates were
entitled to their wives' company. But that was not his
chief reason. "It was true many women were very bad,
but it would make matters intolerably worse if the husbands should absent themselves for years in a province,
and *leave the women in Rome to spend money and mix
in love intrigues.*" Drusus, the crown prince, took
Valerius' part, and nothing came of Caecina's disturb-
ing proposition.

It is well known that Cicero divorced Terrentia after
they had lived together more than thirty years. For a
while their letters show there was much genuine affection between them. "Be assured," he wrote during his
exile, "I have nothing dearer than you. At this moment
I think I see you, and cannot restrain my tears." Then
at the end came the divorce, when they had children and
grandchildren. Probably Terrentia had grown jealous
and quarrelsome; but Cicero's main grievance, so far as
we can find one, was that she kept scolding her husband
for wasting money, while trying to fill her own private
purse somewhat to his disadvantage.

After that, at sixty-three years of age, the destroyer
of Catiline married a young girl, Publilia, his ward, in
order—Tiro, his confidential freedman, said—to pay his
debts with her fortune. The alliance was very unhappy,
and ended in another divorce. Then a third marriage

was offered Cicero. He declined it, saying he had no time to attend both to a wife and to philosophy—a truth he should have realized before.

Many an estranged pair hurried to the praetor for divorce as joyously as to their wedding, though Ovid tells the strange tale of a couple who were in the presence of the magistrate, when the young husband ran to his wife crying: "Thy beauty conquers me!" embraced her, and the praetor had nothing left to do.

In fact where there was no restraining motive—such as the need of disgorging a large dowry—divorces were almost incredibly common. It was charged that women were accustomed to reckon the years not by the consuls, but by their ever changing husbands. Juvenal speaks of ladies having "eight husbands in five years"—very possibly one of his exaggerations; but a plausible exaggeration must have some truth behind it. Cicero speaks in a letter to Atticus of "the women of the many marriages." Caesar required separated persons to wait six months before remarriage. Augustus, in his efforts to promote morality by statute, made the interval eighteen months. His laws—presently to be discussed—set a premium on fruitful marriages; and many unions took place as a consequence, which were dissolved just as soon as they proved barren. Then again, Romans of all classes were a roving people. Soldiers, traders, officers, and the like would leave wife and home and wander away. An old law made marriages void at the end of three years. In this way many a household was broken up.

All this, of course, bespeaks something more than mere immorality—the all but degradation of wives to the level of mistresses. It was a dire blow to the cornerstone of Aryan civilization—the monogamous home. When a savant like the elder Pliny could speak of "celibacy as leading to fortune and power;" when Juvenal could say with even a fraction of truth that "suicide was better than marriage," and that "a good wife was rarer than a white crow,"—it is plain the people of the Empire were not simply very wicked; they were on the high road to moral degeneracy, economic decline, and almost deliberate race-suicide.

3. *Childlessness*.

The well known Belgian savant, Monsieur Willems, has computed that in 179 B.C. there were in the Roman Senate eighty-eight patricians, coming out of seventeen *gentes*. In 55 B.C., there were only forty-three patrician senators from twelve *gentes*. Since the patricians in the second and first centuries B.C., were little more than average representatives of the old landed aristocracy, there is no real reason for thinking that the old plebeian houses were in a different state. The aristocracy of Rome was running out fast, and the wealth won in the later conquests (after 146 B.C.) was mainly in the hands of men of short pedigrees.

Things seem little better under the early Empire. How few emperors left a son to inherit! Julius Caesar's daughter died before him. Augustus' daughter brought him only shame. Tiberius had a son, to be sure, but Sejanus put the luckless prince out of the way. Caligula left no direct heir.[1] Claudius left Britannicus, who never reigned, and whom Nero murdered. Nero perished childless. Galba, Otho, Vitellius left only strangers to avenge them. Vespasian by exception left two adult sons; but Titus' successor was his brother. Domitian had no son to inherit the gloomy vices of his father. Nerva left no son; nor Trajan, nor Hadrian, nor Anto-

---

[1] He left, indeed, a very young daughter, who was put to death soon after he was assassinated.

ninus Pius. At last in Marcus Aurelius we meet the father of a numerous family; though the world has hardly yet forgiven the imperial philosopher for begetting such an heir as Commodus. The average emperor then was either childless, or he left only a daughter. There is little evidence to show that the imperial houses were worse off than the average noble family of the same age. Under Claudius it had been necessary regularly to "create" patricians, that the old religious cults might be maintained.

The shameful truth was that to a large part of the upper classes, and to a hardly smaller fraction of the lower, the maintenance of children was confessedly an intolerable burden, to be avoided as much as possible. In the earlier stages of antiquity there had been few greater calamities possible than for a man to die childless; his ancestral house, and still worse his ancestral cult, would perish with him. In the last stages of antiquity such a lot was confronted with perfect equanimity.

One of Plautus' characters in the *Miles Gloriosus* puts the case as a good many of the middle class saw it, and Plautus—be it remembered—wrote before the days of the Empire. He says that without children he can live happily, surrounded by attentive friends; "before daybreak they are at the door, asking if I have slept well." He knows they only want his money. What matter? What matters it, who gets his money when life is over? And if the childless man were passing rich, all manner of good things flowed his way. He had more invitations than he could accept. Fine morsels and finer gifts came to him from everybody. The ladies went to all lengths to please him. The older and feebler he was, the greater their assiduity—so much sooner would come the opening of the will! Mothers thrust their daughters on him; unscrupulous men their wives.

Pliny the Younger—childless himself, but one who really craved for children—speaks with bitterness of his time "when the devotion lavished upon the childless makes a man regret that he has a son." Nearly three hundred years later Ammianus Marcellinus thus delivers himself as to the attitude of the Romans. "Some persons look on everything as worthless which is born outside the walls of the capital, save only the childless and the unmarried. Nor can it be conceived with what a variety of obsequious observance, men without children are courted at Rome."

Of course Juvenal is savage on the subject. Not even a quail, he asserts, will be sacrificed in behalf of one who is a father; but for a rich man or woman who is childless, if they feel a touch of fever, "every temple porch is covered with votive tablets, and some even promise a hecatomb of oxen."

Modern opinion may point out that this childlessness had its favorable side for humanity; that the Roman aristocracy was so artificial and corrupt, it was good it should be peacefully blotted out, to make room for a sturdier, purer stock. This opinion may not be wholly fair. If the younger Pliny had been given sons, they might have done noble service to society, and Pliny's voice is hardly that of an honest, untainted man crying in a wilderness of iniquity. There was still some good in the Roman aristocracy, if a great deal of evil. But the notable thing was that race-suicide was not confined to the upper classes. The chances of it were even more favorable among the proletariat. The masses living on corn-doles could have no true family life. The mortality of children in the unsanitary *insulae* must have been higher than in the worst slums of New York. The population of Rome was maintained, not by any natural growth, but by the inflow of outsiders from the rural parts and provinces. And then again the shameful fact must be stated that prostitution was direfully inexpensive. The victims were frequently slaves of the cheapest sort; the fee was consequently within reach of the extremely poor class.[1] Consequently the opportunity for unlawful indulgence made fruitful marriages the rarer among those very classes whose families are usually large precisely in proportion as their incomes are small. "A quarter of an *as* woman," was what the young fop Caelius, in Cicero's day, called Clodia, his high-born paramour, after they had quarreled; and an *as* or two *asses*, seems to have been a quite sufficient fee.

And under the Empire too, the actual number of women seems to have been less than the number of men. Women slaves were less valuable for field work than men. The vast number of women who became prostitutes were cut off from fruitful marriage; and even in the best families daughters were likely to be exposed, though as a rule sons were fairly welcome. Consequently the number of proper marriages and the normal family increase was reduced. We seldom hear of "old maids" in antiquity; the demand for wives was too great, however unhappy and abnormal the married state in many cases.

Abortion was frequent. Child rearing was expensive. Women shunned the pains and burdens of motherhood. "Rarely does a gilded bed contain a woman about to become a mother, so potent are the arts of the woman who can secure barrenness," says the master satirist, yet the husband should not grieve; if the babe should be born, "you would be sire of an Aethiop; some blackamoor would be your sole heir." And doubt of paternity seems in various cases to have been cause for

[1] Something not always true to-day. It is freely stated that it is not the submerged tenth but the upper classes that are responsible for most of the "vice" of New York, Boston and Chicago.

the alleged father to repudiate his wife's offspring. Augustus caused the child of the second Julia, his grand-daughter, to be killed. Claudius had a babe, alleged to be his daughter, exposed. When this example was set by the Palatine, what was likely to be done by the Esquiline or the Subura?

Finally the current immorality undoubtedly produced strange mixtures of blood, noble and ignoble. Pliny the Elder tells how in one year the two consuls were observed to look wonderfully like two gladiators on display before them. Juvenal claims that many a presumed aristocrat had a gladiator, a harper or a popular flute player for a father. It is impossible to prove such charges; it is equally impossible to say they are wholly unfounded.

Lastly it must be remembered, that legitimate, fruitful marriage was attacked from Augustus' time onward, by concubinage, a condition legally authorized. The consort would usually be a freedwoman; her children would not be legitimate, but such an alliance was much cheaper. It would not cut off the pleasant attentions of legacy hunters, and the mistress required much less in the way of slaves, dress, jewelry, and social display than the wife. The father of the younger Pliny had a concubine and remembered her in his will. Vespasian had a concubine, so did Antoninus Pius, Constantius Chlorus and Constantine the Great. Children would sometimes come to such alliances, but they would seldom be welcomed and often be exposed; so the whole institution was another that aided race-suicide.

4. *Marriage Legislation.*

Tacitus, when speaking of the Germans and how they abhorred childlessness, remarks that "Good habits among them were of greater effect than good laws elsewhere."

The historian was making a thrust at the attempts of the emperors to promote fruitful wedlock by legislation.

That the prevalence of childlessness and the frequency of divorce or of confirmed celibacy menaced the common weal was evident long before the Republic fell. In 131 B.C., Metellus Macedonicus, while censor, delivered what may be styled a sermon on the subject. "If we could, fellow citizens, we should indeed keep clear of this burden [of matrimony]. But as nature has so arranged it that we cannot live comfortably with wives, or live at all without them, it is proper to have regard to the permanent welfare, rather than to our own brief comfort."

Metellus' sermon was not more effectual than other sermons have been. About a hundred years later Augustus, sharing the good consul's sentiments, undertook to reinforce precept with penalty, to end race-suicide by law.

Augustus himself was neither a model father nor husband. Says Suetonius, "His amorous propensities never left him, and as he grew older it is reported that he was in the habit of leading astray young girls, who were procured for him from all quarters, even by his own wife." His family life too was extremely unhappy. Livia, indeed, he loved sincerely, though not faithfully; but his daughter, the elder Julia, was a sore grief to him. When the people begged him to remit some of her well-earned penalties, his only reply was: "I wish you all had such daughters and wives as she is;" and Agrippa, his incorrigible grandson, and the elder and the younger Julia, he called "his three cancers." He was even wont to paraphrase a line of the Iliad and declare: "Would I were wifeless, or had childless died."

Yet this same man, seeing the noble families perishing around him, seeing the great difficulty in getting recruits for the army, seeing whole districts growing waste for lack of people to dwell in them, undertook to invoke the law to re-populate the Empire.

In passing this legislation, Augustus—who ordinarily had his way so easily in all matters of law making and administration—had to struggle hard with the opposition, and to go to the limits of his influence to win his point. In 18 B.C., he first proposed his law to the Senate, where he forced it through for preliminary approval with difficulty; but the Comitia—usually under his regime so docile —would have none of it. The *equites* seem to have made organized resistance. The law was rejected. Augustus was obliged to bide his time. Late in his reign in 3 A.D., he re-introduced his law, its rewards increased, its penalties lightened. In this way he finally conquered; and later still the consuls Marcus Papius Mutilus and Quintus Poppaeus[1] in 9 A.D., carried for the Emperor additional and perfecting legislation. Taking this legislation as a whole, it is interesting to look at its main provisions.

First of all, certain kinds of marriages were absolutely prohibited, especially with actresses and prostitutes; or of senators and senators' children with freedmen or freedwomen. Second, and far more important, celibates were prohibited from receiving legacies under a will unless they were related to the testator at least in the sixth degree. There were naturally a few exemptions from this. One could take the legacy if one married within an hundred days; or again, if an engagement was made to marry and carried out in good faith within two years. Widows were exempt for two years and divorced women for eighteen months. But a later determination of the Senate under Tiberius enacted that when a man became sixty or a woman fifty, they must, if then unwedded, be counted celibates for life, and could not avoid the penalty by any late alliance.

[1] They were only *consules suffecti:* substitute consuls.

Again, persons who were married, but childless, were forbidden to receive more than one half of a legacy unless the testator stood within the sixth degree. A man escaped this penalty by having only one child, a free woman had to have three, a freedwoman four. It was also provided that when a marriage was childless the wife could take only one tenth of what was assigned her by her husband's will.

Likewise an attempt was made to honor a fruitful marriage and make it desirable. It was enacted that other things being equal, the candidates for public office were to be given preference according to the number of their children. Persons with children were exempted from various disagreeable civil duties; and finally the mother of three children (if a freedwoman, four) was entitled to freedom from *tutela*, or guardianship, over herself and property.[1] When we consider what frantic efforts were made in Rome to snatch at legacies and how legacy hunting and childlessness went nearly hand in hand, the drastic nature of this legislation will be evident.

It is customary to say that Augustus' marriage laws were an absolute failure. This judgment is possibly too harsh. It is quite possible that not a few *bona fide* marriages were contracted, and many children born and reared because of the penalties and premiums of this *Lex Julia et Papia Poppaea*. The Augustan poets— Horace and his following—made a laudable attempt to bolster up their imperial patron's efforts, and celebrate laws to which their own lives hardly conformed. But in the main Augustus' whole attempt must be called a failure. Tiberius tried to deal with a few of the most notorious cases of immorality. He dismissed from the

---

[1] This "*Jus trium liberorum*" would even give the Roman franchise to a "Latin" woman, for three children born *out of* wedlock—the strange case of the state encouraging moral laxity.

praetorship a senator who repudiated a wife that he had married only the day before. He also banished women of good family who had deliberately enrolled themselves as prostitutes to escape the penalties of the law for sexual wrongdoing. The Senate, under Claudius and Nero, tinkered with the penalties for evading the statute, in a vain attempt to find something not too lax or too fast; and the laws remained on the statute books until the age of Constantine the Great, when finally the penalties for childlessness and celibacy were swept away.

But laws like these were proven long before the fourth century to be practically non-enforcible. The emperors were themselves often the chief offenders. They were usually almost childless, and had to relax the law in their own favor to grasp the numerous legacies always left them. They could ill afford to refuse such concessions to their friends, until at last no one, who possessed any influence at court, could miss receiving "the rights of the fathers of children." The emperors indeed realized the value of a sturdy stock of young citizens to bear the burdens of the Empire. Augustus, when touring in the rural parts of Italy, would give 1,000 ses. to such of the lower class as presented before him a goodly brood of flourishing sons and daughters. Trajan founded institutions for the rearing of children, that the poor need not fear to raise ample families. Hadrian, when he sentenced criminals, made the penalty heavier or lighter as they chanced to be parents of few or many children. Septimius Severus sharpened the laws against adultery and also the whole *Lex Julia et Papia Poppaea;* and that his measures were not a dead letter is shown by the fact that when Dion Cassius became consul,[1] he found three thousand accusations for violation of these laws on the lists awaiting trial.

[1] Either in 219 A.D., or 220 A.D.

In the crash and tumult of the third century, however, the average emperor was more busy beating off the Goths than chastising celibates. How Constantine's age saw the end of this legislation, has been remarked. Constantine himself was praised in his generation for marrying early, "yielding himself to the laws of matrimony as soon as he ceased to be a boy." For better or worse the Christian age was at hand, when men would refuse marriage and children for the alleged good of their souls. But celibacy, it should be clearly understood, was no innovation in the ancient world when Christians began asking "whether marriage was honorable." Some gain it was when celibacy ceased to be a synonym for sensuality and the celibates sought the Egyptian deserts and lauras, not the Baths of Caracalla.

5. *Happier Marriages.*

Were all marriages thus fragile? Were all the men and women of the Empire thus anxious to defy the laws of their moral and physical nature? Juvenal would make us think so; but we have tried to discover how far Juvenal is to be believed, how far disbelieved. Him notwithstanding, there were beyond doubt many pure and happy homes, with wifely devotion, husbandly fidelity, love of parents and children, before Christianity came with its new law of divine love. It may even be argued that divorce was not more frequent than in those states of our American Union where the marriage legislation and the courts are most lax; that childlessness was not more common than in those "cultivated wards" of certain New England cities, where celibacy or childless marriages seem almost the rule, where a really large family is a surprise, where the Puritan stock is accomplishing its own destruction. Such speculations are highly interesting, but lead to no answers; for we lack reliable statistics as to divorces, birth rate and mortality among the ancients. That wealth, bookishness and an artificial manner of living go with a falling birth rate, France has already discovered, and certain sections of America are now discovering, even as the Roman Empire discovered centuries ago. The increase of the standard of living, i.e., the increased cost of a household on a scale of refinement to which young men and women are accustomed, undoubtedly has contributed to the result in every case. Justice requires, nevertheless, that one dwell on the other side of the picture in the Empire. If most of the aristocratic families were dying out, certain hung on as sturdily as several of the most famous of the "Back Bay nobility" of Boston have done. Marcus Aurelius was the father of a large family; at least seven children were born to him and his Empress Faustina.[1] Commodus himself was one of twins, a fact which may account for some of his peculiarities.[2] And the succeeding emperors, rough soldiers mostly, usually had sons, sometimes several, even if the bloody violence of the times prevented them from founding dynasties.

There were honorable cases, a century earlier, of fathers of thriving families. Asinius Rufus lived about 100 A.D., and was spoken of as a model gentleman. He had a number of children. "Even in this," we are told, "he acted the part of a good citizen, in that he was willing freely to undertake the responsibilities entailed upon him by the fruitfulness of his wife, in an age when the advantages of childlessness are such that many people regard even one son as a burden. He scorned all these advantages, and even became a grandfather."

The younger Pliny, as has been said, earnestly

---

[1] It is hard to trace all his family; there may have been several children more.

[2] The other twin Antoninus Geminus, died at the age of four.

desired children. He looked on his own high station and
that assured by his wife's connections as something not
to be thrown away. He wrote to her grandfather, that
"he could leave [a son] a straight road to office, and a
pedigree of no mushroom growth. Only let [the chil-
dren] be born, and change our grief to joy!" Pliny had
had an illustration of how Augustus' law handicapped
the childless, for when he was candidate for the tribune-
ship, Calestius Tiro—who was a father—had been preferred for the time before him.

Pliny's wish was never gratified; but his love for Calpurnia was pure and devoted, and hers for him. She
used to console herself when he was absent by "embrac-
ing his letters in the place of her husband, and constantly
setting them in the place he was wont to occupy;" and
he in turn, when no letters from her came, would "take
up her old ones again and again as though they were new
ones."

But we can get a fairer example than that of the
polished consular. On the walls of the bedroom of the
"Elephant Inn" in which one night slept a husband—
very humble perhaps—a carter, trader, or farmer, but
whose thoughts were not on his gain or the pleasures of
the wicked, gay Campanian city, is found this scratching
of his: "Here slept Vibius Restitutus all by himself, his
heart filled with longings for his Urbana." We are more
glad that this record has survived the centuries than for
the preservation of the pompous honorary inscriptions
of many a consul or even an imperator, whose names are
only names to us, whose bones are long since dust.

And the stories could be multiplied. Near Laurentum
in Latium was a lake to which the country folk would
point, and show the spot where a husband and wife
drowned themselves. The husband was suffering from
an incurable disease. The wife, to rid him of his misery

and give him courage, deliberately tied herself to him, and together they plunged into the lake. Her act was likened to that of the famous Arria, that high-born dame, who, when her husband was ordered by Claudius to end himself, and was hesitating, stabbed herself, then stretched out the dagger to her husband, saying, "Paetus, it does not hurt." But Arria was a lady of great family; she could die knowing the whole anti-Caesarian literary circle at Rome would immortalize her. There is glory in dying, when defying a tyrant. How much glory is there in dying obscurely, defying another's disease?

Again one can feel with the younger Pliny's friend, Fundanus, when that grave philosopher—already it would seem a widower—saw his daughter, the light of his life, slip from him. Then "all the philosophy he had ever heard from others, or uttered himself, was put one side; all virtues but one were disregarded for the moment—he could only think of his parental loss."

About half a century later Antoninus, the Emperor, wrote thus to Fronto the Orator. "In the discourse you have devoted to my Faustina,[1] I have found even more truth than eloquence. For it is the fact—yes, by the gods! I would rather live at Gyaros [an isle for exiles] than without her in the palace." She was the mother of his four children. After her death he would not marry again, but simply took a concubine—a singular manner of honoring Faustina's memory! But let not one age be too harsh in judging another.

These examples will at least show that normal family love and family life were not dead under the Roman system. It is impossible indeed that they should be dead in *any* society, if that society is to live on. The evidence, however, is reasonably plain that the violations of the fundamental Indo-Germanic law of the monoga-

[1] The elder Faustina, mother-in-law of Marcus Aurelius.

mous marriage have rarely been so frequent and so brazen as in the age of Rome.

6. *Legacy Hunting.*

In speaking of the "advantages of childlessness" and celibacy, it has been necessary to revert to the incessant legacy hunting that went on everywhere and at all times in the Roman age. But it must not be supposed that legacies were only to be looked for from the childless. Everybody who had a sizable property to leave was expected to remember his friends in his testament. It was a cheap way of paying off all manner of favors from an invitation to dinner to a nomination to the consulship. The law forbade, or at least discouraged, the direct payment of advocates. It was therefore a favorite way of rewarding one's lawyer to remember him in the will. When Seneca was informed by a centurion from Nero that he must die, "he called for his tablets to make his will." The officer said that was forbidden; whereupon the fallen prime minister told his friends that he could not requite them for their services, and could only leave them "the fairest legacy he had—the example of his life." Whether the friends were satisfied with that donation is not recorded in Tacitus.

It was not merely friends who left bequests to friends. Insignificant personages left legacies to great men, as a sort of recognition of their public services, and the great men felt no scruples at taking them. Testaments sometimes made strange bedfellows. Cicero and Clodius hated one another as much as two men can hate, yet the day before Clodius was murdered by Milo, both Clodius and Cicero met at the death bed of one Cyrus, a Greek architect, to witness his will, in which *both* were impartially remembered; and Cicero in his speech defending Milo refers to this as if it were a most ordinary sort of occurrence. Atticus, Cicero's correspondent, greatly increased his fortune by many legacies from friends and clients. Cicero himself, in the second Philippic prides himself on receiving 20,000,000 ses. in bequests—a sign, he thought, of how his countrymen valued his statesmanship and patriotism. As for Augustus, he says in his great testament, that he received the huge sum of 4,000,000,000 ses.[1] in legacies, a testimonial to the gratitude of thousands of individuals for the peace and prosperity he had given the Empire. When Junia, the very rich niece of Cato and the sister of Marcus Brutus died —an old woman—in Tiberius' reign, she showed her spite against the imperial regime by leaving legacies to almost all the great men of Rome, but not to the Emperor —who, however, did not manifest any anger. These are sufficient instances of how almost anybody, who could establish any sort of a claim upon a wealthy person, could hope to be remembered in the will. It is needless to say this habit gave rise to practices of a most disgusting kind.

Seneca tells of old men who sought to be courted by pretending to hate their children, and consequently lived in an atmosphere of hypocritical adulation, with crowds around them, like "anglers, whose one occupation is throwing out a bait in hope of hooking a part or the whole of an inheritance: [and] birds of prey who keep an eye on a dying man and hover around his corpse." Seneca's enemies charged him with being one of these very hunters of the childless himself, and swelling his great fortune with legacies; but we cannot dispose of that accusation. Seneca also tells of two men in his day, Arruntius and Haterius, who boasted they had made a regular systematic art of the hunt for legacies. Another such

[1] Considering the relative purchasing power of money, well on to half a billion dollars.

Nimrod was that Regulus, whom the younger Pliny hated so violently, and who combined legacy hunting, delation and the regular work of an advocate so profitably.

Under profligate emperors, it was often dangerous not to remember the Caesar in one's will; otherwise the whole testament was liable to be set aside and the estate swept into the imperial treasury. A righteous emperor would be more or less exempt from these disgraceful bequests. Nero, says Suetonius, deliberately ordered that "the estates of all persons who had not been mindful of their prince in their wills should be confiscated, and that lawyers who had drawn or dictated such wills should be liable to a fine." When one, however, made a bad emperor an heir, there was grave danger of having the centurion come with orders to commit suicide so that the legatee might enter on the estate. Much of Nero's cruelty can undoubtedly be accounted for by his desire to get at the legacies of his victims. But even under the best of emperors the bequests made to the Caesar could with some confidence be counted on as a regular fraction of the imperial income.

When a man was childless, the disposition of his property was of course one huge lottery. Perhaps a favorite freedman, perhaps a concubine, would get the bulk of it; or some nephew or niece. But the chances were it would be broken up into scores of fragments, and this is possibly one of the reasons why from the second century onwards we hear less of those very great fortunes that prevailed in the later Republic and under the earlier Caesars. The hunting of legacies by the suave, insinuating adventurers who infested the atria of the Roman palaces was undoubtedly as exciting, and the stakes quite as great, as the hurly-burly of the modern stock exchanges or the elegant dissipation of Monte Carlo. The atmosphere, the methods, were utterly different; the underlying motive was the same. When "the tablets" of a multimillionaire, a childless patrician, or a freedman merchant prince were opened, the city would hold its breath. Who was remembered? Who cut off? Had Calvinus and Bibulus—the most faithful of flatterers—won his villas? Had Julius, his second cousin and only blood connection, been remembered? How much had he left the emperor? Then the day after, perhaps, Calvinus who had been living in a Subura garret on starving rations, would glide in purple on a gilded litter through the Forum, with Nubian footboys beating back the gaping crowd, while praetors and consulars would seize his hand and bid him home to supper. So can the touch of Midas glorify!

Not every quest was successful. In Trajan's day lived one Domitius Tullus. He was wealthy and eccentric. Legacy hunters beset him. They were certain he would remember them all. But Tullus was shrewder than they. He angled them cleverly, wrung out of them all manner of service, deceived them utterly as to his intents; at last died. The will was opened; he had left as heirs his adopted granddaughter, his grandson, and his great grandchild. Rome could talk of nothing save this will. Some men swore he was a hypocrite; others praised him for the way he had tricked the rascals.

Martial, perhaps making a specific instance out of a variety of cases, tells also of a certain Torgilianus. Ten times he fell sick. Ten times he recovered. The legacy hunters covered their disappointment, and presented him with splendid gifts in way of congratulation. At last he died. The rapacious train flock to the magistrates' office to hear the will read and behold!—he has left them nothing but the right to weep at his tomb.

And so the game for pelf went on. Were St. Paul living to-day, he might well repeat his dictum to Timothy that "the love of money was a root of all evil;" but the Apostle would probably admit that in certain respects the twentieth century has made some slight gains upon the first. Yet it ill becomes any age to wax self-righteous. The ancients did and said many things in the forum, which later generations have done and said in a corner. But the mere concealment nevertheless has not made the acts themselves more lovely.

CHAPTER VIII

SOME REASONS WHY THE ROMAN EMPIRE FELL

ROME was not built in a day; the Empire of Rome was not destroyed in a day. It did not perish in one or two great battles, as did the first Persian Empire, by the fates of Issus and Arbela. The immediate reason why the Empire fell was because her large population were incapable of courageous and concerted effort against relatively weak invaders. The *Pax Romana* brought many blessings; it made possible the greatest luxury, the most active commercial life the world ever saw till the nineteenth Christian century. But one thing it did which in the end was suicidal to the power that maintained it—it taught the inhabitants of the Empire that war was a thing for the government only; that all fighting must be done by a relatively small professional class called an army; that, though a few savage tribes might ravage the frontiers, the quiet interior provinces were destined to perpetual peace and prosperity.[1]

[1] The standing army of the Empire probably did not exceed 300,000 including all *auxilia*. From Augustus' time onward the enlisting for the legions was a work of great difficulty. To make up the quotas it was necessary to draw less and less on Italy, and ever more on the outlying provinces, or even on the barbarian allies beyond the frontiers. The regular pay of the legionary was not high. The term of service, twenty years, was too long to make volunteering attractive. Conscripting was resorted to rather rarely, although considerable pressure was sometimes used to cause enlistments. Soldiers were, until quite late in the Empire, forbidden to form legitimate marriages. It is not surprising, therefore,

The man of the Empire could be expected to pay heavy taxes; if he were rich, to spend money freely for public buildings and festivals; but to shed his blood in behalf of the emperor was not part of the bargain. He was a faithful subject—only let the Augustus defend him without forcing him to quit his loom, his plow, his counting-room!

The Caesars went far to encourage this propensity. A nation in arms is apt to be a democratic nation. It was better to allow the barbarians to make occasional raids, better to have difficulty in finding recruits for the none too numerous legions, than to put arms in the hands of the provincials—arms which could be as likely turned against an oppressing Caesar as a ravaging German.

The army thus became more and more a class apart from the mass of the inhabitants. Even its officers ceased at length to be Roman noblemen. After the middle of the third century A.D., it was no longer necessary to serve in the cavalry in order to hold high civil office. First Roman senators, then under Diocletian the nobles of the provinces,—decurions and their sons—and all rich persons eligible for city office, were excluded from the army. The provincial militia, once of some slight value in suppressing local riots, became more and more inefficient. When once the shell of the Empire—the line of legions on each exposed frontier—was penetrated, a barbarian tribe might advance and devastate almost at will, hardly a

that the emperors found their armies too small for the great tasks assigned them, and that the soldiers, enlisted commonly from the lowest classes, were ready to mutiny or follow any leader promising booty or a huge *donativum*. It is usual to speak of the Roman imperial army as very large. As a matter of fact it was extremely small for its task of beating back the Picts in Britain, the Germans on the Rhine and Danube, the Parthians and Persians on the Euphrates, the negro tribes in Nubia and the Moors in Africa, as well as for holding in quietness the provinces. That it accomplished this for two centuries well, and for two more centuries partially, is the best tribute to its admirable organization and leadership.

sword flashing against it. It was thus the Goths plundered the Balkan Peninsula and Asia Minor in the third century; it was thus in the overwhelming disasters of the fifth. The citizens of the Empire in short presented a strange similitude to China in the helpless passiveness of the masses of their population.

But the immediate insufficiency of the professional army will not account for the decline of the Empire. Something more than the discouragement of the Caesars was necessary to deprive their subjects of the military spirit which animates every modern nation, when the national life is in danger. The Caesars themselves were partly responsible for the frittering away of their army's strength and their subjects' treasure. Dacia was a very doubtful acquisition by Trajan, and possibly ought to have been abandoned long before Aurelian recalled its hard pressed garrisons. Britain—though it presently became a very loyal province—cost far more than it returned in either commerce or tribute. "The Romans have not cared to subdue the rest [the north] of Britain, the part they have being already practically useless to them," says Appian, writing in the second century A.D. The same was probably true of Mauretania, part of Spain, and some regions in the Balkans. Such incapable rulers as Nero, Commodus, and Caracalla of course did a great deal to make the way for future invaders easier. Yet in justice to the Caesars, it should be said, they impress us, as a class, as being able rulers, alive to the needs of the hour, practical statesmen who gave their subjects quite as good government as they deserved. The trouble lay with the men of the Empire themselves, and the preceeding chapters have been to little purpose if the undermining evils are not made fairly evident.

A monk of the twelfth century relates that when in 267 A.D., the Goths took Athens, they collected all the books in the city, and were about to burn them, when one of their chiefs forbade, saying: "Let us leave the Greeks these books, for they make them so effeminate and unwarlike." The story is largely true in substance if not in fact. The old days of Rome and Greece, when every citizen had his shield and spear above the fireplace, and could take his place in the city *taxis* or legion at a moment's notice, were indeed centuries past. Peace had become the normal, the expected thing. Military drill was seldom taught now in the gymnasium. The only weapons most city folk could see would be those of the arena gladiators, or rarely those of a cohort shifting from one frontier to another. The Roman Empire and the Roman order of things were considered indestructible, eternal. The Palmyra insurgents in the third century went on, striking coins with the head of Aurelian on one side and of Vaballathos, son of Zenobia on the other, almost up to the moment when Aurelian marched against them. The reigning emperor's men might rebel against him—the Empire never. And so in this dream of the absolute fixity of the Roman system, men went on getting, studying, enjoying, dissipating—doing everything except to prepare for fighting—until Alaric sacked the Eternal City. Then too many realized that steel had its value as well as gold; and that it was sometimes as profitable to be a stout swordsman as to possess a goodly balance at the banker's; whereupon in their agony men looked for the causes of disaster. "The sins of the Pagans," cried the Christians; "the coming of the Christians," cried the Pagans. Men fled to the deserts to expiate as anchorites the sensualities of the thermae, the gloatings over the butcheries of the amphitheater. The government vainly issued reforming edicts. There was no lack of worldly wisdom and of sermons from austere ecclesiastics. Nearly all the complaints were justified.

The outcry came, however, four centuries too late. The Roman Senate had been a servile body of flatterers since the rule of Tiberius. The middle classes had been almost extinct in Italy since that time when Augustus tried to raise two legions from among them, and had to eke out the levies with slaves and freedmen. In the provinces things had been little better; a small class of rich, a large class of poor, often practically serfs, and only a weak, dwindling element between. The slave supply had almost ceased, forcing a painful readjustment of farm labor and of industry. The supply of precious metals from Spain and the Carpathians had run low. Much of the gold had been drained away from India for useless luxuries. There was, therefore, a lack of circulating medium, a prime essential for healthy economic life. The increasing difficulties of the government had driven it from one measure of oppression to another. Commerce, industry and agriculture were becoming stagnant. If there had been no Goths, Huns, or Persians, the Roman Empire would still have drifted during the two centuries following 180 A.D., into such a condition that some radical alteration of its social structure and political life would have been inevitable. Left to its self the old machinery might have required another century before ceasing to work. Diocletian and Constantine had effected temporary repairs of doubtful usefulness. The coming of Christianity did not destroy the Empire; but Christianity did little to save it. The Christians were, after all, Romans. They thought and acted as Romans in all things where their new religion did not sway them. St. Jerome and St. Augustine were no more able to afford a panacea for the evils of the Empire—social, economic and military—than Arcadius and Honorius. Christianity in the fourth and fifth centuries was perhaps able to teach men how to die. It was not yet sufficiently developed to teach large masses of men how to live.

Commerce and trade had on the whole expanded under Hadrian. They probably held their own under Antoninus Pius. Under Marcus Aurelius commenced the decline. From this time onward the repeated abatements of the taxes show how the pinch was coming, both in Italy and in the provinces.[1] The examples of public benefactions by individuals grow rarer. The complaints begin to be heard of the great burdens of holding the city magistracies. Freedmen are more frequently admitted to full citizenship in order to compel them to spend their wealth on the community. And thanks to the great plague the population of Italy seems to have declined more than ever.

In fact the Empire, in the centuries following the passing of the "Good Emperors" reminds one of a large and luxuriant garden running to seed. The plants no longer bear; the petals drop from the flowers; the autumn is advancing; on the sunnier days, thanks to the efforts of skilful and solicitous gardeners, Septimius Severus, Aurelian, Probus, Diocletian, Constantine I, Theodosius I, a few blossoms are produced which convey some reminders of the old time profusion and beauty. But the end cannot be postponed indefinitely. If no marauding interloper appears to root up the plants and pluck the last blossoms, still the winter will come at last. It really is of little matter. The trespasser actually does come—a little before the winter. In the western half of the garden he destroys almost everything; the next season all must be planted afresh. The eastern half of the

[1] In Egypt, at least, the complaints that taxation was too heavy began under Antoninus Pius. In 154 A.D. a praefect had to issue a proclamation ordering all who had fled their village to escape the "liturgies" to return, and promising remission of debt to all who would obey. The "Bucolic Revolt" of 172 A.D. in Egypt probably had discontent over the taxation as part of its basis.

garden—the part known as the East Roman Empire—containing a hardier, healthier race of plants, and better protected by high walls, defies both marauder and winter, though not unscathed. It lives a thousand years more, thanks to its peculiar plants, its sheltering walls and the special genius of its gardeners.

That the gardeners—the Caesars and their assistants—were in the main skilful, it is difficult after tracing down Roman imperial history to deny. Yet they had only the mental light of their own age to go by, and that light was often feeble. Their task was a hard one; a certain short-sightedness on the part of rulers and ruled made it more difficult. Especially no attempt was made seriously to enlarge the scope and volume of human energy by mechanical devices. The physical force that built the Flavian Amphitheater was applied in essentially the same way as that which built the pyramids. The ancients give lessons in philosophy, art, and literature which we humbly receive to-day; but for the ancients themselves it was a misfortune that they did not spend less time on forming theories of the cosmos, and more on physical inventions which should increase the economic efficiency of each workman; bring cities closer together; make communication speedy; make town life sanitary; make the rapid multiplication of books easy; make the spears of the barbarians harmless, by learning how to combine sulphur, niter and charcoal. The amount which the men of the Empire contributed to their own ultimate destruction by refusing to devote their attention to physical inventions cannot be estimated. They continued to the end to attempt great projects in the hardest possible way. To take a simple example: the maximum legal burden for a four-wheeled cart in Constantine's time was only 326 kilogrammes for eight horses—forty-three kilograms per horse. The roads, excellent for durability, and for marching soldiers, were extremely rough for wagons. The construction of carts was poor. The horseshoes found in the excavations show that the draught horses must have been very small. Yet good carts, smooth roads and strong horses would have done a vast deal to make the transit of provisions—and consequently the prevention of famines—easier; also would have aided the movement of troops and the defense of the frontiers.

The attitude of the government in such matters was well illustrated by Vespasian, when an engineer offered a mechanism for conveying some huge columns into the capital at very small expense. This wontedly parsimonious Emperor refused the invention, saying: "Let me find work for the maintenance of the poor people." The workmen, no doubt, applauded their Emperor, but posterity will applaud such a policy less.

Mechanical inventions indeed would not have saved the Empire forever. Sooner or later the Germans would have learned to make rifles and cannon. Telegraphs and railroads cannot halt the spread of moral rottenness; but these devices would have tended vastly to ward off the evil day—perhaps until Christianity could have wrought a genuine regeneration. But the age that had so much interest in the theories of the Stoa and the Academy, the new doctrines of Christianity and the mysteries of Mithras, had no interest in the mysteries of boiling water and thunder-storm—and so deliberately added to its handicap.

As time went on, as in the third century A.D., the supply of precious metals ran low, as the coinage became more and more debased until the alloy vastly outweighed the true metal, we find a clear sign of a decline in civilization, e.g., in reversion from payments by money to payments by kind. In Egypt comparatively few coins

21

are found for the whole period from Constantine to Justinian; while the evidence of the papyri shows that small amounts were commonly paid in kind. Claudius II, while a military tribune under Valerian, was appointed the following salary: "3,000 modii[1] of corn, 6,000 of barley, 2,000 lbs. of pork, 3,500 sextarii[2] of old wine, 150 of good oil, 600 of oil of second quality, 50 lbs. of silverware, 150 large gold pieces, 160 smaller gold pieces, besides salt, wax, hay, straw, vinegar, fruits, skins for tents, three horses, ten camels and nine mules annually—the government here was clearly collecting its taxes in kind and found it easier to allot the supplies direct from its storehouses to its officers than to pay the full salary in cash.

The condition of Egypt—the province of which we have the most detailed knowledge—grew steadily worse. In the third century revolts, invasions by the "Blemmyes" and the general disorder of the government caused great retrogression. A record of the Fayum district shows that one sixth of the arable land there had passed out of cultivation. The burden of taxation was increasingly grievous. The canals became choked and disused. Probus employed his soldiers to clear them out again. The middle classes seem to have been practically exterminated. The whole government of an Egyptian village would pass, under the later Empire, into the hands of one rich proprietor, who was practically supreme, except for the collection of taxes. The government legislated in vain against this "patronage." When the Arabs at length overran the Nile valley, they conquered a country that was beginning to present some phases already suggesting feudalism.

[1] A modius was nearly a peck.
[2] A sextarius was about a pint.

As the pressure of the barbarians and the difficulty of raising revenue increased, the government was driven to ever harsher expedients. The grinding taxation system of the later Empire need not be detailed here. It was not so much a system of taxes as a system of requisitions, made by the general of a besieged city upon the inhabitants. Under such conditions personal convenience is likely to give way before military necessity. The government found the noble and propertied classes exceedingly convenient subjects to press money from. It sweetened the bitterness of taxation by the bestowal of divers privileges. It is too often complained to-day that in the courts there is one law for the rich man and another for the poor. By the third century A.D. this distinction had been deliberately and avowedly set up by the Roman government. When men stood before the judge, the first question would be: "To what class do you belong?" Are you one of the *honestiores,*—a municipal official or ex-official, a great landowner—are you rich? Are you of the *humiliores*—a laborer, a small tradesman, an artisan, a petty farmer? In the latter case you can be beaten with rods, crucified, flung to the beasts, or suffer other cruel punishment; if you are rich, no matter how guilty you are, no such fate can befall you; the law will deal with you gently. Thus at last the power of mammon enthroned itself within that invention of which Rome should have been most proud—the Roman law.

As the decay within and the attack without became more deadly, men began to wish to escape even from the "Eternal Empire." Salvian, writing about 440 A.D., tells how the poorer classes actually fled to the barbarians, despite their savage habits. Men preferred the uncouthness to the cruel treatment at home. Under the Germans there was actual freedom with nominal slavery;

under the Empire was actual slavery for possessors of the boasted Roman citizenship. Priscus, a messenger from Constantinople to Attila in 448 A.D., met an outlaw from the Empire in the camp of the Huns. The outlaw hardly felt his loss. He said the Romans were forbidden to use arms, and consequently were exposed to every attack. In peace they were still worse off. The law discriminated between the rich and the poor; the taxes were fearful; and if a poor man got into litigation, no matter how good his cause, he was ruined by the law's delays.

It is usual to put down these evils to the blundering statecraft of the later Empire; it is juster to charge them to the social system which made this statecraft possible—even necessary. The causes of the fall of the Empire run far back into the history of the Republic. They were merely glossed over during the times of the early Caesars and the "Good Emperors." After that, the inherent weakness of the much praised imperial system became every day more evident.

Foremost among the causes why the Empire was weakening was the constant decline in population. It is impossible to say how many millions less the Empire contained in 400 A.D. than in 14 A.D., but everything indicates that the shrinkage was enormous. The process of depopulation had been going forward in Italy since the Second Punic War, when fifteen thousand of the flower of Italian youth fell at Trasemene, fifty thousand at Cannae. The census shows that it took thirty years to repair the loss on paper; nothing could make good in reality the slain thousands and their lost posterity. The wars of the Republic were fearfully bloody, and probably did more than to reduce the population. If we may reason from the analogy of France after the drain of the Napoleonic wars, the actual physique of the Italian people was reduced. The strong had been killed off, the weaklings had been left to propagate. In France in 1789, the average military height was 1.65 meters; in 1832 only 1.56 meters, and it would be hard to say that the wars against Carthage, Macedonia and finally the civil wars two generations later, were less exhausting than those of the French Revolution and first Empire. As early as 185 B.C., Consul Spurius Postumius, while making a judicial tour in Italy, had found to his surprise that colonies on both Italian coasts—Sipontum on the Adriatic, Buxentum on the lower Tyrrhenian sea, had alike been abandoned by their inhabitants, and new levies had to be sent out to replace the old inhabitants. And Italy was not alone—otherwise the Empire might still have fared well. "In our days," says Plutarch, "Greece would be unable to muster three thousand heavy infantrymen;" and two and a half centuries before him Polybius bewails the decline of Greek population, attributing it to the decline of marriage "through debauchery or sloth. If children are born of transient unions, only one or two of them are kept, in order to leave them as rich as their parents."

The imperial government was quite aware of the decline; and we have examined Augustus' measures to promote fruitful marriages. In his day the opinion was expressed that not merely in Italy but in all the Empire a new army of 45,000 men would be very hard to raise. Under Tiberius the shrinkage of the free population gave statesmen constant anxiety. Lucan, writing in Nero's day, complained that in many Italian towns most of the houses stood empty, most of the fields lay waste, because there were no persons to dwell in them or till them. Under Titus it was related as a kind of marvel, that in the best days of the Republic, Italy could bring 780,000 men into the field. A century later we see

Marcus Aurelius settling the conquered Marcomanni on Italian lands—something impossible had there not been vast uncultivated tracts in the peninsula.

Despite the efforts of the emperors the process went on. The failure of the slave supply favored it. The growth of luxury, "the advantages of childlessness," the low cost of prostitution, likewise the spread of asceticism, probably also the fact that the Graeco-Roman stock was at best reaching its autumn, that its physical fruitfulness was running out, all favored the shrinkage. Ateste in Venetia was a large city under Augustus, but the numerous inscriptions of the first century find no duplicates later—a sign that the city was being deserted. Vercellae (in Lombardy) had once been great, but in the fourth century was thinly populated. So the infection that had earlier desolated South Italy crept into the more prosperous north and out into the provinces. Even Rome itself, whither the nations flocked, where immigration would seem to make good all natural loss, was declining in population. Figures as to the grain supply seem to indicate that in Septimius Severus' time only half as much wheat was needed for distribution as under Augustus. Certain provinces, e.g., Egypt and Africa, were noted for their large birth rate and relative increase, but even here the growth was slow. Large tracts in the African imperial domains lay fallow for lack of laborers, while in Egypt it has been attempted to prove that in Vespasian's day, despite great and prolonged prosperity, the population had only increased half a million since the flourishing period of the Ptolemies—a long span of nigh three hundred years. According to Dio Chrysostom (in the reign of Trajan) Euboea was becoming depopulated, though it was a region probably touched as little as any in the Empire by desolating wars. The learned M. Duruy thinks that Alexandria declined by half under the later Empire. There is no reason why Antioch should not have fallen away also.

Added to the havoc wrought by the forces previously mentioned, came the general epidemics—a general pestilence in the time of Marcus Aurelius and another from 250 to 268 A.D.—that raged almost continuously in the provinces. At one time in Rome and in Achaia four thousand per day are said to have died, and in 258 and 259 A.D., Valerian's army was decimated by the plague before Sapor's Persians attacked it.

A far lesser drain, but a real one, came from the gladiatorial games. Every netter and swordsman slain was a laborer, a carpenter; an artisan lost to a society that sorely needed laborers; a potential father of a family lost to a society that even more needed fathers. In the famous sham fight on Lake Fucinus before Claudius, we are told that 19,000 men contended; stout youths, no doubt; a large fraction of them deliberately destroyed by a policy as short-sighted as it was barbarous—deliberately creating the miseries of war in a state of peace.

The Jewish wars of Vespasian and Titus wasted the lives of a race that could have given much to the Empire; the more so as the Jews possessed a fecundity that was clearly lacking to the Graeco-Romans. Josephus—of course exaggerating—declares that 1,100,000 Jews perished in their great revolt. More specifically he says 97,000 were made prisoners. Some of these were sold; some were sent to die in the Egyptian quarries; some were reserved for the fights of the amphitheater. Hardly any of these could have left posterity. From the standpoint of worldly wisdom, this destruction of the Jews was "worse than a crime—it was a blunder." And yet in Hadrian's day the Jewish wars broke out afresh in Cyrene, Egypt, and Cyprus (where many Jews were working the copper mines). Dion declares that during this war in Cyprus alone 240,000 persons perished. In Cyrene, Orosius says almost the whole population were killed off; the land would have been utterly desolate if Hadrian had not sent colonists; while in Judaea, Julius Severus, the Roman general, slew 180,000 Jews who followed Bar Kokaba's ill-starred rebellion of 132 A.D.

When the barbarians at last began to press hard, the losses in population were inevitably grievous. And these losses began in the very first wars, when the invaders were flung back and the Empire seemed to emerge unscathed and triumphant. For example, the Jazyges, who fought Marcus Aurelius so desperately along the Danube, when they made peace, surrendered 100,000 prisoners taken in the Empire. If they *surrendered* that number, it must be left to conjecture how many prisoners they sold away during the furious war, and how many of the peaceful dwellers on the frontier provinces they slew. It was the same with the Quadi and Marcomanni whom Marcus Aurelius combatted. In the third century, when from Frisia to the Euphrates the enemies of the Empire beat ceaselessly against it, the losses by mere war alone doubtless rose from the thousands to the millions. Already by Pertinax's time, the imperial domain lands were becoming desolate; and Herodian tells how this emperor found time in his brief reign to order that these *agri deserti* be given away to any one who would occupy them—with remission of taxes for ten years to the new possessors.

Finally, as time advanced, the use of downright barbarians in the legions became a necessity—if the legions were to be recruited at all. The Roman army which at first had been composed of taxable Italians, then after Marius' reforms of non-taxable Italians, then of provincials—Spaniards, Gauls, Asiatics—at last came to be officered and manned largely by persons who had never crossed the frontiers (except as invaders), until they were enrolled under the eagles. The names of many of the Roman army officers of the third century A.D. that come to us, show how complete was this process of Germanization. We find Probus enrolling 16,000 Alamanni —after they had been defeated in battle—in his legions. Doubtless they were useful troops; but when a nation, much less an empire, has to rely on mercenaries of dubious fidelity for its defense, its future is problematical even if this mercenary army continues to win battles. The day when Gothic and Frankish kings as patricians, consuls, and *magistri* of the emperors should be actually conquering the Empire piecemeal, was clearly foreshadowed in the third century.

We lack an adequate treatment in English of the peaceful Germanization of the Roman Empire; and yet the reality and importance of this process should not be lost to mind. The constant, semi-peaceful influx of northern barbarians went on for centuries, and did much to lessen the final shock and crash of the conquest. In Augustus' own day the process may be said to have begun when his stepson Tiberius transported 40,000 Germans, who had submitted, into Gaul, and assigned lands near the Rhine. Similar instances under other early emperors may have escaped us. The practice was harmless while the Empire was strong, and its native population relatively ample. But we have seen how Marcus Aurelius' settlement of Germans in Italy connoted the depopulation of the peninsula. An hundred years later Probus was settling 100,000 Bastarni in Thrace, as well as many other tribes. This meant more than the occupying of so much waste land. It implied that the process of Romanizing the provinces from Italy outward had ended; that the process of Germanizing the provinces from the frontiers inward had begun.

And so the barbarians at length destroyed a society that was more slowly destroying itself. *Latifundia,* slavery, the uprooting of the small farmers, bad systems of tillage, the excessive desire for wealth without regard to methods or to duty toward posterity; the desire to avoid the cares and expenses of child rearing, and down-right sensuality were accomplishing their perfect work. *The economic evil was at the bottom.* First Italy, then a vast Empire, devoted itself for centuries to a feverish effort for getting money by any means, and to spending that money on selfish enjoyments. Other things went for little. The great benefactions to the public usually implied—not philanthropy—but effort to win the praise and honor of men. In this art of getting and enjoying, it must be said the men of the Empire seemed to win some marked success; yet in the end the experiment proved itself hardly worthy of repetition.

A vast deal has been written on the fall of the Roman Empire. Yet one additional suggestion may be haz-arded. The Empire fell because the ideals animating its builders and its continuers were low and unworthy. No race ever possessed the much vaunted quality of com-mon sense more than the architects of Rome. "Give and get" should have been blazoned on their civic ensigns, seals, coinage. The Aemilii, Cornelii, or Fabii never followed chimeras, never allowed themselves to be betrayed into impracticable enterprises, never shunned hard work whether in the corn field or in the battle field. Painfully—acre by acre almost—Rome won the hege-mony of Latium, then of Italy. Very cautiously—misled by no blatant Alcibiades—she entered upon foreign con-quests. The pressure of the enemy at first had made the Roman patriotic through self-interest; he fought that his own hard-won farm might be safe from the enemy, and that he might add new acres. When Hannibal threatened destruction, his enemies could indeed count no sacrifice too dear to defend their own precious homesteads. When the era of wide conquests came, the governing faction for a while would embark on no war that did not promise direct remuneration, not merely to the state, but to themselves. Thus they destroyed Corinth and Carthage because those cities interfered with their growing commercial system; they spared Alexandria because Alexandria was in the main an aid and ally to their gains. Presently their own selfish interests clashed. There followed political tempests, civil wars. Lands, slaves, money-bags became insecure, thanks to the inefficiency of the old republican government. Therefore came the Caesars—owing their power really to the fact that under their regime men could buy, sell, grow rich, enjoy themselves under extremely favorable conditions.

The Caesars were before all things "practical men." The first Caesar, the great Julius, had indeed been a seër of visions. He had been ambitious, intensely ambitious to be master of a world in which he saw much to rectify, and believed himself capable of rectifying. He was not nice about his means. He was not conscious of the weakness of a benevolent despot; yet he appears to have been a man with an ideal—of a well ordered society in which men are to be justly treated, in which they were to pursue civilized happiness guided, aided by the intelligent *deus in terra* of which he himself was to be the prototype.

Julius Caesar fell under the daggers of men who preferred the weal of a few Roman families to the weal of a world empire. Octavius, his successor, was a man of wide practical ability, but of very humble ideals. To found a workable system of government, to let the future care for the future—that was his task. Augustus (as we commonly know him) may fairly be called the greatest opportunist in history. He merely scratched the surface of the social and economic problems that demanded sooner or later a settlement. He gave his Empire a fair show of stable prosperity. His adopted son Tiberius followed his main policy—shunning innovations, pretending to be only "first citizen," when really a sultan; and governing in the main ably, but with an eye merely for the passing hour. Caligula, who followed, was a madman. His rule was a mere interregnum. Claudius had not a spark of genius, but a certain amount of conservative ability; the Empire prospered under him—another sovereign of eminently "practical" ideals. Then followed the exception in Roman history. Nero was not a madman; he was not an innate monster. He *had* ideals. Unfortunately his ideals were those of a devotee of voluptuous pseudo-Hellenic art and esthetics, not of just laws and human brotherhood. Surrounded by scheming sycophants, by prosing and pliant philosophers like Seneca, by every temptation that can attack a youth of highly erratic impulse, no marvel that he drifted to shipwreck. Nero harping upon the public stage was not a hopeful spectacle; yet if he had waged bloody wars on the Danube, and won victories of not the least real gain to the Empire, would Tacitus and Suetonius have so arraigned him? It is not the least count against the Roman system that a man with the tastes of Nero—a would-be poet, and after his feeble manner an idealist—should be so out of touch with his age as almost perforce to become a monster.

But Nero perished. After a brief civil war, "practical men" succeeded him. Vespasian, Titus, Domitian, Nerva, Trajan, Hadrian, Antoninus Pius, Marcus Aurelius, all governed ably and well—for the moment. Some of them at least had leisure and power to introduce revolutionary reforms; but not one—not Nerva who wrote poetry and whom flatterers likened to Tibullus; not Hadrian, the world-wandering Hellenist; not Marcus Aurelius, the purple-clad Stoic—let any high idealism express itself in their public policy. Marcus could indeed compose his *Meditations*. They are the injunctions to a strong man, telling him how to endure passively the tumults of an evil world. But what the Graeco-Roman world required was, not passivity, but action—not the peace for lucre, but the bloodless war for righteousness—and the bravest emperor never drew sword in that battle. In vain we look for a zealous man of the type of Joseph II of Austria—a man who failed in his ideal of reformation, but who at least failed nobly.

After Marcus Aurelius indeed, the idealist would have been out of place in the Empire. The evil days were at hand; desperate temporary expedients were needed. It is no time to discuss the proper structure of fire-proof buildings while one's very roof is burning. Only thirteen years after the imperial philosopher died at Vindobona, is recorded the crowning triumph of the commercial spirit in the Empire—the purchase of the rights of Julius Caesar and Augustus by Didius Julianus at auction from the praetorian guard. After that— however quickly a Septimius Severus came to punish this overbold exhibition—what hope remained for a society where these things were even possible?

Yet long before 193 A.D. the money power had received formal recognition as a controlling factor. Propraetors, proconsuls, procurators, legates regularly were rated, not according to the respective honor of their posts, but according to the size of their salaries. "One hundred thousand sesterce men," "two hundred thousand," "three hundred thousand," etc., we read even on tombstones, as well as elsewhere, as inscriptions of honor.[1] So did the Roman government, in importance rating its dignitaries as it might the value of its state farms. The society of the capital which gave its tone to the government, the society of the provinces which followed the capital, hardly had higher standards of judgment.

And thus in the West the Roman Empire, built on a policy of low ideals and opportunism, perished. Why not also in the East? Not the strength of Constantinople saved the East Romans: the Queen of the Bosphorus was less inaccessible than behind her marshes was Ravenna, the last stronghold of the western Caesars. Not the absence of barbarian attacks—no nation ever beat off so many foes as did the East Romans. Rather was it not because the men of the eastern Empire were by tradition, and largely by race, Greeks more than Romans? And if Italy was the land of the practical common sense, Greece was the land of ideals. The Arian, the Monophysite, the Monothelite heresies and tumults in the church of the East showed that *there* men could still fight—if needs be die—for ideas and ideals, albeit not always worthy ones. And more, the difference persists to this day. The Church of the East still calls itself "The Orthodox," the true, the church that has grasped the right ideal. The Church of the West is still "The Catholic," the all-embracing, the holder of the entire spiritual property in this world and the next, of the merits of the saints, of the souls of the just, of the treasures laid up in heaven. We have the terms of commerce, of the merchant's balance sheet, translated into the language of the theologians. The Roman

---

[1] A public office to-day is sometimes described as e.g., "a three thousand dollar job," but the holder seldom makes public boasts as to this feature.

Empire of the Papacy surely is not yet dead; perhaps this is one justification of history for the plowing, plodding farmers of old Latium, and for their worldly wisdom, and for the opportunism of the system of Augustus.

But the Roman Empire of the Caesars has long been dead. So many have pronounced its eulogies that another seems needless. No state ever excluded the ideal from its national and social life so strictly as did Rome. It taught its prosaic commercialism to all its provinces. It died a slow, lingering, painful death, after achieving the greatest seeming success in history. Its citizens served Mammon in the place of God with more than usual consistency. The power they worshipped carried them a certain way—then delivered them over to their own rottenness, and to the resistless enemy. Their fall was great—for their Empire with its social structure still looms as the greatest fabric ever reared by human ingenuity; while the lesson of their fall lies patent to the twentieth century.

INDEX

22

WILLIAM STEARNS DAVIS'S HISTORICAL NOVELS

A Victor of Salamis

A TALE OF THE DAYS OF XERXES, LEONIDAS, AND THEMISTOCLES

"A really moving narrative, with figures of flesh and blood in it, and a broad vitality that touches the reader's imagination. The thing is astonishingly human . . . and as unaffectedly dramatic as though he had drawn his material from the modern world."

—The New York Tribune.

"The novel reproduces Greek life, and the events of the Persian invasion brilliantly and with correctness. . . . Mr. Davis has even surpassed his previous efforts in highly imaginative work."—*Boston Budget.*

Cloth, 12mo, $1.50

A Friend of Caesar

A TALE OF THE FALL OF THE ROMAN REPUBLIC

"As a story . . . there can be no question of its success. . . . While the beautiful love of Cornelia and Drusus lies at the sound sweet heart of the story, to say so is to give a most meagre idea of the large sustained interest of the whole. . . . There are many incidents so vivid, so brilliant, that they fix themselves in the memory."—*The Bookman.*

Cloth, 12mo, $1.50

"God Wills It"

A TALE OF THE FIRST CRUSADE

"Not since Sir Walter Scott cast his spell over us with 'Ivanhoe,' 'Count Robert of Paris,' and 'Quentin Durward' have we been so completely captivated by a story as by 'God Wills It,' by William Stearns Davis. It grips the attention of the reader in the first chapter and holds it till the last. . . . It is a story of strenuous life, the spirit of which might well be applied in some of our modern Crusades. While true to life in its local coloring, it is sweet and pure, and leaves no after-taste of bitterness. The author's first book, 'A Friend of Cæsar,' revealed his power, and 'God Wills It' confirms and deepens the impression made."—*Christian Endeavor World.*

With Illustrations by Louis Betts
Cloth, 12mo, $1.50

PUBLISHED BY
THE MACMILLAN COMPANY
64-66 Fifth Avenue, New York

An Outline History of the Roman Empire

By WILLIAM STEARNS DAVIS, Professor of
History in the University of Minnesota

A comprehensive review of the progress and fall of the Roman Empire
such as is a necessary pre-requisite to an intelligent study of the history
of the Middle Ages. The volume is brief and, considering its condensation, of unusually interesting style.

Cloth, 65 cents net

A History of Rome to the Battle of Actium

By EVELYN S. SHUCKBURGH

The author has presented in a vivid manner the story of the gradual
extension of power of a single city over a large part of the known world.
The countries conquered and the details of the conquest, the internal
development of the state, and the constitutional changes that resulted,
are all clearly set forth in the narrative along with a discussion of the
development of literature and the social life. The book is grounded
throughout upon the old writers.

Cloth, $1.75 net

A History of Greece

By J. B. BURY, Regius Professor of
Greek in the University of Dublin

"Excellence in a historical work by this scholar was to be expected,
but the charm of his literary style and clearness of expression have
placed this volume at the head of single volume texts. The history of
Greece is considered in great detail from the political and constitutional
sides, but special emphasis is laid on the literature, art, and social life."

Cloth, $1.90 net

A Student's History of Greece

By J. B. BURY. Revised by EVERETT KIMBALL

"This volume, a condensation of Professor Bury's larger work, presents in a scholarly manner, such details of Greek history, life, letters,
and art as are necessary for an elementary understanding of the
subject."

Cloth, $1.10 net

PUBLISHED BY

THE MACMILLAN COMPANY

64-66 Fifth Avenue, New York

Greek Architecture

By Professor Allan Marquand

"Professor Marquand makes his ideas and theories perfectly clear. Each statement made helps to prove a point. . . . He begins by describing the building materials employed by the Greeks and their methods of construction. He then descants on architectural forms and on proportions. He devotes much space to decoration, explains the principals of composition and style, and ends with an account of the various types of monuments of Greek architecture."

—The New York Sun
Cloth, Fully Illustrated, $2.25 net

Social Life at Rome in the Age of Cicero

By W. Warde Fowler

A notable example of the kind of history that deals with men rather than with institutions and events. This is the only book in the English language that supplies a picture of life and manners, of education, morals and religion, in the intensely interesting period of the Roman Republic. The age of Cicero is one of the most important periods of Roman history, and the Ciceronian correspondence, of more than niue hundred contemporary letters, is the richest treasure house of social life that has survived from any period of classical antiquity.

Cloth, $2.25 net

The Monuments of Christian Rome

By Arthur L. Frothingham

"The first part gives an historical sketch of Rome from the times of Constantine and Honorius to that of 1305, when the popes were in exile at Avignon. The second part is an exhaustive classification of the monuments, together with an index of illustrations and of churches. . . The book is interestingly written, and as its author was at one time associate director of the American School at Rome, it has the authority of first-hand knowledge to give it standing."—*Boston Transcript*.

Cloth, Fully Illustrated, $2.25 net

PUBLISHED BY

THE MACMILLAN COMPANY
64-66 Fifth Avenue, New York

Periods of European History

General Editor, ARTHUR HASSALL

The object of this series is to present in separate volumes a comprehensive and trustworthy account of the general development of European history, and to deal fully and carefully with the more prominent events in each century. The volumes embody the results of the latest investigations and contain reference to and notes upon original and other sources of information. No such attempt to place the history of Europe in a comprehensive, detailed, and readable form has previously been made, and the series forms a valuable continuous history of mediæval and modern Europe.

Period I—The Dark Ages, 476-918. By CHARLES OMAN, Professor of Modern History in the University of Oxford.

$1.75 net

Period II—The Empire and the Papacy, 918-1273. By T. F. TOUT, Professor of History at the Owens College, Victoria University.

$1.75 net

Period III—The Close of the Middle Ages, 1273-1494. By R. LODGE, Professor of History in the University of Edinburgh.

$1.75 net

Period IV—Europe in the Sixteenth Century, 1594-1598, By A. H. JOHNSON, Historical Lecturer, Oxford.

$1.75 net

Period V—Europe, 1598-1715. By HENRY O. WAKEMAN, Tutor of Keble College, Oxford.

$1.40 net

Period VI—The Balance of Power, 1715-1798. By ARTHUR HASSALL, Student of Christ Church, Oxford.

$1.60 net

Period VII—Revolutionary Europe, 1789-1815. By H. MORSE STEPHENS, Professor of History at Cornell University.

$1.40 net

Period VIII—Modern Europe, 1815-1819. By W. ALISON PHILLIPS.

$1.60 net

PUBLISHED BY

THE MACMILLAN COMPANY

64-66 Fifth Avenue, New York